In time for tom...

the Carbon Conversations Handbook

Rosemary Randall and Andy Brown

The authors

Rosemary Randall is a psychotherapist and group facilitator who has been involved in the environmental movement for many years. She writes and lectures widely on the psychological aspects of climate change.

Andy Brown is an engineer with a background in the social sciences. He works in research for the built environment and has been a lifelong supporter of environmental causes.

This edition first published in 2015 by
The Surefoot Effect Community Interest Company
17 Victoria Place
Sitrling
FK8 2QT

www.surefoot-effect.com
info@surefoot-effect.com

Previously published as The Carbon Conversations Handbook: Six Meetings about Climate Change and Carbon Reduction in 2007 with revisions in 2009, 2010, 2011 and 2013

Copyright © Rosemary Randall and Andy Brown, 2015

The moral right of the authors has been asserted

Carbon Conversations™ is a registered trademark

ISBN 978-0-9931211-0-4

Design by Sam Masters, **www.2dgraphic.com**
Printed by Big Sky Print **www.bigskyprint.com**

carbonconversations.org

Contents

Preface and acknowledgments ... iv

Introduction ... 1

CHAPTER 1 Looking for a low-carbon future ... 5

CHAPTER 2 Energy at home and at work ... 31

CHAPTER 3 Travel and transport ... 49

CHAPTER 4 Food and water ... 103

CHAPTER 5 Consumption and waste ... 131

CHAPTER 6 Talking with friends, family and colleagues ... 161

CHAPTER 7 Moving on ... 187

Notes ... 193

Index ... 207

Preface

In Time for Tomorrow? *the Carbon Conversations Handbook* will help anyone who is concerned about climate change and carbon reduction understand their own powerful and ambivalent responses to the subject. It can help you make a practical difference to your carbon footprint, find your way around tricky conversations on the subject with family or friends, and help you think about the political and social changes that are needed.

The book is also part of a package of materials which supports Carbon Conversations groups – facilitated groups of six-eight people who meet in the community or at work over a period of three to six months to explore and reduce the impact which their personal lives have on the climate. This programme is run by the Surefoot-Effect Community Interest Company, and arose from the realisation that although people need information in order to reduce their carbon impact and act on climate change, their greatest need is for a supportive milieu in which to do this. Climate change is not an issue that you can face on your own. Drawing on insights from support and therapy groups, Carbon Conversations is a project that takes account of people's psychological needs in grappling with their carbon footprints. The group setting is one in which the practicalities of carbon reduction can be examined, while the feelings which this provokes can be explored and understood.

Surefoot trains and supports volunteer facilitators and the groups are run in communities and workplaces across the UK. Other elements of the package include a *Workbook*, a detailed *Facilitator's Guide* to running the groups and a set of three games exploring home energy, travel dilemmas and food footprints, and a website where calculations about carbon emissions can be made. A separate guide to using Carbon Conversations in the workplace is also available.

We ran our first Carbon Conversations pilot groups in Cambridge in 2007 and 2008. In 2009 Carbon Conversations became a national project. Now, in 2015 we are re-launching with **In Time for Tomorrow?**, the new version of our original handbook, a new *Workbook* for participants and updated versions of the games, *Facilitator's Guide* and *Guide to Using Carbon Conversations in the Workplace*.

In our original version of the materials we kept most of the psychological explanation in the *Facilitator's Guide*, and in the training we provided for facilitators. Our view was that psychological knowledge is best acquired experientially. We concentrated on equipping our facilitators to offer group experiences that would help participants to face the personal dilemmas of carbon reduction in a supportive and non-judgmental environment. Many people told us that they would like to see more about the psychological dynamics in the main handbook, but also that they would like to see the handbook available separately from participation in a Carbon Conversations group. If you are familiar with previous editions of Carbon Conversations these are the main changes you will notice. There are new sections on the disavowal of climate change, the process of personal change and the experiences of ambivalence, grief and resistance that may be involved. Each chapter contains a section on 'getting stuck', and discusses our common resistance to making changes that are difficult for us. There is also a new chapter on how to talk to friends, family and colleagues about climate change and carbon reduction. The group activities and the forms for monitoring your footprint are now in the separate *Workbook* and we have tried to bring the factual information up to date and in line with the best research – a daunting task in an ever-expanding field of knowledge.

Much has changed since we ran our first groups. Internationally, the prospects for agreement on climate change look bleaker. Public interest in climate change has fallen. Funding for community projects is harder to come by. In these circumstances we feel that the approach of Carbon Conversations is more important than ever. Research by Southampton University confirms the project's effectiveness, with participants typically making reductions of over three tonnes CO_2 to their annual carbon footprint. We are delighted that Surefoot remains committed to the project and hope that this new edition of the handbook will see many more people taking part in Carbon Conversations groups.

Rosemary Randall and Andy Brown, December 2014

Acknowledgments

Many people have helped to make this new edition of the materials possible. We are particularly grateful to the Patsy Wood Trust whose generous funding has helped us to meet the costs of the redesign. Top of the list for their indefatigable, thoughtful and consistent support are our fellow Surefoot board members, Pamela Candea, Jane Orton and Tony Wragg. Their many hours of hard work on training facilitators and organising the marketing, finances and management of the wider project give this new edition its purpose. Without their sharp, well-informed and insightful comments on drafts, this new edition would not have seen the light of day.

Peter Harper from the Centre for Alternative Technology has generously contributed his work on carbon footprinting, and we are delighted to be able to feature a version of his calculator on the Carbon Conversations website. Andy is particularly grateful to Peter for many hours of technical conversation and discussion of numerical modelling. Rosemary is indebted to Paul Hoggett, Renee Lertzman, Sally Weintrobe and colleagues from the Climate Psychology Alliance for extending her understanding of the psychology of climate change. Shilpa Shah's work for the Akashi project has left its stamp on the book in the stories she collected, and in our continuing commitment to represent the many voices of those concerned about climate change. Milena Buchs and colleagues at Southampton University's Third Sector Research Unit, contributed many insights from their ongoing research into the groups and their effectiveness. Rebecca Nestor from Learning for Good drafted the material on action in the workplace. Caroline Roaf volunteered her skills as copy-editor and prepared the index, Amanda Stibrany led our small team of proof-readers and Lucie Stevenson spent many hours checking and shortening the urls. Cardiff University's Energy Biographies project kindly gave us permission to use stories from their website, http://energybiographies.org/, and The Superhomes project introduced us to some of the people whose houses feature in Chapter Two.

In addition a multitude of people advised, discussed, read and critiqued the original drafts, fact-checked, did picture research, proof-read and generously contributed their own stories to the book. Thank you to: Alex Randall, Ali Wood, Allis Karim, Ammar Waqar, Anne Augustine, Astrid Horward, Azeeza Ghani Mohammed Ismail, Barbara Nestor, Belinda Ellis, Catherine Cherry, Charles Whitehead, Charlotte Scott, Chris Groves, Christine Suffolk, Claire Melling, Daniel Welch, Denzel Gordon, Derek Evans, Dr Rong Shu, Elaine Wilson, Elena Blackmore, Emma Burnett, Euri Vidal, Frances Platt, Glenor Roberts, Gomathy Sethuraman, Hannah Baker, Iain Webb, Ivan Cicin-Sain, Jackie Argent, Jacqueline Gonzalez, Jean Langhorne, Jem Whitely, Jo

Bowlt, John and Elaine Riley, Jonathan Baldwin, Jonathan Cooke, Judith Secker, Julian Cooling, Julie Pickard, Karen Henwood, Katherine Simpson, Katie Thornburrow, Keiko Saito, Kiran Malhi-Bearn, Kirsty Wayland, Lorna Edwards, Luthfa Khan, Mary Evans Young, Meg Clarke, Nicholas Hall, Padma Bhuva, Rebecca Miller, Rich Hawkins, Robbie Nestor, Sarah Ravenscroft, Sarah Wragg, Sharon Boyd, Tanya Hawkes, Tina Shah, Venerable Samitha.

Picture credits

Grateful acknowledgment is made for permission to reprint the following images. Cover, primary school, designed to PassivHaus standards, Architype Ltd/ Leigh Simpson. P. 5, Coal-fired power station, Greenpeace/Steve Morgan. P. 8, Planetary Boundaries, Azote Images/Stockholm Resilience Centre. P. 8, Doughnut, Kate Raworth (2012) *A Safe and Just Space for Humanity: Can we live within the doughnut?* Oxfam Discussion Paper, Oxfam International, http://www.kataraworth.com. P. 32, 'Good house and bad house', Chris Fairless. P. 80, electric car, R-Eco, www.r-eco.coop. P. 92, bus protest, South Wales Evening Post, www.southwales-eveningpost.co.uk. P. 107, La Via Campesina, Ian Mackenzie, Creative Commons, CC BY-NC/2.0/ http://bit.ly/Ian_MacKenzie. P. 131, E-waste in China, ©Greenpeace/Natalie Behring. P. 133, Moynaq, Aral Sea, Arian Zwegers, Creative Commons, CC-BY-2.0, http://bit.ly/zwegers. P 145, Mining in Kailo, Julien Harneis, Creative Commons, CC-BY-SA-2.0, http://bit.ly/harneis; P. 149, The Circular Economy: The Ellen Macarthur Foundation.

Introduction

Information has long been the chosen tool of educators, campaigners and activists. The belief that telling people what is wrong with the world will lead to change, dies hard. It remains in place despite decades of experience showing that most people do not respond to tales of disaster with the energy to transform the situation, but with indifference, despair or the shrug of 'what do you expect me to do?'

Telling people is the easy bit. Creating the situations where they can hear you, and are willing to change their own lives or the society of which they are part, is much harder. People fail to act, not because they are selfish or unwilling but because they feel they have no power, because the things that are wrong are part of complex social and political systems and because as individuals we are each a complex mix of competing desires. Altruism is mixed with self-interest, compassion is tempered with frustration, duty conflicts with pleasure. We want life to change but we don't want to suffer in the process.

Faced with unwelcome news the human mind is good at suppressing awkward facts. We are skilled at only seeing what we want to see, and have many tricks for maintaining our illusions. We screen out information that doesn't fit with our world view. We rationalise our part in systems that cause harm. We reject ideas that challenge our sense of our own identity. We turn a blind eye to anything which clashes with our feelings that we are basically good people. We repress the facts that make us feel upset or guilty. We do much of this unconsciously. We don't notice ourselves do it, and we can be surprised and offended if someone points it out.

Meanwhile, our ideas about what is right and good and natural are formed in the societies of which we are part. It is hard to think outside the box of common experience. The UK in the 21st century is a society where individualism is strong, the market is seen as a natural force, and increased consumption of material goods is seen as desirable and good. This way of life seems normal and inevitable to many, despite having developed over a remarkably short time.[1] The collective solutions and personal restraint that climate change may require, can feel hard to contemplate and even harder to achieve.

Carbon Conversations was created as a response to these dilemmas. How can individuals play a part in the changes demanded of society by climate change? How can they not just 'talk the talk' of carbon reduction and low-impact lives but actually live those lives now? If the goal is a world where we are each responsible for a mere 10% of the current, individual emissions of today, how do we get there? How should we be trying to live in 2015, 2020 or 2050?

Our answer to these questions was that three things are needed. The first is an understanding of the part that individuals can play. It is clear that many players are needed in the social transformations that are demanded by climate change. As well as individuals who accept that their everyday lives will need to change we need: leaders who are not afraid to speak the truth; citizens and social movements who are forceful in their demands; businesses that are prepared to rethink their role in society; industry that is prepared to be inventive and take risks; states that are prepared to act in the collective interest; politicians who will plan for the long-term.

It is important to be clear that individuals on their own cannot make the changes to society that are required, and that there is no equality between the various players who need to act. We live in relationships of deep inequality. Programmes of behaviour change can all too easily shift responsibility away from the powerful, and dump it on people whose only offence has been to live in conformity with the norms of society. In the same way that obesity is often framed as an individual weakness, it can also be convenient to blame unsustainable consumption on individual greed. With obesity it is the issues of poverty and the promotion of cheap, unhealthy food that are often ignored. With unsustainable consumption, it is the built-in obsolescence, the relentless pursuit of profit, and the complex social practices that grow up around goods and services that get side-lined. Vested commercial interests, weak politicians and structural deficits in the provision of public transport, housing, and sustainable manufacturing all need to be addressed.

Nonetheless, as we describe in more detail later, we think that most people can halve their individual carbon footprint. The rest of the reductions needed to create a low-carbon society have to come through political, social and technological change. Halving an individual footprint is likely to take some effort. It is a far cry from the trivial 'top ten tips to save the planet' that frequently emerge from behaviour change initiatives. This is where our second two factors come in.

The second factor – despite what we say above – is reliable information. You can't live a low-impact life if you don't know why your current life is high-impact; you need to understand how your carbon footprint is made up. We have met many concerned individuals who have not realised that their cruise through the Norwegian fjords is as damaging as a flight to South Africa, or that the size of their house has an effect on their carbon emissions. Many people have no idea that a high income has a strong correlation with a high carbon impact, and it is news to others that meat is so damaging.

For information to be useful however, it needs to come at the right time, in the right place, in the right amount and with the right support. People need to be open to it, ready to consider it and willing to grapple with its implications. It took Andy many years of advising the building industry on low-energy construction to realise that it wasn't the information he provided that was critical, but his skills in persuading the entire team to agree to a process of change. Even when people are eager for information, it may not be easy to absorb. When Rosemary first read that the average UK footprint needed to reduce by 80% from its current 15 tonnes, she found this unimaginable and reacted with disbelief. How would we live? Surely, we'd freeze in the winter and have to walk to the seaside if we wanted a holiday. I didn't want these facts to be true. As the disbelief passed, I felt criticised. The information seemed to accuse me of profligacy and selfishness. I wanted to reject it and see the author as partisan or puritanical. Only gradually did I become able to disentangle the facts from my strong, emotional response and find a way of acting on them.

If you are not ready to process information of this kind, then your defences will kick in. You will shunt the unwelcome facts to a separate part of the mind, knowing and not knowing them at the same time. You will embrace views which tell you that the unwelcome facts don't matter, are wrong, can be dealt with later or are someone else's responsibility. As we suggested earlier, this is the explanation for the common indifference with which climate change is greeted. We do not deny the reality of climate change outright. We simply park it somewhere so that it doesn't bother us too much, and get on with life as usual.

So the third factor that is needed is help in understanding our complex reactions to climate change, and a milieu where these can be explored and worked through. Reducing your carbon footprint means confronting your feelings about what makes a home a home, your assumptions about holidays, cars and the daily commute, your attachment to particular foods and your right to do what you like with the money you earn. We need to untangle the complex web of social forces, practical constraints and individual desires that keeps our lives as they are. We need to uncover what we think about a future that is likely to be quite different from the present. We may need to explore our personal values, our relationship to nature and our sense of justice. As we try to make changes to our lives we need to recognise that we are likely to make advances and retreats. We need to accept that at times we will respond defensively, feel anxious or hopeless, want to give up or wonder if it is worth trying at all. Challenging the status quo is difficult, whether you are doing this politically or by trying to alter the fabric of your day-to-day life.

There is a long history of using groups as a milieu for support and change. Making bonds around a common challenge – whether it is pregnancy, weight loss, bereavement or delinquency – can bring comfort, new knowledge and the determination to find new solutions. When the group feels safe enough, free from harsh criticism, welcoming to those who are uncertain and tolerant of those who are confused, then people open up. They question old assumptions. They reflect more deeply on the past. They explore their feelings. They admit to vulnerabilities. Their attitudes shift. They try something new. Such groups come in all kinds of shapes. Our experience of running the first pilot groups of Carbon Conversations led us to concentrate on a model of time-limited, facilitated groups. We learned to use activities that would help people explore their feelings about climate change, understand the facts about their personal impact and grasp the possibility of doing something different.[2]

You may be reading this book because you are part of a Carbon Conversations group, in which case we hope that it will give you the company, support and understanding that you need, and that you enjoy the journey you make. There are many other ways to use this book. You might just want to understand the issues better, reflect on the defences and obstacles in moving towards a low-carbon life or find practical advice on how to reduce a particular part of your carbon footprint. Groups are not for everyone, but if you are reading this book alone, think about joining or starting a group. You may be surprised by the difference it makes. Details are on the Carbon Conversations website.

Chapter One takes you through an explanation of the basic facts about climate change and discusses why we can find it hard to take in these facts, often closing our eyes to them and carrying on as if they were not important. Chapters Two to Five, discuss the four component parts of an individual carbon footprint that you can have an effect on: home energy, travel and transport, food and water, purchases and other consumption. As well as outlining the scale of the changes needed and the practical ways to have an effect, we talk about the difficulties people encounter. Ordinary life is not organised in ways that make low-carbon living easy. Everything can seem to conspire against us, from the organisation of transport and patterns of work, to the way supermarkets sell food and the way we do the laundry. In addition we all have our blind spots and resistances, our passionate desires and obstinate sticking points. Understanding these difficulties and working with them is often the key to achieving change. Working with our feelings of anger, disappointment, resentment and hopelessness can help us to leave these feelings behind, and feel better about a future that needs to be quite different from the past or present.

Chapter Six explores how to talk about climate change and carbon reduction with friends, family and colleagues. Many people find that this is a flashpoint in their struggle to reduce carbon emissions. Although many people find good support from those closest to them, the opposite is also true. Teenagers object. Partners protest. Friends are offended. Colleagues tease or mock. People feel misunderstood and pigeon-holed. Finding strategies to deal with this is important, and we offer some pointers that may ease your path. Chapter Seven considers the actions you can take in your local community or in the wider political sphere. Although the focus of this book is on individual action, carbon reduction is not just about individual lives. Most of us have other roles too – as workers, citizens, business owners, political activists or community organisers, to name but a few. Acting in these wider spheres can strengthen and complement what we do in our personal lives.

We have tried to present the factual information in as unpartisan a way as possible but inevitably our personal biases creep through. We hope you will read the rest of this book in the spirit in which it is written – one of hope, reflection and encouragement - and make up your own mind about the conversations you want to have and the actions you want to take.

CHAPTER 1

Looking for a low carbon future

"Thinking about climate change frightens me. We share one world and we are all connected. My dream is that we will sort this out."

Drax coal-fired power station: a major contributor to climate change

Climate change has moved up and down the political agenda in the UK since the late 1980s. Internationally, the world has struggled – and for the most part failed – to agree what should be done.[1] Surveys show that most people are aware that it is a serious issue.[2] It is also clear that it is a complex one. Our way of life is dependent on fossil fuels and the changes needed are huge. Climate change raises questions about justice and equality, economic growth, and our relationship to the natural world. In this chapter we explore some of the broad issues and also some of the practical, personal ones:

- What is climate change?
- Who is responsible for tackling it?
- What might a low-carbon future look like?
- Why do we find it so hard to act?
- What is a carbon footprint and how can we contribute to the changes needed?

Climate change: the basics

In order to understand the problem we need to grasp some basic facts about what is causing climate change and what is likely to happen if it goes unchecked.[3]

Carbon dioxide matters

Life on earth depends on there being carbon dioxide (CO_2) in the atmosphere. Without it, planet earth would simply be another lump of rock hurtling through space. Along with other 'greenhouse' gases and water vapour, CO_2 traps the sun's heat, creating the conditions for plants and animals to thrive. We need the amount of CO_2 to stay stable. Too little brings on risky cooling; too much and the earth overheats.

CO_2 is the main 'greenhouse' gas. Other important greenhouse gases are methane and nitrous oxides. Their levels can be expressed as 'CO_2 equivalents' or CO_2 e, for easy comparison.[4]

Since the start of the industrial revolution – about 250 years ago – the amount of CO_2 in the atmosphere has been steadily rising. The main cause is

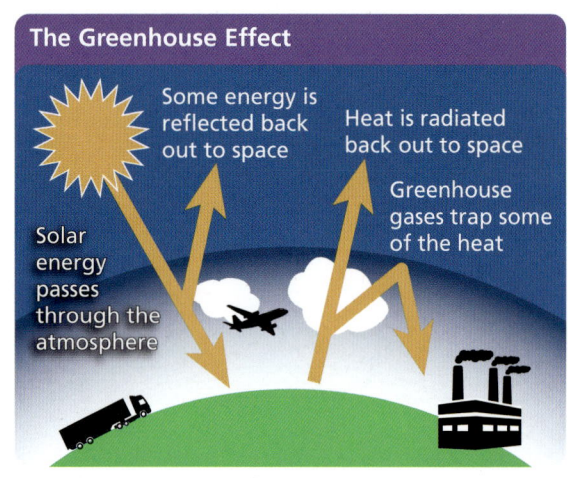

the burning of large amounts of fossil fuels – coal, oil and gas. Deforestation, agriculture and how waste is managed also contribute. Since the 1950s, when global industrial production ramped up, the problem has rapidly increased. As CO_2 has risen so has the average global temperature as you can see in the graph 'CO_2 and temperature rise'.

2 °C or even 6 °C isn't much when you're turning your central heating up or down but it's a different matter with global temperatures. Here, a rise of just a few degrees can have a huge effect, destabilising the climate.

Fossil fuels make modern life with all its comforts possible. But sadly, their use is destroying the natural world that we depend on. Scientists have no doubt that human actions are the cause of global warming. They also agree that the climate has started to change in ways that could be very damaging for human, animal and plant life.

- The planet could warm by as much as 6 °C above pre-industrial levels by 2100.
- Sea level rises could make some islands and coastal areas uninhabitable – for example the Maldives and the delta regions of Bangladesh, home to 110 million people.

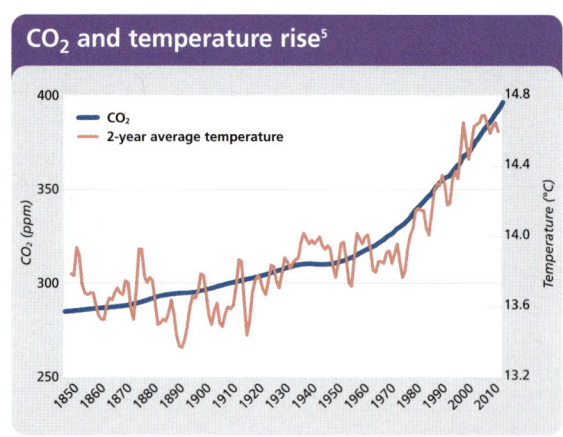

- Rainfall patterns will change, causing more droughts, storms and floods, and more variability, making agriculture more difficult in many areas. Crop yields will suffer.
- Changes to the availability of fresh water, increased heat stress, and the spreading of infectious diseases could all damage human health.
- Many plants and animals will disappear if they are unable to adapt to changing conditions.
- Social and political unrest are likely, as countries compete for resources and struggle with local effects such as droughts, storms and floods.

Scientists are worried

Climate change may not happen evenly or slowly. Scientists are worried about feedback effects that could bring runaway climate disruption. For example, rising temperatures could release methane now locked up in Siberian permafrost or cause rain forests to die back. Either would accelerate the heating of the global atmosphere dramatically.

In 2014 the world had warmed by 0.85 °C since pre-industrial times. With a rise of 2 °C the world will probably still be stable enough for human life although we can expect serious problems. Wet regions will become wetter and dry ones dryer. The Arctic will be ice-free in summer. Sea level rise will affect many communities. Agriculture will be adversely affected. With a rise of 3 or 4 °C life for both people and the rest of the biosphere looks increasingly problematic. In general the poorer regions of the world are the most vulnerable and will find it most difficult to adapt. If 6 °C is reached the outlook looks grim indeed.

Serious floods are more likely as climate change worsens

Is it too late?

CO_2 emissions and average temperatures are both still rising. The temperature increase is currently on course to reach 2 °C by 2050 and 4-6 °C by 2100. We can't stop climate change but swift action could stop the worst effects. Emissions need to peak before 2020 if there is to be any chance of limiting temperature rise to 2 °C.

In wealthy countries like the UK, this means that emissions need to reduce by somewhere between 3% and 10% a year.[6] This is an unprecedented task. The challenges are economic, political, technical and personal. The solutions are likely to involve a combination of:

- development of a low-carbon economy;
- social and political changes;
- better energy efficiency;
- reducing the demand for energy;
- use of new technologies;
- personal and behavioural changes.

The bigger picture

Climate change is not the only problem. It is part of a bigger picture. Work by Johan Rockström and colleagues identifies nine 'planetary boundaries'.[7] These describe the conditions that have allowed human civilisation to flourish for the last 10,000 years. Currently three of these boundaries have been breached: climate change, biodiversity loss and the nitrogen cycle.

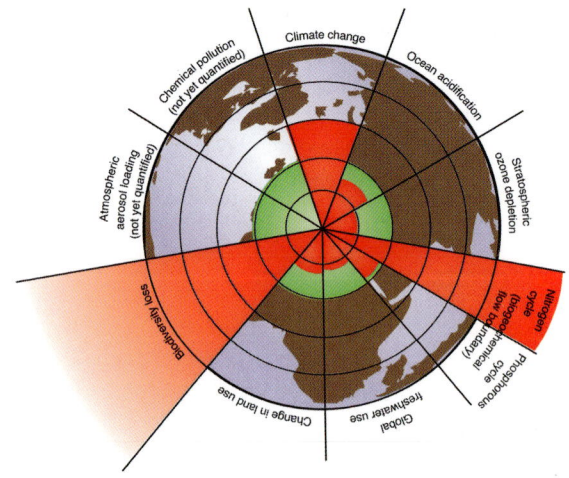

Johan Rockström's planetary boundaries

Rockström emphasises the interdependence of these systems – degrade one and you undermine the others. Since the 1950s all these systems have been under pressure. Oxfam researcher Kate Raworth extends Rockström's ideas, arguing that humanity needs more than an environmentally safe space.[8] At present, some people are putting more pressure on the planet than others: around 50% of the world's carbon emissions are created by just 11% of the world's people. Raworth argues that the environmentally safe space also needs to be socially just. Her doughnut diagram adds people's needs for food, water, energy, health and education.

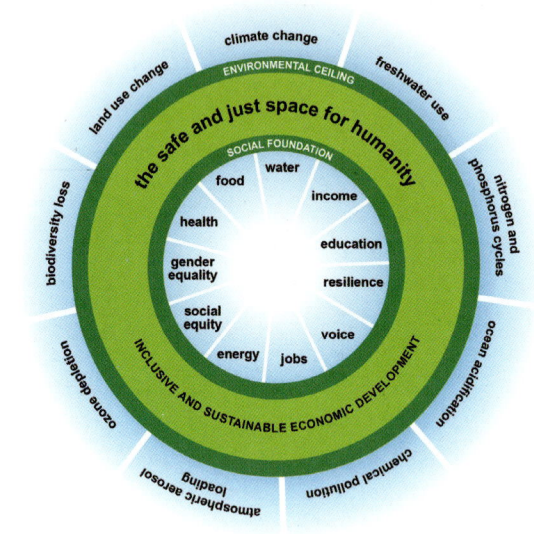

In her view, inequality is the key problem. She makes a good case that dealing with most of the problems on the inside of the doughnut would cost

Kate Raworth: a safe and just space for humanity

very little in terms of carbon emissions if inequality was tackled. The lives of the world's richest consumers would have to change the most, but the lives of people on average incomes in the UK would need to change too. In global terms many of us are wealthier than we think.

The economic system that drives these pressures also needs to change. Capitalism has brought innovation and progress but it is deeply implicated both in threats to the natural world and in inequality. Exactly how it should – or could – change is a matter for debate, as we explore in Chapter Five.

In the meantime your carbon footprint is a good measure of your impact on the world. If you can lower it, you will also lower your impact on the rest of the earth's resources.

Why is change so hard?

Surveys show that most people are concerned about climate change.[9] When you ask people whose responsibility it is to take action however, their replies are mixed. Most people think they have some personal responsibility but as you get specific and ask them what they might do, the number prepared to act drops. Most prefer to see national governments or the international community, as mainly responsible.

Perhaps we all secretly hope that someone else will carry the can. Perhaps – as we see the changes needed – we are overwhelmed. Maybe we are unwilling to give up a lifestyle we enjoy. Maybe our lives are so enmeshed in high carbon use we just can't see a way to change. Maybe we feel that our lifestyles are modest and not to blame. Maybe the whole subject makes us so anxious we would rather not think about it at all.

Shared responsibility

The reality is that action is needed from many players. The diagram 'Shared responsibility' shows one way of thinking about this.

Globally, governments need to make international agreements. At home, they need to set national policies and enforce them. They need to invest in things like new public transport systems, upgrades to the housing stock and upgrades to the national grid. They need to set frameworks that will encourage business to develop low-carbon alternatives and make it easy for householders to adopt them. Business needs to learn how to live without fossil fuels. It needs to invest in the technologies that will deliver the low-carbon goods and services that people will need in the future.

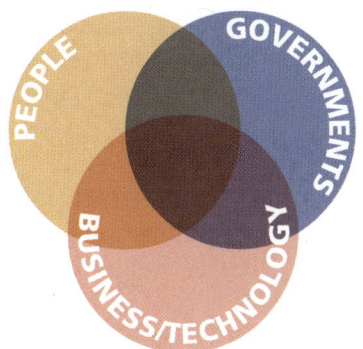

Shared responsibility

But people also need to change. Figures from the International Energy Authority show that in the developed world individuals and households are responsible for almost half their country's emissions.[10] We have to shift our expectations and reduce our demands. A new public transport system is no use if people refuse to use it. And no amount of policy or technology change can get over the fact that most people in the UK need to lead lives that have less impact. People and their lifestyles matter.

❝ The last time I went to Jamaica I was in my teens. It sounds so different there now – the weather is so unpredictable and people find it harder to get fresh water. We were so worried about my Gran when the last hurricane happened, as she lives up in the hills and might not have been able to get help. The phone lines were down too. She was fine, but I worry about next time. People need to see that what we do here and what happens to people we love back home is linked. We live in only one world and it's all connected.

Denzel Gordon

carbonconversations.org

Harm is not obvious

Many people find it difficult to accept that their lives will have to change. One reason is that the impact of our lifestyles is not obvious. We don't see the consequences of our everyday actions. For example, it's unusual to be aware of:

- the wars fought in the Congo, caused by mining the minerals used in our mobile phones;
- the devastation of the Aral Sea, which dried out as the water was taken to grow the cotton for our T-shirts;
- the air pollution caused in China as a result of manufacturing our fridges, TVs and furniture.[11]

Another reason is the intricate way in which our personal lives are entwined in global systems. It can feel as if you don't have much choice. For example:

- modern jobs often demand flexibility and a long commute;
- there are few food shops apart from the big supermarket chains;
- it's hard to know where the raw materials that make up products have come from;
- a normal social life often depends on high levels of consumption.

The facts hurt

But a third reason is that it is painful to take in the information. When people are made aware by a tragedy hitting the news, they are usually appalled. When a factory in Bangladesh making cheap clothes for UK shops collapsed in 2013, killing over 1,000 of the workers, there was widespread shock and revulsion in the UK. Most people had not asked themselves how their clothes could cost so little.

As the news passes, people quickly return to normal life. It's easy to feel defeated by the complexity of the systems we are caught up in and the lack of alternatives. Most of us neither change our shopping habits, nor become involved in campaigns to change the clothing industry. It is hard to be reminded every time you buy a pair of socks that someone has suffered to make them for you. Most of us prefer not to think about these difficult problems for very long.

❝ I cried when I heard about the recent cyclone in Bangladesh. On the news I saw families whose homes were under water, huddled on the roofs waiting to be rescued. Sometimes they get bitten by snakes living in the roofs and many children have died from this. The people who lose their lives, homes and jobs are usually the poorest – haven't they suffered enough? Climate change is making lives so difficult all over the world. We shouldn't just send money and forget about it – we need to ask what we can do every day to reduce the impact of climate change.

Luthfa Khatun

❝ We are worried about climate change in China. The River Yangtze flooded recently, but there are areas in the north which are so dry they will become desert soon. Yet now, like the West, we care more for economic growth than the land and water around us.

Dr Rong Shu

Climate change is no different. It feels distant. It's not happening now. It's not happening on my street. It's a more abstract worry than how to put dinner on the table or pay the gas bill. If you allow yourself to think about it deeply, it is likely to make you anxious and troubled. You may worry about the future for yourself, your children or grandchildren. You may feel angry at the global systems that hold everything in place. You may feel guilty about your own comfortable lifestyle. You may feel powerless to have much effect. Faced with these kinds of feelings most of us look for ways of feeling a little bit better.

Avoiding the truth

When people talk of climate change denial, they are usually thinking of people who believe that climate change is not occurring. But there are more subtle forms of denial and most of us use them, at least some of the time, to protect ourselves from a painful truth. You may be familiar with this state of mind. When something happens which is disappointing, alarming or downright life-changing you seem to simultaneously know it and not know it at all. One part of your mind acknowledges the reality. Another part behaves as if it isn't true. Therapists call this form of denial 'disavowal'.[12] The awkward knowledge is placed in a separate box and treated as if it can be forgotten, is unimportant or insignificant. For example amongst teenagers who have failed an important exam one may start by saying that it can't be true and then try to convince herself the result is a mistake. Another may tell you that she doesn't care, that it doesn't matter or that she didn't need the qualification anyway. If you try to raise the subject they will become irritated or avoid the conversation. Similarly people who are threatened with redundancy may try to persuade themselves that they won't be one of those affected, carry on spending as if it's not true, say they don't really care or minimise the likely impacts. With climate change people will typically acknowledge the facts but:

Deny their meaning: "I don't think it's that serious."

Deny the implications: "People have coped with worse in the past. I doubt it will affect us much in the UK."

Deny the connection to their own lives: "It's not my responsibility – it's down to government."

Deny their emotional significance: "I'm not bothered – I've got more important things to worry about."

Deny the practical significance: "I know it's happening but I can't change my life because of it."

Deny the irreversibility: "I'm sure it can be sorted out later/we can adapt/science will find an answer."

> ❝ I remember sitting in a lecture about climate change and feeling overwhelmed. I felt afraid, it seemed surreal, like a Sci-Fi film. It took me several weeks to accept the reality. I didn't want to believe it. I did my own research, hoping I could find something which showed that there was a solution in hand. It was the severity, the scale, the certainty of the impact and the realisation that we weren't doing enough that was so frightening. Coming to terms with it meant thinking about the skills I had which might make a difference – finding a way to do something instead of being overwhelmed.
>
> Pam Candea

carbonconversations.org

Often people overestimate the changes they are making, or try to strike bargains with themselves:

- "I do eat meat, but it's all organic."
- "I know my flights are bad, but I cycle to work, so I'm sure it equals out."
- "The car's bigger than we need but it means I can collect manure for the garden."

People on low incomes, who have small footprints, may feel furious that those who have enjoyed a high-carbon lifestyle are stamping on their aspirations:

- "I've saved all my life for this cruise and now these green idiots are telling me I shouldn't go."
- "Why shouldn't I have a nice car, a decent home and a foreign holiday? I've worked hard for this."
- "People like me struggle to put food on the table – why should I suffer to clear up the mess other people have created?"

Anxiety, guilt and identity

When we interviewed some people about how they tried to live low-carbon lives, their replies were interesting. Several of them avoided simple behavioural changes because they were a reminder of their painful feelings about climate change:

- "Doing this kind of stuff makes me feel anxious – it makes me think about climate change and then I can feel that it's all hopeless. Frankly, if I'm truthful, I'd rather not think about it and constantly remembering to do things like not overfilling the kettle reminds me."
- "What about the times I forgot? I'd just feel so guilty. I'd think about all that carbon dioxide whooshing up into the atmosphere."

❝ Understanding what climate change meant was a two-stage process for me. It was part of a general political awakening at university – reading Naomi Klein's No Logo and attending lectures on international environmental law – and I remember feeling angry but otherwise it was quite an intellectual understanding. It was only later that I realized how serious it was, when I read a paper by Kevin Anderson and Alice Bows, two climate scientists from the Tyndall Centre. I remember literally rolling around on the office floor groaning and feeling overwhelmed and powerless. I felt despair at that point and it took a while to find my focus again.

Rich Hawkins

❝ My concern about climate change is deeply connected to my feelings about social justice and people's well-being. Mostly I don't think too much about how it makes me feel but it can catch up with me. Deep in your heart there's a great sadness and once you begin to talk, it all comes out. Mostly, I compartmentalize, I intellectualise. It protects me and helps me to carry on. You have to keep going. I find encouragement from people's responses to the work I do with Common Cause and from the rewards of seeing small changes.

Elena Blackmore

Others found that apparently simple behaviours were meshed with their sense of themselves or were a way of coping with another problem. One man always filled the kettle to the top when he was at work. This was a way of getting a slightly longer break from his desk – stealing a few extra minutes from his employer. Putting in just the right amount of water removed his daydreaming time or left him hanging around in the kitchen feeling anxious that he would be challenged. An older woman overfilled the kettle in order always to be sure there was enough for anyone who happened to turn up. Putting in just the right amount of water made her feel she was being selfish. Her behaviour was deeply connected to her sense of herself as a generous person.

More complicated actions – such as choosing to holiday in the UK instead of abroad, or using savings to upgrade the house – involve negotiations with family or friends. One woman told me sadly that she and her husband had agreed to holiday separately this year – he would not forgo his foreign holiday and she did not feel she had a good reason to step on a plane. Few people go this far. They are more likely to find themselves mired in, or avoiding, difficult conversations. We discuss this further in Chapter Six.

It can help to acknowledge that it is painful to face climate change and complicated to alter your lifestyle. Some people feel ashamed that they are not living up to their ideals. Some people feel resentful of others who they think are judging them. Some people feel upset by a critical, inner voice that tells them they ought to do more than they easily can. Guilt is often a cruel and paralysing emotion. It can be more useful to think in terms of mobilising your concern. Empathy for others, a sense of your relationship to the rest of the natural world and a proportionate sense of responsibility are likely to be more helpful than a punishing sense of being weighed down by the wrongs of the world.

Finding motivation

Exploring your positive motivations for acting on climate change can help you move away from feelings of guilt and shame. Discussing motivation with others can help you appreciate the many different sources of strength people use.

Connection to the natural world

Some people's motivation comes from a sense of connectedness to the rest of the natural world. They may feel a deep sense of awe and wonder at nature. Sometimes this is a spiritual or religious connection. They may draw on beliefs about stewardship of the natural world or about people's rightful place in the universe. Sometimes the connection is an ethical one. Some people feel that all living creatures have an equal right to life. They see nature as valuable in its own right, regardless of its use to people. Sometimes the connection is an aesthetic one, combining a sense of wonder with appreciation of nature's power and beauty.

> *I loved being outside as a kid. I grew up surrounded by forests. Age 17 I went to Costa Rica and the cloud forest and the vibrancy of nature blew my mind. It was nature on steroids – energy and life everywhere you looked. If you sat down for a week the forest would have grown you into it, covered you in moss, taken you over. I came back obsessed, with a passion for nature and knew I wanted to be a conservation biologist*
>
> Rebecca Miller

Justice and equality

Some people's motivation comes from a sense of justice and the desire for equality. Sometimes this draws on existing political views and desire for change. For some people the connections to poverty and exploitation make climate change a natural field for concern. For others the focus is more on a sense of one's own good fortune and the desire to help others.

Enlightened self-interest

Some people's motivation arises from a sense of enlightened self-interest and the feeling that it would be stupid not to act on climate change. Who on earth would want a 4 °C world? The desire for security is often part of this, as is a concern for one's children and future generations. Being able to imagine and empathise with the lives of others is a powerful influence for some.

Challenge and creativity

Some people may see creative openings or business opportunities – the win-win of "good for me and good for the planet". Others may enjoy the sense of purpose that comes with a new project, the pleasure of rising to a challenge and the satisfaction of a task well done.

What about you? Reflect for a moment on what draws you to act on climate change.

Most people find they have a mix of motives pulling them to act on climate change, alongside a mix of motives that make them turn away from action. Principles and values can be hard to live up to. Most people experience conflict between their ideals and other factors in their lives. The conflict may be between:

- a value and a desire ("I care about the natural world but I love to travel and see it for myself");
- a value and the way society is organized ("I care about the environment but I can't get to work without driving)";
- two opposing values ("I want to reduce my footprint but I need to visit my mother in Pakistan").

> Islam teaches that we are all 'khalifas' or 'stewards', responsible for the welfare of the earth. But to me, saying we should take care of our environment is just common sense.
>
> **Allis Karim**

> It's about justice and equality – these things have always been important to me politically. I want to preserve a world for my children and other people's children too. Losing the richness of the natural world is about losing a human experience.
>
> **Tony Wragg**

> All living things are interconnected. We are part of nature and nature is part of us. There is no separation. We must live more simply and act in harmony with other people and species.
>
> **Venerable Samitha, Buddhist monk**

carbonconversations.org

Thinking about a low-carbon future

Technology, governments and individuals should all play a part in a low-carbon future, but one of the key issues to consider is fairness. Are there countries, organisations or classes of people who could easily use less fossil fuel? Are there some who need to catch up and burn a little more? Who are the big polluters?

What is a fair share?

Different countries produce different amounts of CO_2. People in the developed world are the biggest polluters. The United States, has 5% of world population, but is responsible for about 25% of global CO_2 emissions. Here are some figures for average CO_2 emissions per person each year:

Annual per capita emissions	
USA	20 tonnes
UK	15 tonnes
India	1.5 tonnes
Tanzania	0.3 tonnes
World average	**4 tonnes**

You will see both lower and higher figures than these for per person carbon footprints.[13] Many of the lower figures don't take account of the emissions associated with international transport and with importing consumer goods and food. We've chosen to use some of the higher figures because we think they give a more realistic picture. Within countries, personal carbon footprints can vary a lot between different people. Income and wealth have a big impact – wealthier people usually have bigger footprints – but there are also variations with household size, age and region.[14]

At present, the world can absorb an estimated 2.5 tonnes of CO_2 per person each year. As the world population grows, this figure will fall to 1 or 1.5 tonnes per person per year. The UK's Climate Change Act commits the country to reducing carbon emissions by 80% from 1990 levels, by the year 2050. If this is achieved it should get the average carbon footprint down to around 2 tonnes. However, many scientists and environmentalists say these reductions need to happen sooner. They suggest we should aim for an individual limit of 1 or 2 tonnes per person, by 2030 at the latest.

Does carbon reduction mean giving up everything that makes 21st century life comfortable? No. But it does mean accepting some changes. Technology should be able to solve some of the problems but a low-carbon future will probably mean:

- fewer consumer goods;
- less travel;
- almost no air travel;
- highly insulated buildings;
- more local production of food and other goods;
- carbon taxes or carbon rationing.

What's in an average footprint?

The graph opposite shows what makes up the average, individual, UK carbon footprint.[15] What would you change to reduce it?

What is your carbon footprint?

If you join a Carbon Conversations group your facilitator will calculate a rough footprint with you. Then, as you go through the sessions, you will learn how to make a more accurate assessment of each of the four areas you can affect directly. If you're not part of a group, you can do the calculation yourself, using the program on the Carbon Conversations website. See More Information at the end of this chapter for details.

Will technology save us?

A lot of hopeful, technological ideas have been suggested for solving climate change. Some are realistic but…

Some are scientists' pipe-dreams

Impractical ideas include: increasing CO_2 take-up of the oceans using iron filings; reducing the effect of the sun by scattering tiny mirrors in the upper atmosphere; building solar-power stations in orbit that beam microwaves down to earth. Despite the risks of these geo-engineering solutions, they are being seriously considered by some.[16]

Some are a long way in the future

Carbon capture at coal-fired power-stations, new nuclear power stations, and huge solar power stations in the Sahara connecting to northern Europe by a new high-tech grid may all help, but not soon enough.

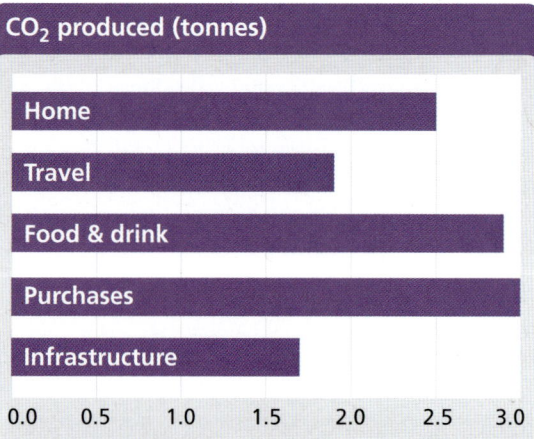

CO_2 produced (tonnes)

Home (UK average: 2.5 tonnes)
Someone who lives at high temperatures in a large, un-insulated, under-occupied home with old appliances, might be responsible for 5 tonnes CO_2. Someone who lives in a highly insulated, fully occupied home with efficient appliances used carefully, might be responsible for only 0.5 tonnes.

Travel (UK average: 3.5 tonnes)
Driving 10,000 miles per year will produce 3-4 tonnes of CO_2. A return flight to New York will create 3 tonnes of CO_2. Cycling to work and using trains may produce less than 0.5 tonnes.

Food & drink (UK average: 3 tonnes)
Eating a diet heavy in meat and dairy, using a lot of processed and imported food might create 5 tonnes of CO_2. A non-meat, non-dairy diet with no processed food, 75% from local sources (with the rest imported by sea only) might produce only 0.5 tonnes of CO_2.

Purchases (UK average: 3.5 tonnes)
Spending £5,000 a year on carbon intensive purchases such as a new car or home improvements will produce 5 tonnes CO_2. Spending the same amount of money on less carbon intensive purchases such as clothing, services (cleaning, gardening, education, health services) phone calls and IT will produce 1.5 – 2 tonnes CO_2.

Infrastructure and public services (UK average: 2.5 tonnes)
The government emits CO_2 for you by building roads, hospitals, schools etc.

Some bring their own problems

Biofuel is a good example of a solution with unintended consequences. Biofuels from plant sources such as corn and palm trees can be used instead of oil to make diesel. Wood chips can be used to replace coal in power stations, as is being done at Drax in the UK. There are problems however.[17] Most countries cannot grow enough biofuels to replace oil. Providing biofuel for UK road transport alone would require four times more arable land than the UK has in total. Sourcing biofuels overseas doesn't help either. Felling tropical forests to plant palm oil for biofuel results in an overall increase in greenhouse gas emissions as CO_2 is released from the soil. Large-scale wood-burning is polluting in itself and is causing damage to the ecosystems of the forests that are being felled to supply the wood. Meanwhile, world food prices have been pushed up as US farmers have switched from growing food to growing biofuels. Biofuels could play a helpful role in a low-carbon future, if they were limited to a small percentage of current demand.

Some might help

High-quality insulation materials, solar thermal panels, photo-voltaics, wind and wave power, more efficient cars and electric cars all show real promise. The difficult issue that has to be faced however is our high demand for energy. Technology can only help if we reduce this.

Finding the right policies

Regulation in one form or another will be necessary in moving to a low-carbon future.[18] Poor countries need help to reach a decent standard of living for their people. Rich countries need help to curb their excess consumption. Some schemes need to be international. Others can be imposed by individual nations. CO_2 can be controlled:

- upstream, i.e. close to where fossil fuels are extracted or burnt in power stations; or
- downstream, i.e. close to the end-users (the people putting petrol in their cars or heating their homes, and the companies making goods for people to use).

Many of the schemes proposed for tackling climate change rely on energy efficiency and the power of markets for their effects. Energy efficiency rarely delivers all it promises because of the rebound effect while market-based systems don't tackle the underlying problem of unchecked economic growth. These are often hot topics for discussion in Carbon Conversation groups and we explain them further below.

Taxation

Taxation can encourage companies or individuals to be more fuel-efficient and the proceeds can be used to fund big projects (like wave or wind power or public transport). Taxation can be imposed either upstream, on oil companies and coal mines, or downstream on individuals and companies.

Investment

Many of the technological solutions need investment. Work by the New Economics Foundation suggests ways of doing this that would bring much needed work to local communities.[19]

Carbon budgets, rationing and caps

The 2013 report of the Intergovernmental Panel on Climate Change gave an estimate for the first time of the amount of carbon that can safely be burned if the world is to keep within a 2 °C limit.[20] Their estimates suggest that most of the known coal, oil and gas reserves need to be left in the ground. This suggests that the right to emit CO_2 needs to be rationed. Rationing can also be done upstream or downstream. Upstream rationing is usually referred to as a cap on the production of oil or coal, or a cap on the amount of CO_2 that an industry is allowed to emit.

The moment the idea of carbon budgets and rationing is introduced every country, industry and individual has their own idea of what a fair system would look like. Who should use less? Who should be allowed more? What is just? What is fair? Arguments about what a fair system would be and who should pay for it have bedevilled international negotiations for years.[21]

Carbon trading and individual allowances

Caps and rationing can be made more palatable, and possibly more efficient, by allowing carbon allowances to be traded. In carbon trading schemes a cap is placed on the amount of pollution allowed, firms are allocated a certain number of credits and have to buy more if they pollute above their allocation. Firms who do well can sell their credits. Such schemes are dependent on the cap being accurate. The example of the European Emissions Trading Scheme has not been encouraging so far.[22]

You will also come across proposals for individual tradable carbon allowances. Here, each person would be given a carbon budget. Any purchases of petrol, gas, electricity or airline tickets would use up some of that person's allowance for that year.[23] The complexity of such schemes means that so far they have not found favour with governments.

Paying for nature's support systems

Another market-based solution places monetary value on nature's support systems, such as forests, as a way of recognising their importance, encouraging their protection and reducing the emissions that come through their misuse or degradation.[24] This is seen as a way of providing help to the Global South whose forests are often at risk of destruction. Critics make ethical objections to this but also practical ones. While it may be possible to put a price on the timber itself and on the forest's role as a carbon sink and flood defence, it is harder to price the forest's intrinsic value. Putting a price on it may actually be the next step towards further exploitation as these hard-to-measure benefits are ignored.

The problem of rebound

Many technical and policy solutions rely on energy efficiency as their key mechanism. The assumption is that increased efficiency will reduce the use of energy. In practice however, increased efficiency often leads to greater use. This phenomenon is called the rebound effect.[25] A simple example of direct rebound is the fact that as engines become more efficient, cars go further for the same amount of petrol and so drivers are happy to make longer journeys. Another example at the domestic level happens when someone saves money through insulating their house and then uses that money to take a flight. This is usually referred to as indirect rebound. Slightly more complex examples see industry making larger cars as they become cheaper to run and markets for consumer goods expanding as their falling prices make them accessible to more people. In both cases, the overall amount of energy used in the economy may not reduce as a result of the efficiencies. Occasionally energy savings are completely wiped out by increased use. This is usually called 'backfire'.

The extent of the rebound effect is hotly debated, but there is no doubt that it exists and that it is one of the reasons why improvements in efficiency have not seen the reductions in CO_2 that were hoped for.

Growth, contentment and GDP

Increasingly researchers are connecting environmental issues with wider global problems. Inequality, climate change, the financial crisis and numerous other problems seem to be connected. Some see economic growth itself as the problem: in a finite world, how can we go on expanding our use of natural resources?[26] Some focus on justice and equality. They argue that the economic system has unfairness built into it, allowing some countries and some people to prosper at the expense of others.[27] Some blame out-of-control global companies. The enthusiasm of oil giants like Shell and Gazprom for exploiting tar sands and the oil beneath the arctic, certainly suggests that market mechanisms may not be enough to deal with them. We discuss these issues further in Chapter Five. For now, take a look at the graph. High-spending, materialistic societies – the ones with high CO_2 emissions – don't produce contented populations.

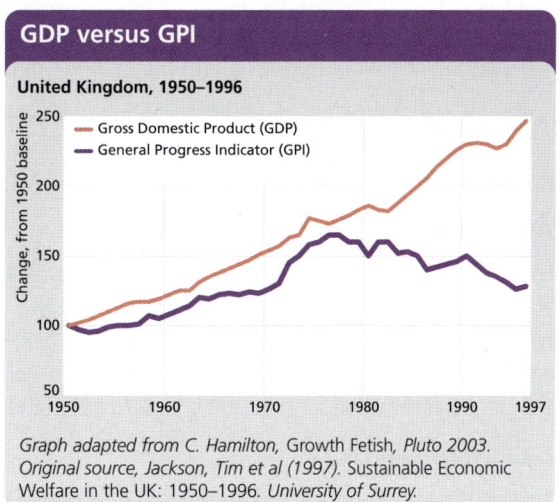

Graph adapted from C. Hamilton, Growth Fetish, Pluto 2003. Original source, Jackson, Tim et al (1997). Sustainable Economic Welfare in the UK: 1950–1996. University of Surrey.

CO_2 emissions are closely linked to a country's Gross Domestic Product (GDP). The more economic activity, the more CO_2 is produced. An increase in GDP is usually seen as a good thing, bringing more jobs, better goods and services and greater happiness. However countries with high GDP don't necessarily score well when quality of life is measured. A General Progress Indicator (GPI)[28] or Measure of Domestic Progress (MDP) score adjusts GDP by correcting it for costs that do not improve wellbeing or the health of the environment. The costs of dealing with pollution, road accidents or health problems like obesity are usually counted as part of GDP because they are part of the country's economic activity. When you take them out, the picture changes. The graph shows how GPI and GDP have changed in the UK since 1950.

Visions of the future

Since people started telling stories, we have frightened ourselves with dystopias – tales of impending doom – and comforted ourselves with utopias – dreams of an ideal future. The utopias often express longing for a lost past which it is hoped will return or at least provide inspiration for the future. The Romans dreamed of a Golden Age. Christianity mourned the loss of the Garden of Eden. The 18th Century Romantics yearned for pre-industrial rural life. More recently, you will find people who turn to a Palaeolithic diet or to other pre-industrial cultures for

> *I would like to have children and I've been thinking about the impact that each new life brings to the planet. The way that I have my children will be driven by my environmental thinking. I'd like to have one of our own – it's strong, that urge, I couldn't miss that out – and to adopt two.*
>
> Rebecca Miller

carbonconversations.org

inspiration. There is a desire to find a way of life more in tune with nature, a belief that it existed somewhere in the past, and a powerful desire to re-create it, that runs through our culture.[29] The dystopias often represent the dark sides of ourselves that we fear will escape and do harm, or our sense of powerlessness in the face of forces stronger than ourselves.

When people look to the past as a model for the future they often make this same split. Remembering my own childhood, I tell one story about the freedom to play out, the lack of traffic, more abundant wildlife and a slower pace of life. In another story I put the sexism, the misogyny, the slum housing, the racism and prejudice that feed my more dystopian imaginings.

It can be difficult to think about the future without bringing in both the longing for a lost ideal and the fear of horrors to come. The insecurity that climate change brings can push us to focus too much on our dreams and nightmares and make it hard to think realistically about what we want and about what might be feasible in a low-carbon future.

In the section below we describe some practical attempts to think about low-carbon futures. They are too detailed to describe fully here but all are available online and you may find it helpful to explore them further.

2050 pathways

The government's *2050 Pathways Project*[30] looks at how to produce an 80% reduction in CO_2 by balancing energy supply and demand in the UK. A tool on their website allows you to play with different combinations of fuels such as nuclear, renewables, gas, coal and oil and different amounts of building renovation and reduction in demand. There is a simple tool which anyone can use, a version for schools and a detailed explanation for professionals.

A self-sufficient UK?

Also on the national scale, the Centre for Alternative Technology has published a series of reports called *Zero Carbon Britain: Re-thinking the Future*.[31] Their main focus is to explore how Britain could become carbon neutral and self-sufficient, but they are also concerned with long-term sustainability and biodiversity. They look at land use, diet, energy supply and transport. They describe a world of much reduced demand which nonetheless maintains a high quality of life. This Britain is powered by renewable energy, imports little food, eats a low-meat diet and travels much less than at present. *Zero Carbon Britain* makes it clear that there will be losses in a low-carbon future as well as gains. Most people won't fly, parts of the landscape will change and some goods and services will be more expensive.

Five global scenarios

The report *Climate Futures* from the charity Forum for the Future[32] deals with a number of 'what-ifs'. What would the world be like in 2030 if:

> **❝** I think a carbon neutral world could increase economic equality. Small cities and towns could become renewable energy hubs that create jobs locally, rather than spending revenues on foreign oil imports. These new 'clean' revenues could be spent on important issues such as care services and education. There is the potential to create a truly global village, a more altruistic, tolerant and welcoming world for everyone.
>
> Euri Vidal

- We make a rapid, high-tech transformation immediately?
- Carbon became the most expensive commodity in the world?
- Progress is redefined as well-being?
- Action is left very late?
- International agreements fail?

The five scenarios analyse current trends and look at different ways in which climate change, public attitudes, business, the global economy, natural resources, technology and political responses might interact and produce quite different futures for the world. Some of the scenarios create an individualistic, consumerist society while others do better at tackling inequality. Some feature high-tech solutions. Others go for low-tech options. Some are more stable than others. Some threaten civil liberties. One sees the breakdown of international co-operation followed by resource wars. Some of the scenarios have quite negative features, but they will help you think about the seriousness and complexity of the situation.

Teasing out the detail

If you are interested in the details of how the world might quickly make the reductions in carbon that are needed, the report from the Tyndall Centre's *Radical Emission Reduction Conference*[33] is a fascinating read. Here you will find experts from economics, housing, transport, technology, psychology and many more disciplines discussing what needs to be done. The collection of articles in *Living in a Low-Carbon Society in 2050*, edited by Horace Herring is also good on the detail and features four short stories as well as more academic responses.[34]

What do *you* imagine?

Thinking about the future matters because it helps you to have a political voice. There are difficult choices to be made and most of us resist changes we fear will disadvantage us. Do you prefer wind turbines or nuclear power? How do you feel about the countryside changing as different crops are grown? How do you feel about being priced out of flying somewhere warm for your holidays? How would you feel if regulations brought restrictions on civil liberties?

Sometimes a feature that one person sees as an advantage fills another with horror. Would you welcome a reduction in travel because it would bring quieter streets and closer communities? Or would you hate the restriction on your freedom and the parochialism of small-town life?

In any future there are likely to be winners and losers and it seems to be human nature to bury ourselves in unrealistic dreams or terrifying nightmares. Try taking a look at the reports we suggest, talking with friends, family and colleagues and deciding what you think would be a realistic future you could live with.

> **❝** *I grew up in the 1950s which was roughly a four-tonne world. Holidays were camping or caravanning and felt very exciting. At six I could walk to school with a friend and at eleven, cross Bristol by train and bus. A birthday party meant a few friends to tea with cake and jelly. There are some things from that period that I would have in my low-carbon future – more public transport, less pointless consumption and a slowing down of life. There are some things I wouldn't want – cold lino, no showers, the small-mindedness, sexism, racism and homophobia.*
>
> **Jane Orton**

- How do you imagine a low-carbon future?
- What would you look forward to in it?
- What would you dislike about it?
- What would you miss from the present?

Setting a realistic goal

The rest of this book is concerned with the changes that individuals can make now – their contribution to the 80% reduction in emissions that needs to be made. Government and industry need to supply:

- changes in energy supply, switching from coal- and gas-fired power stations to renewable sources;
- energy-efficient workplaces, and longer-lasting, more efficient goods;
- better public transport;
- a halt to road-building and airport expansion;
- reductions in emissions from government activity.

Individuals, families and communities need to do the rest.

Aim to halve your footprint

We suggest you put to one side the 2.5 tonnes that the government emits on your behalf. Then – if you have an average footprint – aim for a limit of about 6 tonnes in the rest of your life – and see how close to that goal you can get. Divided evenly, this would give you a target of about 1.5 tonnes for each of the four areas of your footprint – home energy, travel and transport, food and drink, and other purchases.

If your footprint is larger than average, ignore the 2.5 tonnes of government-related emissions and try to halve the rest. For example if your starting point is a 25 tonne footprint you should aim for about 11 tonnes.

If your footprint is smaller than average, you are already on the journey. Aim for 6 tonnes.

Don't expect to achieve your goal immediately. Many changes need to be planned and can't all happen at once. People who take part in Carbon Conversations groups typically achieve a three tonne reduction fairly quickly. There is then a slower process of organising the harder changes. Four or five years would be a reasonable time-scale for reaching these targets.

If you take part in a Carbon Conversations group you will be able to get support in making these changes. The rest of this book provides the background you need in order to measure your emissions accurately and make some realistic reductions.

How to count carbon

The average carbon footprint is made up of:

- direct emissions – which come from burning fossil fuels like oil, gas or coal in you boiler, your stove or your car;
- indirect emissions – which come from burning fossil fuels to make electricity;
- embodied emissions – which come from the fuels used to make manufactured goods, services and food;
- CO_2 equivalents for the other greenhouse gases, nitrogen oxides (which come from burning fuels), methane (which mostly comes from agriculture) and fluorocarbons (found in some parts of industry and some refrigeration systems).[35]

It's relatively straightforward to measure your own direct and indirect emissions. Reading your gas and electricity meters, checking how much petrol you buy and counting the mileage from journeys made by train, bus, ferry and plane will give you quite an accurate figure. If you're taking part in a Carbon Conversations group you will find detailed advice in your *Workbook* on how to monitor these emissions.

It's a little harder to calculate the impact of food and other goods and services. Researchers have two ways of going about this. These are sometimes called 'bottom-up' or 'cradle to grave' analysis and 'top-down' or 'input-output' analysis.

A bottom up/cradle-to-grave analysis looks at each stage in the manufacture of an item and works out the energy used at each stage. Accuracy is limited if the emissions of some components are not known. There tend to be underestimates where good data is not available. As more and more products have their emissions calculated, the process becomes easier and more accurate. This method is particularly useful for showing the differences between similar products.

A top down/input-output analysis starts from national and industry statistics for the inputs to each industry sector and uses this to work out the total amount of fuel and emissions that belong to their outputs. Estimates have to be made for the emissions from imported goods and added to the totals. It's harder with this method to distinguish between the emissions from similar products but it's less prone to missing emissions.

This book uses results taken from both approaches. The data on food is mostly from bottom-up analyses of the CO_2e embodied in particular products. For the rest of the goods and services you buy, our main source is top-down, input-output analysis.

Star ratings

As you go through the book you will come across charts with lists of possible carbon-reducing actions each with a star-rating against it. People often ask: "How much carbon will I save by insulating my loft/giving up meat/taking the train instead of the car?" It is very difficult to give an accurate answer. The carbon saved by insulating a loft will be different depending on the size of your house, the amount of insulation already present, other energy-saving measures taken and how you deal with the rebound effect. Our solution to this is to show the relative merits of different changes by giving each one a star rating. One star is a small saving, five stars is a big one. Remembering to turn appliances off stand-by makes a small saving. Giving up meat makes a big one. In general, each extra star doubles the savings.[36]

The process of change

You're probably clear by now that the changes required by climate change are serious ones. They involve more than just changing a few light bulbs or taking the occasional trip by train. We may not always like change but life is full of it and most people have their own ways of approaching it. It may help to think about how you have handled:

- **Transition points** – such as changing school, leaving home, starting a new job, getting married, a new baby, children leaving home, retirement;
- **Crisis points** – such as financial difficulties, illness, divorce, redundancy, family conflict, bereavement;
- **Good resolutions** – such as working harder at school, doing a fair share of the housework, weight loss and exercise programmes, reducing alcohol or drug use.

You will probably find that the way you handled the change depended on:

- the amount of control you had over it – whether the change came as the result of choice, necessity or coercion;

- who else was involved – the opposition or support you received;
- the social pressures for or against the change.

Where the change was a chosen one, your success was probably dependent on:

- the strength of your motivation;
- how you prepared for the change, anticipated and planned how to deal with difficulties;
- how you managed your mixed feelings about making the change and dealt with your own resistance;
- the amount of support you had and the way you used this;
- how you negotiated conflicts and pressures from others, both those who supported you and those who may have opposed you.

Change often involves coming to terms with loss. This is obvious with bereavement or redundancy where change is forced on you. Here, shock, anger and the slow, painful processes of grief are inevitable. But it is also true in changes you welcome or plan. Taking one path means letting go of another and there is often a lingering regret for the path not chosen. The new path may be difficult. Sadness, anger and frustration can be likely accompaniments as well as a sense of satisfaction and achievement.

In the Carbon Conversations groups we try to create a safe space where people feel free to talk, without fear of judgment. We encourage people to talk about the strong and mixed feelings prompted by taking carbon reduction seriously. It's important to acknowledge that these mixed feelings exist. You may feel upset to realise the extent of your contribution to climate change. You may feel very sad if you decide to give up flights to places you've loved. You may feel anger towards friends and colleagues who remain unconcerned. If you push these feelings aside they will return in other forms. You may find yourself unable to stick to the changes you've planned, arguing yourself out of them or giving up in despair at the difficulties. If change is to stick, it has to be approached with recognition of what is involved practically, emotionally and socially too. Our experience is that when people are able to do this, then the outcomes are good.

❝ When I started thinking about this I felt it would be a steep hill. However, as time went by, I stuck to changes because they were good for me in some way. I think that change that happens gradually is more likely to last. There is nothing I do today that feels hard or unpleasant. I think it's important to start with the things that seem more appealing and stick to the things we enjoy, otherwise trying to change might backfire and we could tire and give up altogether.

Euri Vidal

❝ Making changes to reduce my carbon footprint makes me feel better but at times I feel overwhelmed – I have a big, draughty house and am limited financially. I tend to deal with this on my own but am inspired by the ideas of permaculture because it is such a positive philosophy. I can't let carbon reduction completely rule my life - it's a juggling act – but I have to feel OK that I am doing what I can. I will carry on because I feel that there isn't any other option.

Belinda Ellis

What about at work?

Although our main focus in this book is on people's personal carbon footprints, many of us also work and can be involved in helping to reduce carbon emissions at work. This can be both rewarding and frustrating but we hope you'll find some ideas and support in the section on workplaces in each chapter.

The core activities of some organisations contribute directly to climate change, for example, coal mining, oil and gas extraction, and electricity generation. Others emit a lot of CO_2 through their operations. All organisations have buildings and delivery costs. Global networks mean that many companies frequently fly staff to conferences and meetings abroad.

People working in some organisations may struggle to find alternative ways of working. Sometimes it's hard to envisage how products or services could be delivered in low-carbon ways. If a high-carbon activity is central to the organisation's purpose, it may feel quite impossible. Similarly if your sense of professional identity is bound up in the organisation you work for, being asked to consider that organisation in a completely different shape may make you feel deeply uncomfortable. You may resist making the imaginative leap. At the day-to-day level too, power, division of responsibility and rules at work can create frameworks in which people struggle to make a difference. Even working out how to turn the thermostat down in some workplaces can be a baffling experience and leave you feeling powerless and cynical.

However most organisations do have plans for reducing their emissions. Large organisations – e.g. supermarkets, water companies, banks, local authorities and all central government departments – are part of the Carbon Reduction Commitment Energy Efficiency Scheme under which they must monitor and report on their energy use, and pay a fixed amount for each tonne of CO_2 emitted. The scheme provides a financial incentive to reduce the emissions from direct use of energy in the organisation's buildings (though it doesn't cover travel, or the emissions from purchasing decisions, or the emissions from goods manufactured overseas). In part because of this incentive, most large organisations have published plans and strategies for reducing emissions. Smaller organisations may not be required to publish their emissions, but they can get advice and support from bodies like the Carbon Trust.

Some organisations go well beyond the legal requirements. Marks and Spencer, for example, has adopted 'Plan A'. This is a comprehensive corporate sustainability plan that includes challenging targets on waste reduction, fair trade, customer, employee and supplier involvement, and the use of natural resources.

The need for new technologies and business structures that will help reduce carbon emissions has created a growing green jobs sector. Here, small companies and social enterprises are being established in fields such as renewable energy, local food production and distribution, and green tourism.

Many of the jobs people did 50 years ago have disappeared and new ones have arrived. Some of the jobs we do today won't exist in the future and others will be transformed.

- What might your job look like in a low-carbon future? Will it exist? How might it have changed?
- What commitments has your workplace made to carbon reduction? Can you find out? What progress is being made?
- What changes would you most like to see in your workplace? Can you talk with colleagues about what you want?

 # Frequently asked questions

Hasn't the climate always changed? Isn't it just showing normal variation?

It's true that the climate has always changed. Scientists learn about changes over hundreds of thousands of years by studying ice cores from Greenland and Antarctica. Most of these changes have been caused by shifts in the sun's activity. The changes of the last 200 years are different however. They are much more extreme. Scientists have no doubt that they are caused by human activity and that they are dangerous.[37]

Are the devastating hurricanes, typhoons and droughts of recent years due to climate change?

We can't say definitely that a particular weather event is due to climate change but we can be sure that we're going to see more extreme events over the next decades. Hurricanes, typhoons, droughts and floods are likely to be more severe.[38] The capacity of governments to respond is critical. The 2011 drought in East Africa is thought to have been partially caused by climate change, but the effect on war torn Somalia was much more severe than on Kenya and Ethiopia where aid agencies were able to organise help.[39]

Why should we bother when the government is planning to build more airports and roads?

Government policy is certainly worrying. You may want to take political as well as personal action. Carbon Conversations often helps people find the confidence to speak up. Add your voice to those who are objecting.

Why should I bother when my neighbour drives an SUV?

Answers we have heard include: "because it's the right thing to do"; "because it makes me feel better"; "to live by example"; "to be prepared for changes that will have to come"; "to show I'm serious"; "to walk the walk, as well as talk the talk". Try talking to your neighbour!

Isn't China now producing as much CO_2 as the USA?

Yes it is. But per person their emissions are similar to the European average. A lot of China's emissions arise from manufacturing goods for Western countries, so really belong to our footprints, not theirs.[40]

What about the USA?

The US government has been a problem, as have the influential oil companies and the well-funded climate change deniers who have been very successful in influencing US opinion. But many Americans want to do something about climate change. Many US cities have signed up to the 'Mayors' Initiative' which aims for significant local reductions. In June 2014 President Obama's National Climate Assessment[41] set some limits on CO_2 emissions from power plants.

What's the difference between an ecological footprint and a carbon footprint?

An ecological footprint measures the amount of the earth's resources your lifestyle consumes.[42] It measures this in hectares, or by telling you how many planets would be needed if everyone in the world lived like you. UK lifestyles typically consume about three planets. A carbon footprint measures only the amount of greenhouse gases you are responsible for. It is measured in tonnes of CO_2 equivalents.

carbonconversations.org

Isn't 'Peak Oil' more important?

It's true that the world will eventually run out of oil and that we are currently passing the peak where more oil has been produced than can ever be produced again. The decrease in production this will bring won't happen quickly enough to solve the climate change problem however. As production from the most accessible oil fields slows, production from more difficult sources becomes profitable. Many of these, like the Canadian tar sands and the Arctic oil fields, carry huge environmental risks. There are also other fossil fuels to worry about. There are huge reserves of coal left and reserves of gas that can be extracted by the damaging process of hydraulic fracturing. Solving the climate change problem will deal with the peak oil problem but we can't expect peak oil to fix climate change. Fossil fuels need to be left in the ground. In order to prevent dangerous climate change 50 – 75% of the proven reserves need to be abandoned.[43]

Could 'fracking' for natural gas in the UK help reduce our emissions and provide energy security?

Natural gas has lower carbon emissions than coal but it is still a fossil fuel. We need to move quickly to genuinely low-carbon sources of fuel. Fracking for gas will divert investment from the renewables that need to be developed. The fact that the gas is produced in the UK is unlikely to make it cheaper or provide security as it will be sold on the international market.

I was shocked to see how tiny the Tanzanian footprint is. Surely they need to be using more energy not less?

You are right. There are big questions of justice and equality to be considered. One reason the West needs to reduce its footprint so much is to allow countries like Tanzania to catch up and create a decent standard of living for their people.[44]

Will climate change bring more immigrants and refugees to the UK?

There are connections between climate change and the movement of people but also a lot of myths. Most people who are displaced due to climate change will move within their own countries. There are unlikely to be sudden mass exoduses and the UK is unlikely to be a major destination for people who do need to move.[45]

Surely the big problem is population growth?

The relationship between population and climate change is complex. The key factor is not population itself but the resources that the population consumes. Countries with high population growth also tend to be poor. They contribute little to climate change because their resource use is low. Globally the rate of population growth has been falling for some time. Under current trends world population should stabilise at around 10 billion within the next hundred years. The critical factor will be achieving low-carbon lifestyles worldwide.[46]

Surely the real problem is the grip of fossil fuel companies over the government?

Research by the World Development Movement reveals a 'revolving door' between government, fossil fuel industries and big financial institutions. The lobbying power of the fossil fuel industry is enormous. So far, most fossil fuel companies have preferred to protect the status quo rather than face the need for radical change. There are also concerns about the way companies such as Exxon Mobil have funded climate change denying think-tanks like the US Heartland Institute. You are probably right to be concerned.[47]

# More information

This section lists a small number of books and websites with good, accessible information that will help you fill in the background and follow up facts you are not clear on. You will find more detailed sources and a wider selection of reading in the Notes.

I'd like to know more about…

…calculating and reducing my footprint

Use the Carbon Conversations calculator at http://carbonconversations.org/ to get a rough idea of your personal carbon footprint.

How Bad are Bananas? The Carbon Footprint of Everything, Mike Berners-Lee, Profile Books, 2010, gives detail about lots of products and a good sense of the scale of the problem.

…climate change

The Age of Stupid. Film and DVD, director Franny Armstrong, Dogwoof Studio Ltd, 2009, is a scary, compelling argument about the need to act.

The No-Nonsense Guide to Climate Change, Danny Chivers, New Internationalist Publications, 2011, is a clear, factual guide.

Weather Reports from the Future is a series of short videos, created by the World Meteorological Organisation, fronted by weather presenters from around the world. They show what the weather could be like in 2050, what effects climate change is having now and explain why this is happening, http://bit.ly/wmo-2014.

…international issues and the politics of climate change

This Changes Everything, Naomi Klein, Allen Lane, 2014, sets out clearly why capitalism finds it so hard to deal with climate change.

A Safe and Just Space for Humanity: Can We Live within the Doughnut? Kate Raworth, Oxfam 2012, is a good introduction to the issues of equality and justice. http://bit.ly/Raworth-2012.

Kyoto2: How to Manage the Global Greenhouse, Oliver Tickell, Zed Books, 2008 sets out the dilemmas of international agreement.

…people's attitudes

A New Agenda for Climate Change: Facing up to Stealth Denial and Winding Down on Fossil Fuels, Jonathon Rowson, 2013, RSA. http://bit.ly/Rowson-2013.

…policy and low-carbon futures

Heat: How We Can Stop the Planet Burning, George Monbiot, Penguin, 2007, remains a good introduction.

The Burning Question: We Can't Burn Half the World's Oil, Coal and Gas, So How Do We Quit? Mike Berners-Lee and Duncan Clark, Profile Books, 2013, brings the story up to date.

…quality of life

Growth Fetish, Clive Hamilton, Pluto Press, 2003, remains one of the best arguments about how economic growth fails to bring happiness.

...tradable carbon allowances

Energy and the Common Purpose: Descending the Energy Staircase with Tradable Energy Quotas (TEQs) David Fleming, The Lean Economy Connection, 2007, is an easy guide by one of the originators of the idea.

...what's happening in Scotland

Details of the Climate Change (Scotland) Act and the Scottish Government's policies and plans are at: http://bit.ly/SGov-CC.

CHAPTER 2

Energy at home and at work

"I'd like my house to be more energy efficient. What stops me? A mixture of ignorance, confusion, and the hassle of builders and DIY."

Home energy is responsible for about 25% of your carbon emissions

Houses are very personal places. We make them into homes and have strong feelings about them. Energy used in the home accounts for about one-quarter of our CO_2 emissions.[1] This is probably the area of our lives where we have most control over our emissions – particularly if we are home owners. Homes offer some of the easiest and cheapest ways to reduce emissions and also some of the most complicated and expensive. In this chapter we:

- explore the meaning of home;
- explain what needs to be done to UK houses;
- suggest how you can make your home comfortable and energy efficient while taking account of your feelings and desires;
- take a quick look at energy-saving at work.

This chapter contains a lot of technical terms. Most are explained in the A-Z of Home Energy at the end of the chapter. Use it to check anything you are unfamiliar with.

carbonconversations.org

Low-carbon housing

British houses waste an enormous amount of energy. Many UK homes are also cold, damp, draughty and uncomfortable. They are hard to heat and bad for people's health. The average UK house uses 26,000 kWh of energy each year and emits 6 tonnes of CO_2.[2] Much of the heat used to keep houses warm goes straight out through their walls, roof, floors and the gaps round doors and windows. Meanwhile we buy more and more electrical appliances. Some of them are more energy efficient than in the past but many are also larger.

Typical UK house now

26,000 kWh energy in ▶ **6 tonnes CO_2 out**

✗ draughty doors and windows
✗ solid brick walls
✗ unfilled cavity walls
✗ poor insulation
✗ ancient boiler
✗ single glazing
✗ lights left on
✗ inefficient appliances
✗ uninformed owner or tenant

Much UK housing is old and around 87% of it will still be here in 2050. So, although there are now higher standards for new houses, something has to be done about the old ones. All houses built before 2008 will need to be upgraded so that the average UK house emits less than 1 tonne of CO_2 by 2050. Upgrading these homes isn't just good for climate change. It will provide more comfortable, healthier homes as well.

Low carbon house in 2050

5,000 kWh energy in ▶ **1 tonne CO_2 out**

✓ everything draught-stripped
✓ super-thick insulation
✓ triple glazing
✓ heating from a renewable source
✓ heat recovery ventilation
✓ solar panels
✓ LED lights
✓ smart meters
✓ efficient appliances
✓ energy-conscious owner or tenant

How can we get there?

There are two ways of reducing the carbon footprint of housing.

1. Reduce the demand for energy by insulating houses, producing more efficient appliances and adopting less wasteful behaviour.
2. Generate the energy in ways that use less carbon – with renewables such as wind, solar, hydro, tidal and geothermal, and with low-carbon options such as combined heat and power.

Both are essential: neither is enough on its own.

Two reports from the Environmental Change Institute at Oxford University, *Home Truths*, and *Achieving Zero* describe what needs to be done.[3] Government, industry and individuals all need to play a part.

- The Building Regulations need continuous upgrading so higher standards are enforced both for new homes and for renovation.[4]
- Energy Performance Certificates (EPCs)[5] need to be used to limit the sale and renting of the worst houses.
- The worst houses – about 3 million of them – need to be demolished or completely redeveloped.
- Almost all other houses built before 2008 – about 20 million homes – need to be upgraded.
- All gas and electric appliances need to be gradually replaced with energy-efficient models.
- All houses need to be fitted with 'Smart Meters' so that people can easily monitor the energy they are using.
- The energy supply needs to be de-carbonised. More electricity needs to be generated from renewable sources such as wave and wind-power, hydro schemes and photovoltaics. More biogas from landfill and anaerobic digesters needs to be fed into the gas grid. Coal-fired and natural gas-fired power stations need to be closed.

What might government do?

We can hope for Government policy along the lines of the Oxford University reports and as citizens, we can press for that if we think it is a good idea.

As individuals we can expect to be offered both 'sticks' and 'carrots'. The sticks may be: more regulation, personal carbon allowances, carbon taxes, higher energy prices, minimum standards for renting, selling or extending houses. The carrots may be: grants and loans such as the Green Deal for insulation and for installing renewable energy systems; tax relief on energy-efficiency measures; lower taxes for selling more energy efficient homes; schemes such as the Feed-in Tariff for householders selling renewable electricity back to the grid. We should also expect the government to spearhead better communication about housing, stressing comfort, health and efficiency over money-saving.

What might industry do?

Industry may also need some sticks and carrots from government to produce:

- better trained architects, builders and installers;
- more sustainable building materials, windows and doors;
- more efficient appliances;
- smart meters and clear energy bills which users can easily understand;
- a growing retrofit industry;
- a growing renewable energy industry;
- decarbonisation of electricity production.

What can we do?

In this Chapter we discuss many things that people can do – both home-owners and tenants – and how to make a long-term plan. Some people are keen to get started, but others feel daunted. It's quite common to feel:

- annoyed at being told what to do with your home;
- worried about how complicated it seems;
- confused by conflicting advice;
- anxious about cost and disruption.

In general people renovate their homes to solve a problem. A tatty kitchen, a lack of space or broken equipment can all be the impetus. Home improvements also allow people to express their identity. The style of decoration, the furniture and the use of space all help us say something about ourselves. This means that it's important to keep in mind what you want from your home apart from making it climate friendly.

The meaning of home

What does home mean to you?

- "Closing the door, shutting out the day's stresses and difficulties..."
- "Running down the street in freezing rain, shedding my dripping clothes and slumping on the warm sofa..."
- "When I'm away, conjuring up the picture of family, gathered round the kitchen table..."
- "Someone to hug, someone to listen to me, someone to love..."
- "Privacy, solitude and silence..."
- "Looking at colour swatches, choosing paints, making this place feel it's ours..."

For most people, home means emotional security. Home is where we start from in childhood, venturing out bit by bit into a tougher world. At home, we expect to be able to relax, to feel ourselves, to get support and to have control. It's somewhere to retreat to, the secure base which makes everything else possible.

This is, of course, an ideal. Home is also the place of family conflict, domestic violence, loneliness, neglect, problem neighbours, irresponsible landlords and substandard buildings. The ideal has power however. Everything else is matched against it. Our longing for the ideal home drives TV makeover programmes and fuels an industry of 'must-have' household goods. The importance of home to our sense of security also means that it is easy to feel violated when someone else suggests change.

When people think of moving house or altering their existing home, their first thoughts are usually about how it will feel. Sometimes this is conscious. Will an extra bedroom stop the kids

> ❝ My home is a place of happiness and security. It's filled with things that are familiar to me and connected to me and my family and our lives. It's warm and lived in. There's lots of light. I grew up in Kenya, where a family of eight lived together in a small apartment, so I really appreciate the space.
>
> **Tina Shah**

squabbling? Is the living room big enough for a family party? Can I squeeze in Granny's lovely old chest of drawers? More often it is just a question of gut feeling – this is what feels like home. Anything that disturbs this will be resisted.

More than we realise, we are also caught up in social practices that define the 'right' way to do things at home.[6] In the 1950s bathing your children twice a week and putting them in clean clothes on Mondays was the sign of a good mother. In 2014, a bath or a shower and a clean outfit every day are the norm. Central heating, plentiful hot water, easy-care fabrics and washing machine technology all contribute to systems that seem natural but which actually arrived within living memory.

Some of the changes demanded in our homes by climate change do not fit easily with existing social practices or with people's aspirations. For example, drying clothes out of doors, living at lower temperatures and lighting only the rooms in use, can all upset people's deeply-held feelings about what makes a home a home. When change demands building work as well we can feel invaded at a very deep level. For weeks, home doesn't feel like home. The mess and disruption upset our basic feelings of security, causing anxiety and stress. Although we may be pleased with the result, the process is painful and we demand a trade-off. Borrowing thousands of pounds for a new kitchen may feel worth it. It's easy to anticipate the pleasure the kitchen will bring and to imagine showing it off to admiring friends. Borrowing thousands for solid wall insulation has little of the same attraction. There's nothing to show for the disruption and though the house will be warmer and heating bills lower, it rarely produces the same anticipatory thrill. And of course if you are struggling with a mortgage or living in substandard rental accommodation, the thought of spending thousands on anything will be a distant dream. You may simply feel irritated at the suggestion that there is anything that you can do.

So, before thinking about the detail of what you could do it may help to explore how your feelings about home connect to the features of the building and its location.

Home comforts

What makes a home feel right for you? Think about:

- the fabric of the house and its technical systems;
- space;
- location and community;
- design and style.

> **As a child I lived on a farm with no neighbours apart from my grandparents in an adjoining cottage. It was isolated and isolating – some of this was psychological not geographical as we were on the edge of an industrial town. The farm was the centre of gravity for me and the wider family. My grandmother ruled with a rod of iron, dictating when other family members came. I still think of home as a centre of gravity for our own children but I don't want coming home to be compulsory like my grandmother made it.**
>
> **Tony Wragg**

carbonconversations.org

The fabric of the house and its technical systems

The fabric of a house refers to its walls, floors, windows and roof and what they are made of – usually, brick, stone, timber and tiles. Its technical systems are the plumbing, heating, electrics and IT. If a house is well-constructed and its technical systems work well, most people don't pay much attention to these aspects of their homes. When a house doesn't work well, you will notice problems like high gas and electricity bills, damp, draughts, condensation, noise, dark and dingy rooms, heating systems that don't warm the house and hot water that runs out before everyone has showered. Houses like this are hard work to live in and people often struggle to understand the cause of the problems.

- How much do you know technically about your current home?
- Were these technical aspects a factor in your choice of home?
- Do you know its Energy Performance Certificate (EPC) rating?

Space

Space is a big issue for a lot of people. Some people live in cramped and over-crowded accommodation. Others crave more space for leisure activities, a home office, a spare room or simply somewhere to store an increasing number of possessions.

Over the last 30 years households have got smaller.[7] Divorce and separation are one reason but rising expectations also play a part. Larger houses are more expensive to heat and light. If small houses are well-designed with good storage, size may feel less of an issue. Ask yourself:

- How much space do you need?
- What kinds of space do you need?
- Could better layout and storage solve any of your space problems?
- If you are stuck with a large house, could you share it with others?

Location and community

If the location of your home isn't right for you, you probably won't feel comfortable. For some people it's a garden that's important. For others, schools, shops, a 'good' neighbourhood or access to urban life, parks or the countryside are what matters.

There are energy issues here as well. Some people have little choice about where they live: they rent or buy where they can afford. Others make choices which have big impacts. Choosing a neighbourhood that is a long way from work or family means big travel bills and high CO_2 emissions.

- What do you like best about your current home's location?
- How close is it to your ideal?
- What would be the energy implications if you moved?

> *I'm an urban nomad. I have lived in more than 20 places in 30 years. What matters to me is that there's a roof over my head. In Japan, space is a hugely precious commodity, so it's nice to have some room! The windows and having good light are important to me too.*
>
> **Keiko Saito**

Design and style

Design and style can give you practical comfort and also make you feel good about yourself. They are often powerful reasons for choosing a particular house, its furnishings and appliances.

Good design can bring down energy costs but there are also times when fashionable design and energy efficiency clash. Recessed halogen spotlights, open fires and floor-level curtains that cover the radiator will all reduce your home's efficiency.

- What do you like best about your current home's design and style?
- How close is it your ideal?
- Have any past decisions turned out to be energy nightmares?

Planning for a low-carbon house

All houses can be improved but they vary in how easy this is to do and how low-carbon they can become. Some can be turned into zero-carbon homes. Others will be a challenge to get down to 2 or 3 tonnes and the work may be expensive.

Increasingly, houses have Energy Performance Certificates which tell you how energy efficient they are. These are now issued whenever a house is sold. Landlords must also supply them to prospective tenants. A qualified energy surveyor inspects your house, makes some complicated calculations and rates it on a scale from A to G. Houses built after April 2008 should get an A rating. Most existing houses will get E or D ratings and need to be improved to at least a C.[8] An average-sized house with an E or D rating emits around 6 tonnes of CO_2 per year. Getting this down to 2 or 2.5 tonnes is a realistic target and would give the house a C or B rating. Some houses will be able to aim for a target of 1 tonne or lower.

There are four steps to making a plan for a low-carbon home:

1. monitor your energy use;
2. get to know your house;
3. understand the things you can do;
4. draw up a plan.

Do you rent or do you own?

People who rent often think that there is nothing they can do to lower their energy use. Although they have fewer options than home-owners there are still actions they can take.

- The way you use the house can make a big difference.
- You have choices over which appliances you purchase.
- You can talk to your landlord about upgrading the house and inform him or her about the government schemes, financial help and tax relief that are available.

> "People often think they need an extension when actually some better design of their existing space would solve their problems and be more energy efficient.
>
> **Katie Thornburrow, architect**

The case studies later in this chapter show how much can be achieved when tenants and landlords work together.

People who own their own homes do have more options but not everyone is keen on home renovation. People are more likely to think about renovation if:

- space is a pressure;
- the house is in poor condition or something breaks;
- they see their home as a project for self-expression and are open to outside influences.

Surprisingly, money is not a strong factor.

Few people do energy-efficiency renovations without doing other work as well. Most energy-efficiency tasks are piggy-backed onto other projects.[9] This means that it is critical to understand your home, and what it needs to become 'climate-friendly'. If you don't, you will miss opportunities. It will help to make a plan – noting which energy-efficiency measures fit naturally with other upgrades. For instance, insulating a wall is easily done when new windows are being fitted. Adding more insulation than the current building regulations demand is simple when you're having a loft-extension done. If you're re-fitting the bathroom anyway, it's the perfect time to opt for a very low-flush loo, heat-recovery extractor fan and low-water use shower.

There are advantages to undertaking a complete eco-refurbishment but you do not have to do everything at once. Gradual changes can achieve the same result over a five to ten year period if they are well-planned. Try to buck the trend and see energy upgrades as a priority. Keep them front of mind when you are planning any other changes.

Monitor your energy

The first step toward a climate-friendly home is learning how much energy you use. You need to monitor the gas, electricity, coal, oil and wood your home consumes.

> *I grew up in India. In the villages, kerosene lamps were used for lighting at night. The wicks were soaked in vegetable oil, which attracted mice. You could hear them running around and I remember being scared! Now I'm in Cambridge I still don't take electricity for granted. I automatically switch things off. Electricity isn't free, we should stop treating it as if it is!*
>
> **Padma Bhuva**

> *I have an energy efficient washing machine and I hang out my wet washing on the line in the summer months. It's one of those things I find a pleasure rather than a chore. But what to do in the winter months? The feline approach to life – find a sunny spot to lie down for a snooze – is also the way to dry clothes. Place a rangy clothes-hanger in front of the window in the sunniest room in the house, and the tumble drier can be out of a job much of the time.*
>
> **Karen Henwood**

If you monitor your fuel use, you can:

- see exactly how much you use;
- set some realistic targets for reduction;
- see the difference you can make.

Many factors affect how much fuel you use, such as:

- the season, outside temperature and number of daylight hours;
- the location, orientation and altitude of your home;
- the construction of your home and its insulation;
- the systems used for heating, hot water and lighting;
- how many electrical appliances you have, how efficient they are and how much you use them;
- the number of people in your household and how much time they spend at home;
- the choices you make about the temperature of the house and your hot water use.

In order to get a clear idea of how successful you are in reducing your energy use, you need to monitor over a long period, ideally over a full year or more.

Read your meters weekly for the next four weeks. Then continue by reading the meter once every four weeks after that. If you are taking part in a Carbon Conversations group you will find more advice about this in your *Workbook*.

You can take the hard work out of meter reading by signing up to iMeasure at www.imeasure.org.uk, or to Carbon Account at www.thecarbonaccount.com. These handy sites will do the hard work for you. Simply read your meters, enter the figures and they will keep a record of your energy use and CO_2 emissions.

Finding your meters

Modern houses often have a meter box outside. You will need a special key to open it. If you don't have one, a hardware shop or plumber's merchant should be able to sell you one. In older houses, meters are often under the stairs, by the front door or in the kitchen. In blocks of flats, there is often a separate meter room or cupboard. Ask your landlord or management company for access.

Smart meters

Over the next few years it should get easier to read your meter. It is government policy to install smart meters in every home and business in the UK between 2015 and 2020. Smart meters give you a moment-to-moment reading of your electricity and gas use on a clear digital display. They can show you the surge as you switch on the kettle or plug in the iron. They will also allow suppliers to offer you cheaper deals at times of low demand – suggesting the best time to put on a load of washing for example. Research suggests that smart meters can reduce energy use by between 5% and 15%.[10] The work will be carried out by energy companies at no cost to consumers and the smart meters will replace the old 'dumb' ones. Some homes will get their meters sooner as part of a pilot phase.

In the meantime:

- Some energy companies now offer a service that sends you monthly figures for your actual use of electricity and gas.
- You can buy monitors that hook up to your electrical supply to display continuous readings.

Get to know your house

A proper energy survey is quite technical. A good energy consultant would look at the features listed below, make calculations, give your house a rating, and make recommendations for what you should do. You will find details of how to get a professional energy survey done in the More Information section at the end of this chapter but every householder should be able to get a rough feel for how their home works.

Create a file about your house. Include any architect's drawings, details of building work done, and appliances purchased. Then take a walk around your house asking yourself the questions that an energy surveyor might ask (listed below). If we use terms you don't understand, check them in the A to Z of Home Energy towards the end of this chapter. If you are taking part in a Carbon Conversations group you will also find more guidance in your *Workbook*. Make a note of what you find.

The construction
The construction of your house is fundamental. What are the walls made of – brick, wood or stone? Is it detached, semi-detached, in a terrace or a flat? How old is it and how big? Are the walls and roof spaces insulated? How thick is the insulation? Are the windows single, double or triple glazed? Is there any damp or mould? Are there cold spots? How easy will it be to make changes?

Ventilation
Ventilation allows fresh air into the house and stale air out. How much energy is lost depends on whether draughts can be controlled. Is there any fixed ventilation, such as airbricks? How are the extractor fans controlled? Is there any draught-stripping round doors and windows? How effective is it? Is there any mechanism for heat recovery?

Heating, hot water and cooking
How much energy is used for room heating and hot water hinges on whether gas, electricity, coal, oil or wood is used. How old is the boiler? Is it a combination boiler or is there a hot-water tank? How good are the heating controls? How easy are they to use? Where are the thermostats? How warm is the house kept? What temperature is the water heated to? Are the pipes insulated?

The amount of water used depends on: the number of baths, showers, sinks, basins and WCs; whether these have any water-saving features; and how much hot water they are each likely to use.

CO_2 emissions from cooking are affected by whether gas, electricity, solid fuel or microwave is used as well as the size and efficiency of the cooker.

Lighting and appliances
Energy use for lighting is affected by the number and type of light-fittings; whether these are suitable for energy-efficient light bulbs, how many are already in place and whether they are turned off when not in use.

Energy use by appliances is affected by how many appliances there are (particularly heavy energy users like a tumble drier) as well as their age and energy ratings. Is it easy to turn appliances off when they are not in use? What is the household's pattern of use?

DIY survey

1 Check if your walls are insulated. Cavity walls (left) can be filled with insulation. You can recognise a cavity wall by the brick pattern – every brick is laid in the same direction and appears the same size. In solid walls (right) some bricks are laid end-on giving an appearance of alternating long and short bricks. Solid walls need insulation added on the inside or outside or the house. Most houses built after the 1930s have cavity walls. Most houses built from the 1990s onwards were built with insulation in the cavities. If your cavity wall was filled after it was built you may be able to see the drill holes in the brickwork.

2 Check how much insulation you have in the loft: there should be at least 300mm.

3 Check there is draught-stripping round windows and doors.

4 Get to know your heating controls – and use them!

5 Remember to turn off lighting, appliances and gadgets when you are not using them.

6 Talk about how you use the house. There are huge differences between the most careful and least careful users of energy (even if they live in very similar properties).

7 Check the More Information section towards the end of this chapter if you would like a professional survey done.

carbonconversations.org

Low-carbon living in practice

The charts on the following pages list over 50 changes that could make your home energy-efficient. Many can be done regardless of whether you are renting or own your home. Others can only be done if you are a home-owner or have to be carried out by the landlord. If you are taking part in a Carbon Conversations group you will play a game 'Low-Carbon House' which helps explain them. Many of them are also described in more detail in the A-Z of Home Energy at the end of this chapter.

Each item is given a star rating. This indicates whether it is likely to make a large or a small difference. It is always difficult to say exactly how much carbon any one measure will save. It depends on the existing condition of the house, its size, which other measures are taken and how the house is used. In an average house with average use:

- * Up to 100kg
- ** Between 100kg and 250kg
- *** Between 250kg and 500kg
- **** Between 500kg and 1000kg
- ***** Over 1,000kg
- ✪ Actions that don't save carbon themselves but will increase the carbon saving of other actions

Take a look at the lists, thinking carefully about your home. Be ambitious. Achieving a low-carbon home means making many of the changes on the lists.

Some of the changes may feel inspiring; some may feel boring; some may be expensive. You may worry that some may not fit with the way you live, or worry about getting other household members to cooperate.

- Take a look at what you would like to do.
- Put ticks against each item in whichever column best applies.
- Think about why each change feels easy or difficult, attractive or unattractive.

If you rent your house or are not planning to stay very long in it, you may be restricted mainly to items in the first three charts. If you own your house, or are able to persuade your landlord to do some upgrades, you can also consider ideas from the fourth and fifth charts. A complete refurbishment will require plans drawn up by an architect; but you can use the charts to consider the options you prefer. If you are planning to introduce energy efficiency gradually as money becomes available, plan the best order. Make sure one change doesn't get in the way of the next. Once you have a rough plan, a discussion with a builder may help.

Draw up a plan

In drawing up your plan, you may also find it helpful to:

- read the case studies that follow;
- look at other case studies on the Superhomes site or visit Open House events (see More Information towards the end of this chapter);
- look at the FAQs later in this chapter;
- study the A-Z of Home Energy at the end of this chapter;
- consult some of the books and websites listed under More Information.

If you find you have not ticked many items in the first two columns, or that in six months' time you have not acted on many of your ticks, take a look at the 'Getting stuck' section later in this chapter. It can be hard to put good intentions into practice.

Good housekeeping

These are changes in the way you use your home. They cost nothing to do but could bring savings of up to 20%, depending on your current behaviour.

		I've already done this	I'd like to do this	Don't fancy / couldn't do this
Turn off lights when you're not using them	*	☐	☐	☐
Turn appliances off standby	*	☐	☐	☐
Turn the room thermostat down by 1 °C	**	☐	☐	☐
Turn the room thermostat down by 3 °C	***	☐	☐	☐
Ensure the heating is turned off at night and when you are out or away from home	***	☐	☐	☐
Take short showers instead of baths	**	☐	☐	☐
Halve the ironing you do	*	☐	☐	☐
Review and adjust the settings on thermostatic radiator valves	*	☐	☐	☐
Don't overfill the kettle	*	☐	☐	☐
Run the washing machine at 30 or 40 °C and only run when full	*	☐	☐	☐
Run the dishwasher at 55 °C and only when full	*	☐	☐	☐
Dry clothes outdoors	*	☐	☐	☐
Defrost fridge and freezer regularly	*	☐	☐	☐
Close curtains at dusk and make sure they don't block the radiator	*	☐	☐	☐
Check radiators are off and doors closed in rooms not in use	*	☐	☐	☐
Read your meters monthly to check how much fuel you're using	**	☐	☐	☐

carbonconversations.org

CASE STUDY

Green Impact Student Homes

Green Impact Student Homes (GISH) in Sheffield is an NUS funded project which involves students and their landlords in making positive environmental changes to their housing. It supports students to make changes such as reducing their energy use, improving their recycling habits and following a more sustainable diet. Energy monitors are supplied to participating households so they can track their use.

At the same time, project worker Kiran Malhi-Bearn liaises with their landlords to support the landlords in carrying out the bigger changes – everything from changing the lightbulbs and buying more efficient appliances to installing more insulation, double glazing or PV – providing advice about what needs to be done and the grants and loans that are available.

Weekend jobs

Many of these simple measures can be done as DIY jobs. None of them are very expensive. Some can be seen as temporary fixes while you wait for the right moment to do something more permanent.

		I've already done this	I'd like to do this	Don't fancy / couldn't do this
Replace any remaining incandescent lightbulbs with energy-efficient ones	**	☐	☐	☐
Draught-strip all external doors and windows and seal open-fire chimneys when not in use	***	☐	☐	☐
Fit draught-strip to your letterbox	*	☐	☐	☐
Seal the gaps round cat-flaps and pipes in external walls	*	☐	☐	☐
Check the insulation on your hot-water tank – add or replace it if it's less than 75 mm (3") thick	*	☐	☐	☐
Insulate hot-water pipes	*	☐	☐	☐
Fix shelves above radiators on external walls, put foil behind and adjust curtains to sit on the shelves	*	☐	☐	☐
'Shrink-wrap' all single glazed windows for winter	**	☐	☐	☐
Put up DIY secondary glazing on appropriate windows	**	☐	☐	☐
Increase the insulation in the loft from 50 mm to 300 mm	***	☐	☐	☐
Find out if you have an unfilled cavity wall and (if yes) have it filled	****	☐	☐	☐
Put your fridge and freezer in the coolest places possible	*	☐	☐	☐

Both students and landlords use an easy, informative, online workbook outlining sustainable actions. There are three levels to aspire to with the added incentive of vouchers, competitions and prizes for the best-performing households. In the first year 42 properties took part, competing for the titles of 'Best Landlord' and 'Best Student House,' winning £5,000 for green property improvements and a month's rent respectively. The competition was really close with lots of students and landlords making a tremendous effort and seeing real reductions in energy use.

❝ Something that really motivated me to join GISH was to learn to reduce my bills and push myself and my housemates into being a little more green by being involved in a formal project. I learnt new things – I never realized that the kettle could be a real culprit in the electricity bill! I also started practising everything very seriously after being involved in GISH and would admit that I was a bit careless before.

Our property is moderately well maintained. We had a mix of normal and energy saving bulbs but after GISH we requested our landlord to replace the other bulbs with energy savers which he did. In future I am planning to meet our landlord and enquire whether the windows are double glazed which I have a confusion over and also request him to perform a regular maintenance check on the heaters.

My experience of taking part in GISH has been very useful and enjoyable. Even my housemates have become energy savvy and green! Continuing with the things which I had already been doing like recycling and reusing has been very easy. Switching off appliances when not in use is something we started after GISH. Playing with the energy monitor has been enjoyable and it's been interesting to know tips we weren't aware of before. It has been challenging to get my housemates involved but they are happy with the reduction in our monthly bills and are thankful for how the energy monitor made them aware of the rise and fall in our usage."

Azeeza Ghani Mohamed Ismail

Taking opportunities – appliances

Keep your home's energy performance 'front of mind' when you are buying new appliances.

		I've already done this	I'd like to do this	Don't fancy / couldn't do this
Whenever you buy electrical goods, choose the most efficient based on the EU energy label	*	☐	☐	☐
Buy the smallest appliance you can manage with	*	☐	☐	☐
If appliances are not EU rated (TVs, Hi-Fi for example), ask about their efficiency and choose the best you can find	*	☐	☐	☐
Choose the most efficient 'A' rated boiler, remembering also to upgrade controls, radiator valves and your hot-water cylinder	***	☐	☐	☐
Check that new lamps/side lights can take energy-efficient bulbs	*	☐	☐	☐

carbonconversations.org

> **CASE STUDY**

Upgrading a Victorian terrace home

❝ Our house is a 3 bedroom Victorian terrace with a long back garden, close to the centre of town. It's typical of many houses that need a bit of thought if they are going to be retrofitted well. Andy's motivation had a lot to do with his fascination with solving the technical problems but for both of us the ethical dimension matters. The refurbishment is a way of lessening some of the harm our lifestyles cause and of making a commitment to the future.

When we moved into the house, in the late 1980s, it had a recently built back extension with 50 mm insulation in the cavity walls and roof space. Over the next 18 years we made improvements as opportunities arose, including triple glazed patio-doors, a condensing boiler, a wood-burning stove and lots of draught-stripping and energy-efficient lightbulbs. Despite this, in 2005 the house had a carbon footprint of just over 6 tonnes annually, partly because Rosemary works from home, which means the heating is often on during the day. We made a plan to reduce the emissions to less than 2 tonnes.

Our biggest problems were:

- an attic room with only 75 mm insulation between the rafters and no headroom to add more;
- a loosely boarded ground floor that was difficult to insulate because of the risk of condensation and rotting timber;

Taking opportunities – building work

Keep your home's energy performance 'front of mind' when you are redecorating or having building work done. It's easy to combine energy-saving measures with repainting, having a new kitchen installed or building an extension. The cost is reduced and disruption minimised.

		I've already done this	I'd like to do this	Don't fancy / couldn't do this
Get advice about 'best practice' for energy saving – exceed current building regulations	✪	☐	☐	☐
Choose high-performance double or triple glazed windows and doors	★★★	☐	☐	☐
Insulate solid walls internally by dry-lining at the same time as windows are replaced	★★★★	☐	☐	☐
Ensure all new lighting takes energy-efficient bulbs and upgrade other fittings while the electrician is there	★	☐	☐	☐
Choose a wood-burning stove rather than an open fire	★★	☐	☐	☐
Upgrade central-heating controls	★	☐	☐	☐
Make sure kitchen and bathroom extractor fans include heat recovery	★★	☐	☐	☐
Install a low-water-use shower	★	☐	☐	☐

- a narrow alleyway which runs at ground-floor level only, between our house and next door, making it impossible to insulate the narrow hallway either externally or internally.

The house is not suitable for PV.

Finances and the problems of disruption meant that we did the work over an eight year period bringing the builders back on three separate occasions. We found the disruption difficult each time. It made us aware of how much our personal well-being depends on being able to relax at home. We're pleased with the results but the process was tough.

All the outside solid walls are now insulated either internally or externally with 100 mm of polyurethane. We added 100 mm of insulation to the flat roof of the back extension and solved the problem of the attic by working externally – lifting the tiles, replacing the insulation between the rafters and adding another 100 mm above that, with new battens and some new slates. On the ground floor, we replaced the old boards with a new solid floor, 80 mm of insulation and reclaimed boards. In the alleyway we insulated the ceiling and put solid, draught-stripped doors on either end, bringing it into the envelope of the house and cutting the heat loss from the only remaining single brick wall. The house is now triple glazed throughout, has a high-performance insulated front door, solar water heating, a heat-recovery extract fan, an additional wood-burning stove and a low-water shower to replace the bath.

Emissions are now about 1.8 tonnes a year which we are pleased with. The most important feature is the insulation but our favourite features are the sedum finish on the flat roof of the back extension and the reclaimed wood floor that came from some old French railway carriages. The total cost was £65,000 and was possible because we had finished paying our mortgage. Spread over eight years this £8,000 a year was less than many people pay on their mortgages each year.

If we were doing this again we would try to do all the work at once. Although we would have had to borrow money and move out for a few months it would have been easier to achieve good connections between the different parts of the work, eliminating potential cold bridges and doing a better job of creating an air-tight barrier. We might also have coped better with the disruption."

Andy Brown and Rosemary Randall

CASE STUDY

Working in partnership with your landlord

Tenants often feel there is little they can do but this example shows that it can be worth approaching your landlord.

" Our house was cold in winter and very noisy. You could feel the draughts around the edges of the single glazed, original 1880s windows. We knew that we were losing energy and we needed the house to be warm because we were expecting a baby. It was clear that the windows needed to be replaced.

Tenants sometimes get scared asking for house improvements but we have found that if you ask for things that are reasonable you can be successful. We are good tenants and we approached the landlords in a spirit of partnership. We did some research, got some quotes and offered to organise the work. In the end the landlord realised they could supply better windows than we hoped for at a lower cost than we could find.

The new windows are brilliant. They look lovely, it is much quieter and there are no draughts any more. We've got a long wish-list of other things we would like done, many of which would improve the energy efficiency of the house, make it more comfortable and improve its value. If we stay here we will talk to the landlords about doing some more jobs that will make next winter much more comfortable for us and the baby."

Ali Wood and Julian Cooling – Tenants

❝ I own the house with my two brothers so we all need to agree the decisions about what is done to it. I believe in saving energy and I want anything that we do to the house to be done on a long-term basis. I think you should think in terms of the next 100 years really. One of my brothers is more worried about money but he was OK about this and we were able to go ahead. Happy tenants are good tenants – they pay the rent and they stay! I also want to help them use less energy.

We arranged to do the work while the tenants were away on holiday, otherwise it would have been a bit unpleasant for them. There's a lot of mess

Big changes

These are the changes people often think of when they imagine a greener home. They are major projects that need to be carefully planned. Some are expensive and some may cause disruption. You will need to do some of these if you want to achieve a truly low-carbon home.

		I've already done this	I'd like to do this	Don't fancy / couldn't do this
Install solar panels for hot water	***	☐	☐	☐
Install 2 kW photovoltaic solar panels for electricity	***	☐	☐	☐
Replace all windows and any glazed doors with high-performance, double or triple glazed units	***	☐	☐	☐
Replace front and back doors with high-performance, insulated doors	*	☐	☐	☐
Insulate underneath the ground floor	**	☐	☐	☐
Dry-line all external solid walls	****	☐	☐	☐
Insulate external solid walls from the outside – especially flank walls with few windows	****	☐	☐	☐
Externally insulate flat roofs	**	☐	☐	☐
Install a ground-source or air-source heat pump	****	☐	☐	☐

carbonconversations.org

when you do a job like this – 100 years worth of muck in the old box sashes and a lot of dust and disruption. The windows are Rationel – the opening sash is aluminium clad, the frame is wood. They're a high quality, reasonably priced, double glazed option.

I hadn't heard about the Landlords' Energy Saving Allowance before I did this interview but I'm definitely going to look that up and make sure we claim it if we can.

I would like to do more to the house, in particular to insulate the solid walls."

Jonathan Cooke – Landlord

CASE STUDY

Gradually upgrading a 1960s house

❝ Our house was built in 1968. I've lived there since 1996 with my wife and two children who are now teenagers. When we first moved here I was too busy with full-time work and a young family to do much but more recently I realised that our home was overflowing with stuff and that we could do a lot to lead a more environmental life. I first became interested in environmental issues in my twenties, both because of the connection with a more spiritual and pacifist outlook and for the social connections that come from being part of a group (I'm currently involved with our local Friends of the Earth group).

A 1960s house may look quite modern but most of them need a lot of upgrades. We started by insulating the cavity walls and then topped up the loft insulation which now has insulation both under the rafters and under the boarding between the joists. The next thing was dealing with the central heating. We upgraded to a condensing boiler, put thermostatic radiator valves on all the radiators and installed new controls. All our lighting is low-energy and we've gradually replaced most of our appliances with the most efficient ones. We replaced the windows with uPVC double glazed units and finally installed Photovoltaic panels three years ago.

Since starting the work I have bought a thermometer for the house so we can see exactly what the temperature is and it's made me more likely to put on warmer clothes than turn up the heating. As well as upgrading the house, we have bought a hybrid car, eat less meat and installed water butts in the garden.

We didn't make an overall plan but we did take advantage of grants as they became available and so that drove some of our decisions. We did the work gradually, over a ten year period and spent about £26,000 on it. It is important to me to know that we are doing the right things for the environment. We have hosted two Superhomes open days, and I think the visitors were interested and motivated by seeing what we've done.

The most rewarding aspect is knowing we are using clean renewable energy when the sun is shining."

Ivan Cicin-Sain

CASE STUDY

A stone house in Scotland

"We live in a large, detached stone house in Lanarkshire, which was built about 1900. I first became aware of climate change when I read Mayer Hillman's book *How We Can Save the Planet* and became aware of Aubrey Meyer's ideas about contraction and convergence. This made me aware that something earth-shattering was happening and was the motivation behind the eco-renovation. Originally I wanted to build a new eco-home but we also wanted to remain near family and friends and in the end we settled for renovating our existing home, which we also extended so we could run a small bed and breakfast.

The whole building is massively insulated with high performing insulation panels up to 170 mm thick in places. The windows, doors and skylights in the extension are all wooden framed triple glazed units. Hot water for the central heating is powered by a mix of a new condensing gas boiler, solar thermal and a wood stove, managed by a sophisticated control system. Both the main house and guest area have heat recovery systems so we maintain a healthy, low-moisture atmosphere and don't lose heat.

The lights are all compact fluorescent bulbs or LEDs and there are motion sensors in the entrance and corridors of the guest area. We have a 4 kW photovoltaic solar array which generates electricity when the sun shines. Our appliances all have A+ ratings or above and we try to make sure we use them when the sun is shining! Rainwater harvesting provides water for flushing the loos and for the washing machine and garden. Finally, we've installed electric vehicle charging points to encourage our guests to come by electric car.

We moved out for a year while the work was done. The worst bit was the dust and stress but the best bit is the improved comfort of the house. In winter the kitchen used to be an ice box but it is now a lovely space with a warm floor. Although we've doubled the size of the house and the price of fuel has risen we are spending no more on energy. The extension cost about £130,000 and the renovation of the existing house about £20,000."

John and Elaine Riley

Help and challenge

There are a number of sources of help in upgrading your home. There are also some challenges to be aware of.

Financial help

The **Energy Company Obligation** (ECO) is a government-sponsored scheme which offers help through the energy companies to households with low incomes who receive benefits such as pension credit, working tax credit and income support. The full or partial cost of loft and wall insulation, and replacing a boiler can be met.

For people without savings or access to loans and who are not eligible for ECO, the Government's **Green Deal** scheme may be an option. These loans provide finance for home energy upgrades. The loan attaches to the house not the owner or tenant and is paid back through a charge on your energy bills, which are guaranteed not to rise as a result of the loan.

In Scotland the Scottish Government's **Green Homes Cashback Scheme** offers grants of up to £7,500 to help with measures recommended by a Green Deal Advice Report.[11]

Feed-In Tariffs were introduced in 2010 to encourage people to install renewable electricity-generation. Under the scheme you are paid for any electricity you generate, whether you use it yourself or export surplus to the grid. Technologies which qualify for the scheme include solar electricity (PV), wind turbines, hydro-electricity, anaerobic digesters and micro combined heat and power.

The **Renewable Heat Incentive** (RHI) works in a similar way and covers solar water heating, air-source and ground-source heat pumps, and biomass heating systems. Its introduction has been repeatedly delayed but it will be backdated to cover any installation made after July 2009.

There is now a **reduced rate of VAT** (5%) on energy-saving materials for VAT-registered builders. This covers both the cost of materials (everything from draught excluders to solar panels) and installation. Unfortunately, this reduced rate cannot be claimed by householders – but your builder should pass on the price saving to you.

The **Landlords Energy Saving Allowance** (LESA) allows private landlords to offset the cost – up to £1,500 – of energy-efficiency improvements against rental income.

You may also be able to get a **commercial loan** from your mortgage company, just as you would for other home improvements.

See the More Information section at the end of this chapter for where to find out more about all these schemes, and for websites with more up-to-date information as government schemes change frequently.

General advice

The answers to many questions can be found on the Energy Saving Trust website and on the Centre for Alternative Technology's online information service. Amongst professionals, look for architects and engineers whose training has involved eco-renovation, who are members of the Association for Environment Conscious Building (AECB)[12] or who have completed PassivHaus[13] training.

Heritage homes

Homes built in the nineteenth century or before pose additional challenges. Many can be made extremely energy efficient but care is needed, particularly with listed buildings and with homes in conservation areas. In both cases there may be restrictions on what you can do.

If you own a heritage home it is vital to get advice from architects and to employ builders who have experience of historic buildings and their thermal improvement. A good architect will also have the experience to negotiate with local authority conservation officers and find the best solution for your home.

Many of the features that make older properties interesting can be damaged or destroyed by energy efficient upgrades. Thermal upgrades must also be sensitive to the existing materials. The building may have survived for hundreds of years because it has relied upon cool and well ventilated conditions. Careful use of vapour permeable materials will be needed to prevent condensation inside the walls which will cause mould or decay.

There are an increasing number of specialist materials and components available that may be acceptable to conservation officers, the most important of which is conservation glazing. This double glazing has a mere 4mm gap and can replace the glass in restored window frames. Combine this with the addition of discreet draught seals and the restoration (and use) of the original wooden shutters and you will see a huge improvement to the performance of the windows and comfort of the room.

While it may not be possible to refurbish an historic building to the standard of a 21st century home, all the advice on efficient heating systems, lighting, appliances and good housekeeping still applies. You will find more advice on heritage homes in the More Information section at the end of this chapter.

Fuel poverty

Over 4.4 million households in the UK live in fuel poverty.[14] Fuel poverty is usually defined as needing to spend more than 10% of household income to provide an adequate standard of heating and electricity. The government created a more complex definition in 2013 which redefined some people as no longer fuel poor, but the problem remains.

It is important to realise that dealing with fuel poverty will not bring large reductions in carbon emissions. Most fuel poor households under-use energy. They cannot afford to buy enough to keep warm. Once their homes are properly insulated the amount of fuel they purchase doesn't necessarily change. Better insulation allows them to heat their home for longer and to keep it warmer.

If you are fuel poor and manage to get your home insulated, make sure that you take the gains in warmth and comfort. Don't be disappointed that your carbon emissions only fall by a small amount.

Rebound effects

Sadly energy efficiency may not bring all the energy savings you hope for. The rebound effect means that you may respond (consciously or unconsciously) to lower energy bills by leaving the lights on and keeping the heating on for longer, even though you don't need to, or by spending money you save on other energy-intensive items. If you have been living in fuel poverty it is essential that you now heat your home properly but if not, keep an eye on your behaviour and your spending. It's easy to relax and forget about a radiator left on in an unused room if your bills are falling. It's also tempting to blow money saved through energy efficiency on a high-carbon treat, such as a holiday flight. Work by Mona Chitnis and colleagues[15] estimates the rebound effect for a basket of typical home energy upgrades at 5-15% for an average UK house and household. Most of this is indirect rebound, where money saved through upgrades is spent elsewhere. If you do save money through energy-efficiency, try to spend it on further upgrades to your home or on goods and services with a low carbon intensity. We discuss this more in Chapter Five.

Getting stuck

There are many reasons why a wish to reduce emissions doesn't turn into reality. You may find it helpful to think about each of the following. They can all be genuine reasons for finding it hard to make progress. Sometimes they are also reasons which people reach for rather quickly to explain to themselves why they can't do more.

Relationships

"I'd happily get rid of the second freezer but it's my wife who does the shopping and that's the way she likes to do it."

"I started turning lights off and turning the thermostat down but my teenagers complained that the house was shabby and cold and stopped bringing their friends round."

"My requests to flat-mates to be more careful with hot water and so on just seem to encourage them to do the opposite. They like winding me up. I'm made to feel like a school prefect in my own home."

Unless you run your home like a dictator, you can't impose change on those you share your life with. These examples point to the risk of conflict and the importance of getting everyone's agreement. Your family and housemates need to feel ownership too. Can you find time for conversations with those you love about:

- what makes home feel like home;
- how to monitor the energy you all use;
- the gains and the difficulties of making changes;
- how every household member could be involved;
- energy-efficient changes you can all agree on?

> **❝** Moving back to my parents' house after graduation disrupted my routine of simple tasks such as turning off lights and lowering the thermostat. I found it awkward trying to tell my parents how their house should be run and my attempts almost always led to some form of confrontation. Expressing my feelings about these issues in the Carbon Conversations group helped me approach my parents in a less confrontational way. Borrowing an energy monitor was really useful as it put things into perspective for my parents. Since then they often ask me about ways to reduce their emissions and are making a conscious effort to become more sustainable.
>
> Lucie Stevenson

Chapter Six discusses ways of going about this. Try to see the objections of family and friends as part of the process rather than a permanent roadblock.

Dread of disruption

Major work, such as dry-lining walls and fitting new windows, is always disruptive. Even a minor job such as adding insulation to the loft can falter if the loft is used for storage and the junk of decades needs to be taken out and sorted through. Fitting draught-stripping to windows and doors is often forgotten during the warm summer months which are the best time to do it. Tackled as winter approaches, the open doors and windows make the house cold and the job gets put off for another year.

The only answer to disruption is careful planning. Schedule work for the warmer months. Make sure it doesn't clash with important family events. Organise help from friends and family. Recognise that the work can be stressful and plan for how to cope.

Feeling daunted or confused

Many people find it hard to appreciate the scale of what needs to be done to most UK houses. It's common to see energy upgrades as optional or as coming second to other plans like a loft extension. When you do realise what needs to be done it's easy to feel daunted and, instead of creating a long-term plan, opt for a few easy measures, comforting yourself that you've done your best, or done your bit. Confusion and lack of knowledge add to the picture. It's important to recognise that, if you are going to upgrade your home properly you need to be ambitious and inform yourself fully about what is needed. This takes time. As with any new area of knowledge you will not get clarity immediately. Work through the material in this chapter carefully. Look at some of the resources in More Information.

You may also need to explore your attitude to your home, rethinking the relative importance of energy saving and other uses of your time, effort and money. This kind of change isn't easy and many of us avoid it by hiding behind our ignorance or throwing up our hands in despair at ever finding the right answer. Most people who make the upgrades needed have done so after a slow process of exploration and planning in which the confusion gradually clears. If you can keep your focus, you will get there in the end.

Money and choice

It is expensive to upgrade a typical UK home to an A or B energy rating. Estimates of between £20,000 and £80,000 are not unusual, depending on the size and original condition of the property.

> ❝ We bought our house intending to do a complete eco-refurbishment. When we shared our plans with our neighbours we were taken aback by the level of opposition, which felt quite hostile. Finding a solution was difficult and caused conflict between us: Tim remained focused on doing an exemplary job, whilst I wanted to be more conciliatory. Now, we've reached a good compromise. I think the issue is how far do you push things and at what expense? I feel it is important to bring along those who live around us. After all, this community is part of why we chose to buy the house we did.
>
> Jo Bowlt

While some people simply do not have a spare penny others are making complex choices about what they think is worthwhile.

A culture has grown up which says that energy saving improvements:

- are one spending option to be considered amongst many;
- should pay back their costs in reduced bills;
- can be rejected if they impinge on the style or character of the house.

The idea of payback times started as an attempt to persuade businesses that energy saving measures were worth doing but it has had unfortunate consequences, particularly as it has been extended to the domestic market. Many of the measures needed will not pay back their costs but are essential if we are to deal with climate change. The reasons for doing them are similar to the reasons for upgrading slum housing in the 1960s and 1970s when the government provided grants to install electricity, bathrooms and indoor toilets in homes that didn't have these essential services. We need to see full insulation, triple glazed windows and efficient heating systems as similarly essential. They have to be paid for whether or not the money can be recovered in lower bills.

The emphasis on payback feeds into the idea of choice and the idea that energy-saving is optional – something to do if you have some spare cash. If you think like this, you will do the minimum required by law and spend the rest of your money on something that brings you more pleasure – a beautiful rug, some designer radiators or new kitchen equipment.

Similarly, if you see energy-saving as an optional extra you will try to weigh up its benefits against the costs of losing a feature of your home you value, or paying a lot of money to have it retained. For example a Victorian cornice may be lost or will be expensive to restore if solid wall insulation is installed. Similarly you may feel that new triple glazed windows don't have the charm of old sash windows or you may regret giving up a coal fire.

We need to move to the idea that energy-saving is the first consideration – until it is achieved, everything else has to wait. This is hard. Our feelings about money and about our homes are always complicated and rarely rational.

Resentment, grief and unfairness

Although logically it makes sense to prioritise our common future and get on with upgrading our homes as fast as possible, many of us don't do this.

If we're planning a loft extension, conservatory or kitchen, we're often prepared to use savings or borrow money to fund it. We become engrossed in the detailed plans, enjoy choosing new fittings and paint colours and put up with any amount of disruption to realise a dream. Energy saving measures often feel different and the reasons we give ourselves for inaction can hide some difficult feelings.

> *I still feel there's something unwelcoming about coming to a dark house. I've always liked to leave a light on – interestingly this wasn't a tradition in my childhood family, but took root later. I don't leave a light on now but it doesn't sit well with me. I don't feel I'm welcoming others and I don't quite feel welcomed myself.*
>
> **Tony Wragg**

Resentment, grief, a sense of unfairness or being cheated can all lie behind our reluctance. You might resent your spending money on upgrades, when others are spending theirs on holidays or days out. You might worry that others are saving for goals, such as their children's university fees, which will offer personal advantage instead. You may feel fed up that there's little to show off when all the work is finished. You might feel grief at giving up a favourite feature of your home. You might resent being labelled a 'green prig' by your friends. You might feel cheated because other generations didn't have to deal with these problems.

These kinds of feelings all have one thing in common – they take time to work through and resolve. It will help to see them as problems to be resolved rather than permanent obstacles. It will help to acknowledge them to yourself and reflect on how to deal with them. It will help to recognise them as part of an inner conflict. On the one hand you have a strong motivation to act but on the other you are paralysed by your feelings. Both are true.

It will help to discuss these issues with other people. Realising that others share these feelings means that you are less likely to feel ashamed of them or get stuck in justifying them. If you're taking part in a Carbon Conversations group there will be plenty of opportunities for these discussions.

What about at work?

Not many people feel the same level of responsibility for their workplace as they do for their home. The Carbon Trust estimates that while almost all of us are concerned about energy use at home, less than half of us have the same concern for our workplace.[16] Power dynamics or a poor information flow can all affect how we make decisions about energy use at work:

- Large workplaces often have complex heating, ventilation and lighting systems which are hard to understand and may not have been explained to the managers and staff who need to be able to control them.
- People who feel alienated from their employers may not be motivated to help reduce their carbon footprint.

And we may have other reasons for avoiding taking action in the workplace.

- If the working environment is shabby, chilly, draughty or uncomfortable, turning up the thermostat and leaving the lights on may make it feel more homely.
- When employees are under increasing pressure to deliver more work with fewer resources, stickers exhorting people to turn the lights off may be experienced as a nagging voice from the employer.
- If managers and colleagues don't discuss climate change, people may feel it isn't really a priority.

> *It's the simple things – people open a window rather than turning the heating down, and they don't really think about it. They're hot, so they open a window. And there are radiator controls on every radiator, so it's not that it couldn't be done. I suppose it's a lack of common knowledge in the workplace.*
>
> Julie Pickard

- People who are conscientious about keeping the thermostat low at home, may feel like the workplace is somewhere they are allowed to be irresponsible.
- If people have to wear a uniform or if there is a dress code, then adding a jumper or removing a tie may not be a possible response to feeling too cold or too hot.
- Workplaces often have shared rumours about what the rules say – for example that printers and computers should always be left on so that they can be used remotely.

These feelings are entirely understandable, but if we are to minimise climate change, helping to bring down our employer's carbon footprint is just as important as reducing our own. The Carbon Trust estimates that a typical organisation with ten employees could save a tonne of carbon dioxide a year if employees switch off lights when a room is empty and at the end of the day.

But it's not just about taking individual actions. The first step may be to have a conversation about what could be done. Talking to immediate colleagues is a good start, and this may prompt a more formal meeting. Can you involve managers? Is there a technical expert you can invite in to advise you? Can you discuss what matters to people about the workplace and how it could be made more comfortable while saving energy?

Practical actions

Many of the 'Good Housekeeping' tasks listed earlier may also apply to the building you work in. Which of the following could you do?

- Switch off lights when you leave a room, when there is enough natural light and at the end of the day.
- Close blinds to prevent overheating and open them to provide daylight.
- Switch off computers, printers, fax machines, photocopiers and other equipment, where appropriate, at the end of the working day.
- Only fill kettles with the amount of water needed.

Conversations with colleagues could result in agreements to:

- close external doors and windows in chilly weather – remember to put a sign on doors if necessary to explain to visitors that you are open;
- have coffee and tea-breaks in groups, so that you don't keep boiling the kettle individually.

Moving beyond the simple actions you can do yourself means finding out more about the organisation you work for and the building you work in. Many organisations have an environmental

> **"** Our mistake, as managers, was not starting with talking. I was prompted into action when a young staff member wrote an impassioned memo about why reducing our carbon emissions was important. With the help of the facilities department the management team issued an action plan but staff got annoyed and uncooperative. When we asked people to discuss the plan in their teams, however, there were lots of good questions and sensible suggestions. We began to get support and, even though the thermostat still got turned up occasionally, it was more acceptable to turn it down again and people began to come in with warmer clothes.
>
> Rebecca Nestor

policy with objectives for energy reduction. Some have Corporate Social Responsibility statements with environmental goals. Large organisations have to monitor and report their energy use and many large buildings display Energy Performance Certificates.[17] The buildings themselves may have:

- a Facilities Manager or an Energy Manager who can advise you on how to use the building's systems properly;
- a business owner who might be grateful for some help with their environmental impact;
- a landlord who can be approached and may be interested in improving the premises.

Large buildings are complex. Retail, office, leisure and factory buildings all face different challenges and many organisations will need specialist advice on how to reduce energy use. Often an energy audit is the first step. This identifies how the building works at present and can lead to:

- simple steps such as resetting controls and putting up notices explaining how to use them;
- plans for involving employees in 'Good Housekeeping' measures;
- plans for upgrading heating, ventilation, lighting and IT systems with (for example) more efficient boilers, better controls, LED lighting and automatic switch-off;
- plans for upgrading the building itself with better insulation, windows and blinds.

As an employee you may be able to start the conversations with colleagues and managers that lead to your organisation taking some of these larger steps, but it is just as important to be part of a growing group of people who make it normal to notice how a building is working. Once it feels normal to turn off the lights, fiddle with the blinds or look for the heating controls, everyone will do it. Don't underestimate the importance of this contribution.

👍 Rules of thumb

Small is beautiful

The smallest you can manage with is the best; smaller houses, smaller appliances, shorter showers are all winners.

Monitoring is a must

If you measure it you can manage it. Unless you read your meters regularly you won't be able to see whether the changes you are making are having the effects you hoped for.

Insulation! Insulation! Insulation!

Insulated lofts, walls, floors and pipes are all winners. Heavy curtains and window shutters will also help. It's difficult to overdo insulation. Aim to need no heating at all.

If in doubt, switch it off!

It's never more efficient to leave things running when you're not using them.

Ditch dinosaurs

It's sometimes better to get rid of an inefficient appliance, even though it still works.

Build tight, ventilate right

Draughts are not a good way of getting the fresh air you need. Make sure your house is air tight and also has the necessary ventilation in the form of fans, and windows that can be opened.

Recognise expertise

Look for builders and architects with real experience of low-energy construction. Don't get confused by chat on the internet: use the reliable resources suggested in More Information.

Be kind to yourself

Your green solutions are more likely to succeed if they are also comfortable and convenient.

Talk, plan, do

Talk to the people you live with, make plans together, act on them.

Frequently asked questions

If you can't find the answer to your question here or in the A-Z of Home Energy try the Centre for Alternative Technology's online Information Service http://info.cat.org.uk/.

Which form of home heating creates least CO_2?

Per kWh, going from best to worst: natural gas, heat pumps, liquid gas, oil, coal, electricity. Wood and other forms of biomass are often considered low-carbon because they absorb CO_2 as they grow. However, as wood burns it emits a similar amount of CO_2 to coal so you may want to consider other low-carbon heating methods, combined with super-efficient insulation. Heat pumps and electricity will become better solutions as the grid is decarbonised.

Aren't wood and other forms of biomass a sustainable solution?

Even if you see them as low-carbon, wood and biomass can only solve a small percentage of our national energy needs due to the limited amount of land available for growing them. They may be acceptable as an interim measure, particularly if you have a good source of local timber or scrap wood for your stove.

Is a wood pellet boiler a good solution?

Wood pellet boilers are more efficient than wood-burning stoves and can be used for central heating if mains gas is not available. However, some wood pellets come from unsustainable sources, often from overseas. Make sure you know what you are buying.

I love an open fire – is it a good way to heat my home?

Open fires are one of the least efficient forms of heating. Warm air from the house is drawn up the chimney with the smoke. Turn off any other heating if you use your fire, so you are not sucking already heated air up the chimney. A flue baffle will stop warm air rushing up the chimney when the fire is not lit. An old pillow will do, or you can buy a chimney balloon, but remember to remove it before you light the fire and to replace it afterwards. Coal is a very high-carbon fuel and there are concerns about burning wood as we describe above.

What about nuclear power?

Nuclear power has some strong advocates, including in government. We're not keen because of the time it takes to build new nuclear plants, unresolved waste disposal issues and security risks. We think renewables provide a safer, quicker option.

I buy my electricity on a renewable tariff. Surely it doesn't matter how much I use?

Renewable energy is a scarce resource and shouldn't be wasted. The complexity of the electricity market means that even the best green tariffs do not really provide all your electricity from renewable sources as the renewable aspect of the electricity you buy has been counted and sold several times over. Nonetheless by signing up you help increase the market for renewables and provide investment.

Is it worth fitting a solar water heater?

Yes: when you can afford it and if you have a suitable roof.

Does the feed-in tariff make photovoltaics (PV) a good place to start?

PV could be part of your whole house plan if you have a suitable roof. It's just as important to reduce your demand for energy – make sure you also insulate and draught-strip properly.

Which are the best energy-saving lightbulbs?
The most efficient are modern LEDs. New models are being developed all the time. Compact fluorescents are much better than halogen bulbs. No-one should still be using old-fashioned incandescent bulbs. If you have any left, don't wait for them to burn out. Replace them immediately as you will quickly recover the energy that went into their manufacture.

Doesn't it use a lot of electricity turning lights off and on?
No. This is an urban myth.

I get headaches working under fluorescent lights. Do I have to have them at home as well?
Old-fashioned fluorescent strip lights flickered at only 100 times per second and caused headaches. Modern compact fluorescents generate 40,000 flickers per second. This looks continuous to the human eye. They won't give you headaches.

Is it better to replace my old fridge with a more energy-efficient model now, or wait until it breaks down?
If your fridge is quite old (over 8 years) it is worth checking its energy-performance. Look at its energy-label or check its performance with a plug-in power meter. A new fridge could save 200 kWh per year. This will rapidly make up for the energy used in manufacturing it.

My TV only uses 1 watt on standby. Surely it's not really worth turning it off all the time?
A house with some older equipment, including two TVs, a computer system, a Hi-Fi system and three mobile phone chargers could be using 15 watts constantly. This is almost 130 kWh or 60 kg of CO_2 per year (equivalent to a 200 mile car journey). Sort out your plugs and leads so that it is easy to turn things off.

How should I dry the washing in winter?
Try to reduce the amount of laundry you do and dry it outside when you can. Drying clothes indoors cools the house down and may require additional ventilation to stop the windows steaming up and the house getting damp. Try to dry clothes in an unheated room where you can open a window when needed without losing heat. In a modern, completely airtight house it may be better to use a tumble drier. Make sure you run it for the shortest time possible.

If I stop up all the draughts, won't the house get awfully stuffy?
Be in control of your ventilation. You need a system where you can open trickle vents or windows when you want to, rather than relying on a general draughtiness to get fresh air. Stuffiness is often caused by the air being dry and cold, rather than stale. It often happens when cold, dry air is leaking into the house.

Are there any dangers in stopping all draughts?
Rooms with open fires or old gas fires or boilers need a fixed air supply. This is usually provided by an airbrick or a window ventilator. There is a risk of carbon monoxide poisoning, particularly from gas fires, if you ignore this. If you buy new furniture or carpets or have building work done involving particle board, you may need to ventilate the room to get rid of volatile organic compounds (VOCs) used in their manufacture.

My house doesn't feel draughty. Do I really need draught-stripping round the windows?
It may not feel draughty because the house is generally warm. This doesn't mean that there is no air movement. Heated air will be going out of your windows! Draught-stripping will stop this waste of energy.

carbonconversations.org

My hot-water tank is well lagged. Isn't it better to leave the hot water on all the time, rather than letting it cool down and heat up again?

No. The energy needed to heat up a tank of water is less than the energy needed to keep it warm all the time.

Is it really worth doing all those fiddly things like lagging hot-water pipes, putting foil behind the radiators and putting up radiator shelves?

Yes. You only have to do it once, it is an easy way to save a few watts, and it will make the house more comfortable.

Can I put temporary double glazing on any window?

Almost. You must not cover any fixed ventilation for fires or heaters in the room. You should not put fixed panes over windows that might be used as escapes, in case of fire.

If I fill my cavity wall with insulation, won't it let in the damp?

Not if it's done properly. This used to be a problem with some foams which shrank, cracked and allowed water to run through the gaps. Modern materials are more stable and water repellent.

I'm worried that dry-lining the walls could make the brickwork damp.

This can be a problem with older buildings, so you must take good advice and use an experienced contractor. Breathing insulation is one solution.

I'm worried that dry-lining my solid walls will make the room much smaller. Is it OK to use less insulation?

Ideally you should install at least 100mm of rockwool or 85mm of polyurethane. In most rooms you don't notice the small reduction in size and you gain by being able to use the room fully – putting a bed or chair against a previously cold wall for example. Small rooms with two external walls may be a problem, in which case you should consider external insulation instead. Do not be fooled by companies selling unlikely products like insulating paint and insulating wallpaper or making claims of extremely high performances for thin products.

The new building regulations are so much better than the old ones, my builder says it's not worth doing more than the regulations demand. Is he right?

No. Try to build for the future. Today's standards will soon be out of date. Try to make sure that your house will achieve an 'A' rating on the EPC standards or go for the equally demanding Passivhaus (Enerphit) standard.

My friends say one thing, my builder says another, my plumber has a third opinion and the internet offers a dozen more. How do I decide what to do?

Compared with the rest of Northern Europe, the British construction industry has a poor record in training, in education and in following best practice for energy efficiency. This results in conflicting and poor advice being given by people with insufficient knowledge. Look for people with real experience of low-energy building. This might be a builder or an architect or others who have had low-energy renovations done. Best-practice guides are published by the Energy Saving Trust and the National Refurbishment Centre and your builder or architect should be referring to them – see More Information for details.

More information

This section lists a small number of books and websites with good, accessible information that will help you fill in the background and follow up facts you are not clear on. You will find more detailed sources and a wider selection of reading in the Notes.

I'd like to know more about…

…building control and planning regulations

Contact your local authority. The Planning Department and the Building Control Office are usually run by the district or city council. The Planning Department can tell you about permitted development and whether you need permission for a solar panel or other upgrades you are planning. The Building Control Office oversees implementation of building regulations and can advise on the standards currently in force for projects you are planning.

…examples of eco-refurbishment

Superhomes (UK wide) and the *Green Homes Network* (Scotland) showcase numerous homes that you can arrange to visit, http://www.superhomes.org.uk, and http://bit.ly/EST-greenhomes.

You can also search for Open Eco House or Green Door events in your area. Here a number of home-owners open their houses on the same day, allowing you to compare their approaches and solutions.

…getting an energy survey done

A Green Deal survey costs about £100. You can find a surveyor through the official *Green Deal* website, http://bit.ly/Greendeal-survey, or you can call the *Energy Saving Advice Service* on 0300 123 1234. Some local community groups offer energy surveys and in London, *Parity Projects* are a commercial organisation with a good reputation, http://www.parityprojects.com/.

…grants, loans and financial help

The *Energy Saving Trust* can tell you about the Green Deal, ECO, the Feed-In Tariff and the Renewable Heat Incentive. There is a network of local offices that can be reached via http://www.est.org.uk/ or 0300 123 1234 (England, Wales and NI) or 0800 512012 (Scotland).

Information about the Landlords Energy Saving Allowance (LESA) is at http://bit.ly/hmrc-landlord.

…heritage and older buildings

The *English Heritage* website *Climate Change and Your Home* is a good source of information about how to deal with older properties, http://bit.ly/CC-yourhome.

Historic Scotland's website has a number of guides that deal with Scottish homes, for example *Improving Energy Efficiency in Traditional Buildings* and *Fabric Improvements for Energy Efficiency in Traditional Buildings* available at http://bit.ly/old-building.

Try reading *Energy Efficiency in Old Houses*, M.G. Cook, Crowood Press, 2009, or *Old House Eco Handbook: A Practical Guide to Retrofitting for Energy-Efficiency and Sustainability*, Roger Hunt and Marianne Suhr, Frances Lincoln, 2013.

…monitoring my energy use

Sign up to iMeasure, http://www.imeasure.org.uk/, or *The Carbon Account* http://www.thecarbonaccount.com/.

...policy

The UK government set out their policy here, http://bit.ly/govuk-policies, but for a stronger vision read *Achieving Zero: Delivering Future-Friendly Buildings*, Brenda Boardman, Environmental Change Institute, 2012, http://bit.ly/Boardman-2012.

...renewable technologies

Try the Energy Saving Trust's *Guide to Renewable Technology*, http://bit.ly/est-renewables, or read *The Home Energy Handbook: a Guide to Saving and Generating Energy in your Home and Community*, Allan Shephard et al, Centre for Alternative Technology Publications, 2012.

...retrofitting my home

Eco-House Manual, Nigel Griffiths, Haynes Publishing, 2012 is well-illustrated and practical.

Sustainable Home Refurbishment: the Earthscan Guide to Retrofitting your Home for Efficiency, David Thorpe, Earthscan, 2010, is a technical book with good advice on how to make a plan and achieve a complete retrofit bit by bit.

The Environmental Design Pocketbook, Sofie Pelsmakers, RIBA publishing, 2012 is a technical handbook for builders and eco-renovators

...sources of advice

Online, try the *Centre for Alternative Technology*'s online Information Service, http://info.cat.org.uk/, or the Energy Saving Trust, http://www.est.org.uk/.

If you want to talk to someone, ring the *Energy Saving Trust* 0300 123 1234 (England, Wales and NI) or 0800 512012 (Scotland).

Look for an architect or builder through the *AECB*, http://www.aecb.net/, the *PassivHaus Trust*, http://www.passivhaus.org.uk, or the *Green Register*, http://www.greenregister.org.uk/.

...standards and specifications

The *National Refurbishment Centre* publishes 'Best Practice' guides, http://bit.ly/NRC-refur-bguide. Some others that should be on your architect's or designer's shelves are:

Sustainable Refurbishment CE309 from the Energy Saving Trust, 2010, http://bit.ly/est-refurb.

The Green Guide to Specification(4th edition): an Environmental Profiling System for Building Materials and Components, Jane Anderson et al, Wiley-Blackwell, 2009, http://bit.ly/Anderson-2009.

The Green Building Bible: Essential Information to Help you Make your Home and Buildings Less Harmful to the Environment, the Community and your Family, Keith Hall, The Green Building Press, 2008.

The PassivHaus Handbook: a Practical Guide to Constructing and Retrofitting Buildings for Ultra-Low Energy Performance, Janet Cotterell and Adam Dadeby, Green Books, 2012.

...what's happening in Scotland

Look at the *Greener Scotland* site, http://www.greenerscotland.org/, and at Changeworks who run home energy advice centres across Scotland, http://www.changeworks.org.uk/.

The A-Z of home energy

Not sure what a technical term means? Want to check out the details of different options? Use this alphabetical guide to help you.

Best practice
Doing better than the average. If we are building for 2050, it makes sense to plan for something that will not seem like a dinosaur by then. This means going beyond the minimum requirements of the building regulations. Advice on best practice can be found in the guides published by the National Refurbishment Centre (www.rethinkingrefurbishment.com) or in voluntary codes like the AECB Gold standard or the Passivhaus standard.

Biofuel heating
There are various biomass fuel crops. The one most common in domestic use is wood, in the form of chips or pellets. Wood-pellet boilers work like conventional ones. They are automatic, only requiring the fuel hopper to be filled and the ash to be emptied from time to time. They can be used instead of oil, but take up more room than an oil system.

Burning wood or other biofuels emits a similar amount of CO_2 to burning oil, coal or gas. Biofuels are seen as low-carbon options because the trees or plants absorbed CO_2 as they grew. There are concerns about widespread use of biofuels and many people argue that they should be seen as a transitional solution only while more truly climate-friendly options are developed. Biofuel boilers are eligible for RHI (see below) and are counted as a low-carbon option in EPC calculations (see below).

Boiler types – Combi and System
Combination or Combi boilers combine central heating (hot water for the radiators) and instantaneous water heating (for the taps). System boilers heat the radiators and store the hot water for the taps in a separate hot water cylinder. Combi boilers are popular because they do not need a hot-water cylinder or header tank. System boilers are more suitable for big houses. If you are installing a new boiler, make sure that it has the highest SEDBUK rating (see below) and that it is compatible with a solar water heater, in case you want to install this as well – now or later.

Building regulations
These are legal standards for buildings, set by government and enforced by local authorities. Although they cover the energy efficiency of buildings, you will have to exceed these standards in order to create a truly low-carbon house.

Cavity wall insulation
Between about 1930 and 1982 most houses were built with two skins of brick, separated with a 50 mm (2 inch) gap. Initially, this was seen as a good way to keep the inside walls dry. Now it is seen as a good place to put insulation. This is blown in through small holes drilled in the outside walls. There may be a grant or loan available for this. See Green Deal.

Central heating controls
These should help your system work more efficiently. Ideally the controls will: switch the system on and off at times convenient for you; allow you to adjust individual room temperatures as well as controlling the firing of the boiler, so that it works efficiently. If you are installing a new boiler or having other work done on your central heating system, look at also upgrading your controls.

carbonconversations.org

Code for Sustainable Homes

This is a set of design standards from the government setting out energy and environmental standards for new houses. At the time of writing the government has back-pedalled on promises to make these mandatory.

Cold bridging

When you are insulating solid walls, any steel lintels, window frames and the corners of the house can create cold bridges where heat has an opportunity to escape. The cold bridge can encourage damp. Care must be taken with the detail of these parts of the job. Insulation often needs to be extended around the corners of rooms and into the window reveals.

Combined heat-and-power

This system uses the extra heat created in generating electricity to produce hot water. The old Battersea power station used to do this. Many hotels have small gas-powered engines that generate electricity and heat their water. Blocks of flats or even whole streets can be designed for combined heat-and-power. Units are now available that are small enough for use by a single house.

Comfort

Energy consultants mean something very specific by comfort. They define it as the right combination of air temperature, surface temperature (temperature of the walls, windows, and radiators or other heaters) and humidity. Well-insulated walls have a higher surface temperature and are more likely to make occupants feel comfortable.

Composting loos

These are dry toilets that produce useful compost. They save precious water and remove the need for disposal systems or drain connections. They have to be carefully designed to be convenient and hygienic and are most suited to rural locations.

Condensation and mould

Where warm, humid air from the house permeates into a cold place, such as behind the insulation on a solid wall, it can lead to condensation. Mould can grow on timber and other organic materials whenever the humidity is high even if there is no visible damp. Proper detailing will avoid this problem. This might include a vapour barrier or a ventilated cavity.

Condensing boilers

These are now the standard for gas heating. They achieve high efficiency by extracting so much energy from the burnt gas that the steam condenses. Look for one with an 'A' rating, either a System or a Combi boiler. Oil boilers can also be designed to work in condensing mode but are more expensive as components have to be protected from the corrosion produced by sulphur in the oil.

Conservatories and sun spaces

South-facing walls are ideal for conservatories or sun spaces. Designed, built and used properly, these can make a contribution to home heating by trapping the warmth of the sun, even in the winter. Unfortunately some people install them as a cheap way of extending living space and try to heat them in the winter. Even if the conservatory is double glazed, the amount of energy wasted is huge. Think of your conservatory as a buffer space between indoors and outdoors which is warming the rest of your house.

Controls

Thermostats, time clocks and light sensors can automatically turn things off saving you money and reducing your CO_2 emissions. All are easily fitted by electricians or a heating contractor. Review the times and temperatures from time to time: small changes can make a big difference. See also: Central heating controls, Lighting controls, Radiators.

Curtains and shutters

If you have single glazed windows, curtains are especially important as they reduce heat loss and make the room feel warmer. Make sure they are thick and lined, and that you close them at dusk. A common mistake is to have curtains hanging down over the front of a radiator. This directs the heat straight out the window! A shelf above the radiator will keep the curtain off the radiator and direct heat into the room instead. In Victorian or Georgian houses, restoring the original wooden shutters is an effective option.

Decarbonising the grid

The amount of CO_2 emitted by the UK's power stations depends on the balance of coal, gas, nuclear and renewable energy generators which are operating at any time. As more renewables come on stream the amount of CO_2 per kWh will decrease. This will lower the impact of heat pumps and electric heating, but electricity is likely to become a more valuable commodity.

Defrosting

If you keep your fridge and freezer defrosted, they will work more efficiently. Cleaning the dust off the fins at the back will also improve their efficiency.

DIY secondary glazing

A range of products available in any DIY store will reduce the heat loss and draughts around windows. Plastic film can be taped up, as a temporary measure, for one or two winters. It is cheap and surprisingly invisible. More expensive framed systems can be fitted with clear plastic panels or glass. Be careful not to put unbreakable plastic over a window that might need to be used as a fire exit in an emergency. Check sufficient ventilation is left for any gas fires or stoves.

Double and triple glazing

The best windows have three layers of low-e glass in sealed units. PVC units have a high environmental cost in their manufacture and a relatively short life. Wood needs regular maintenance. On a listed building, or in a conservation area, you may need to get windows specially made. Windows and doors now come with A to G ratings, awarded by the British Fenestration Ratings Council (www.bfrc.org) Look for those with an 'A' rating. See also Low-e coatings.

Draught stripping/sealing

This is one of the most effective improvements you can make. Draughts are responsible for a huge amount of heat loss. Most new windows and doors come with their own draught seals. There are a range of materials to help control draughts around older windows and doors. Look in your local DIY store. Most are simple to fit. If you are redecorating, remember not to paint over existing seals.

Dry-lining

Houses built before about 1930 were usually built with solid brick or stone walls. Dry-lining adds an inner skin to an outside wall, on top of an intervening layer of insulation. The room becomes slightly smaller but, even in small houses, this is rarely noticeable or a problem. In a cold house, dry-lining creates more useable space as it is no longer uncomfortable to sit near external walls. The work itself is disruptive and best done when redecorating or when new windows are being installed. It needs to be done by a competent builder who understands the technical issues of condensation and cold bridges.

Drying clothes

This is best done outdoors! Tumble driers use a lot of electricity and should be seen as a last resort. Indoors, try to dry your clothes in an unheated space: if you have to open a window to disperse the damp, it won't waste too much energy.

Electrical appliances

All refrigeration and laundry appliances, dishwashers, electric ovens and lightbulbs must now carry an EU energy label. These rate appliances from A, A* or A++ for the best, down to G for the worst. Choose the highest rating available every time! If you are buying something without an EU rating, ask about its power consumption.

Embodied or embedded carbon

This is the technical term for the carbon or CO_2 emissions that result from manufacturing items that you buy. You may also hear these referred to as indirect emissions or Scope 3 emissions.

Energy Company Obligation (ECO)

This is an element of the Green Deal (below). ECO provides: means tested funding for the poorest households; grants for solid wall insulation; support for community groups upgrading community buildings. It is funded by a levy on the Energy Companies.

Energy Performance Certificate (EPC)

Whenever a home is sold or is re-let, it needs an EPC. This gives the house a rating from A to G for its energy efficiency. If you are applying for the Feed-In Tariff (see below) you will need an EPC showing that your home is at least a D.

External insulation

Insulation can be attached to external walls and then plastered or boarded over to give an attractive finish. It can be expensive but the work is not disruptive. The detail around windows and doors needs to be well designed.

Feed-in tariff

This is a subsidy for micro-generation (see below). Owners of eligible technologies receive a payment for every kWh of renewable energy they generate, whether it is used in the home or fed back to the electricity grid.

FSC timber

Timber that has been certified by the Forest Stewardship Council (FSC) has come from a sustainably managed source (http://www.fsc.org).

Full loads

Most appliances will use similar amounts of electricity or water whether they are full or empty. Even the clever ones that adjust for the load are most efficient when full.

Green Deal

This is a Government scheme to encourage insulation and energy retrofits of existing buildings. Home-owners and landlords can borrow money to retrofit their home and the money is repaid by an addition to their electricity bills. The so-called golden rule ensures that repayments don't increase the previous gas and electricity bills. This limits the size of the loan which will probably be no more than £10,000. There are some grants available under the ECO scheme (see above). The system is managed by green deal providers who start the process by carrying out a green deal assessment, similar to an EPC survey.

Grey-water system

This uses collected rain water or filtered waste water to flush WC's. It requires extra grey water pipework and a storage tank.

Ground-floor insulation

Insulation can be installed under the floorboards, or under a solid floor, to prevent heat loss. Timber floors have to be lifted. Then, rockwool can be laid over the joists or rigid insulation can be cut and fixed between the joists. Breather paper or plastic sheet placed over the joists before the boards are re-fitted will stop a lot of draughts. Existing solid floors are harder to deal with. It is sometimes possible to install an insulating barrier around the house, against the outside wall above the foundations. These are jobs best done as part of a complete refurbishment, or because the floor needs replacing for other reasons.

Heat pumps

Heat pumps use electricity to extract energy from the air or ground outside and transform it so it can be used to heat the house. Every kilowatt hour of electricity used by the system's heat exchanger and compressor delivers 3–4 kWh to the house. Ground-source heat pumps are more efficient than air-source heat pumps. Ground-source heat pumps use long coils of water-filled pipe buried in the ground; they are expensive to install and require a large garden. Air-source heat pumps look like small air-conditioning units and are fixed to an outside wall or roof. They are cheaper to install and are gaining in popularity in the UK. Heat pumps are most appropriate for highly insulated houses that are supplied by renewable electricity.

Heat recovery

Heat-recovery systems allow stale air out and fresh air in without losing all the heat. They come in the form of kitchen and bathroom extractor fans and as bigger whole-house systems. The best models are quiet and have efficient fans.

Heritage buildings

Buildings with architectural significance are protected from alteration by planning law, administered by the local authority. Many old buildings are listed and require a discussion with the local heritage officer before changes can be made. Houses in conservation areas, national parks and other protected areas also have limitations on the changes that can be made. See also Permitted development.

Hot-water cylinder

Gas, oil, wood and solar water systems can all have hot-water cylinders. New cylinders come with some insulation, but you can get jackets to add more. Stuff old duvets round for a DIY solution.

Hot-water pipes

Pipes are the Cinderella of insulation. Most could do with being wrapped up. If you're having building work done, insist that pipes are lagged. Otherwise, take it on as a DIY job. Use purpose-made pipe insulation (available from DIY stores) and don't forget to tape the joints. In particular, check: the pipes between the boiler and the hot-water cylinder; heating pipes under the floor or in unheated spaces; all hot-water pipes; and any cold-water pipes that suffer from condensation.

Insulation

See Cavity wall insulation, Dry lining, External insulation, Ground-floor insulation, Insulation materials, Loft insulation and Roof insulation.

Insulation materials

There is a huge choice and different materials suit different jobs. The most efficient (by thickness) is polyurethane foam (e.g., Celotex, Kingspan). However it is made from petrochemicals and is not cheap.

The cheapest (for a given level of insulation) is probably fibreglass or rockwool. However fibreglass is an irritant to skin, lungs and eyes and hazardous in exposed areas.

There is a huge range of materials made from organic or recycled materials, such as wood fibre, wool, flax, hemp and cotton waste. Many of these can breathe and help control condensation inside the wall. Most are still more expensive and more bulky than the mineral and oil based products.

Landlords Energy Saving Allowance (LESA)

This allows landlords to offset the cost of energy improvements against the tax on rental income.

Lightbulbs

These are listed below, in order of efficiency, starting with the best.

- LEDs (light emitting diodes): these provide some of the most efficient light sources and are increasingly popular. New lamps and fittings are being introduced all the time.
- Compact fluorescents (CFLs): often called energy-efficient or low-energy bulbs, these are 400–500% more efficient than ordinary (GLS) bulbs, and now come in numerous shapes, sizes and ratings.
- Tungsten–halogen: often used for spotlights in kitchens, some up-lighters and garden lights, these are 30–100% more efficient than ordinary (GLS) bulbs, but the saving is often illusory because more are installed.
- Incandescent or GLS bulbs: these ordinary, old-style lightbulbs are horribly inefficient and are being phased out. Over 90% of their energy is lost as heat.

Compact fluorescents are often labelled to show which ordinary lightbulb they should replace. Manufacturers sometimes overestimate their power which leads people to complain that they are not bright enough. A 20 watt CFL may be labelled as equivalent to a 100 watt ordinary bulb but in fact its output is closer to an 80 watt old-style bulb. If you want the equivalent of 100 watts you need to choose a 25 watt CFL.

Lighting

The light delivered to the surface you are lighting is dependent both on the rating of the bulb and on the light fitting. Recessed lights and dark lampshades waste a lot of energy. Up-lighters, which bounce the light off the ceiling, are not as efficient as direct lighting, especially if the ceiling is not a brilliant white. The best strategy is to provide a warm background light and local lighting where it is needed (e.g. on kitchen worktops or where you sit and read). Always choose light fittings that will take low energy bulbs. These are not always easy to find; you may need to search and be persistent.

Lighting controls
Motion and daylight detectors can sometimes be useful in making sure lights are not left on unnecessarily.

Loft insulation
Many houses have no more than 50 mm or 2" of loft insulation, although the recommended level is now 270 mm or 10.5". This will stick up over the joists so, if you want to store things in your loft, you will have to construct a platform above the insulation. Don't forget to insulate and draught seal the loft hatch. Be careful not to bury any wiring; and leave a small breathing space between the insulation and the roofing felt by the eaves. Fitting more loft insulation is one of the easiest and most effective things you can do.

In an attic room, you can insulate between the rafters and plasterboard over it. In small attics and older loft conversions, it can be hard to get enough insulation in place this way. It may be possible to install external insulation when the roof needs replacing (see Roof insulation).

Low-e coating
A treatment for glass used in double glazed windows, that increases its efficiency by reducing heat loss.

Low energy bulbs
See Lightbulbs.

Micro-generation
A term used for small renewable electricity systems, such as roof-mounted photovoltaic panels or small wind turbines. For the purposes of FIT (see above) heat pumps are also included in this category.

Ofgem
Ofgem is a government body which regulates the gas and electricity markets in the UK. It is the gateway to FIT payments (see above) and RHI payments (see below).

Passivhaus
This is a building energy standard for both new and retrofitted homes with its own certification system which ensures compliance. It is one of the most demanding standards. To comply a building will need 250mm or more insulation, triple glazing, a very high standard of air tightness and a full heat recovery ventilation system.

Permitted development
This is a term used by planners to describe the small changes you are allowed to make without applying for planning permission. It enables solar panels to be installed without obtaining permission (except for heritage buildings).

Photovoltaics

These are solar panels that generate electricity from sunlight. The price is dropping as more systems are installed. Like solar water panels, they are usually fixed to the roof and need a south-facing slope. They are eligible for the feed-in tariff.

Pipe lagging

See Hot-water pipes.

Radiators

These will not be needed in super insulated houses! In older houses, if they are against an outside wall, you should fit reflecting foil behind them. (This is available in rolls from DIY shops). If they are positioned below a window, a small shelf (or an extension to the sill) that sits at least 50mm above the radiator will stop warm air rising straight up from the radiator and going out the window. The curtains can then rest on the shelf and stop cool air next to the window from dropping down and cooling the room. Fit thermostatic radiator valves to allow control of individual rooms.

Renewable Heat Incentive

A government scheme, similar to the Feed-in tariff, the RHI rewards carbon savings made with renewable heating systems. It makes annual payments for systems including solar hot water, biomass heating and ground-source and air-source heat pumps.

Renewable Heat Premium Payment

This small grant can help you install solar water heaters and biomass boilers.

Roof insulation

Flat roofs can be insulated on the outside. This is a good job to do when you are re-felting. It is also possible to insulate a pitched roof on the outside by lifting the slates or tiles, fixing insulated sarking board to the rafters and fixing the tiles back to the board. This may be the solution for houses with loft conversions. The detailing needs to be properly designed.

SAP

This stands for Standard Assessment Procedure and is a calculation used in the building regulations to estimate the energy efficiency of a building.

SEDBUK

This stands for Seasonal Efficiency of Domestic Boilers in the UK, and is the rating scheme for boiler efficiency.

Showers and baths

Generally, having a shower will use less water and therefore less energy than a bath. Typically, a five minute shower will use 35–50 litres and a bath 80–100 litres. However, some power showers can use as much water as a bath.

Shrink-wrap

See DIY secondary glazing.

Smart meters
These are electricity and gas meters that communicate directly with your supply company so you don't need to take readings. They provide clear displays of energy consumption to the home-owner and will allow the energy company to offer variable tariffs, depending on factors like the time of day or the amount of energy available from the power stations. There is a programme to install them in all UK homes by 2020.

Solar-powered hot water
Solar panels on your roof can provide about 50% of all your hot water – almost all that is needed in the summer and a significant amount in both spring and autumn. There are two types: flat glazed panels and groups of evacuated glass tubes. The tubes perform better in winter. Both types work best on south-facing roof slopes. Other situations may be suitable but will need specialist advice. If you have a combination boiler and no hot-water storage, you will need a new cylinder and possibly modifications to your boiler. The system usually needs a larger, specialised hot-water cylinder. This will store a few days' worth of hot water and allow an ordinary boiler to top it up on cloudy and winter days. There are small grants for new installations (see Renewable Heat Premium Payment) and there will be ongoing subsidies under the Renewable Heat Incentive (see above).

Solid walls
The usual term for external walls constructed without a cavity. See Dry Lining.

Standby
Turning things off standby mode saves small amounts of electricity. Appliances tend to be left on standby permanently, so these small amounts quickly add up, especially as homes have more and more equipment powered from small transformers. More efficient switch mode transform-ers may make it acceptable to leave one or two essential devices on.

Thermostats
Turning your room thermostat down by 1 °C will save about 10% of the fuel used (see also Controls).

Turf and sedum roofs
Flat roofs can be covered with turf or sedum moss, which slows the water run-off, attracts wildlife and helps the energy performance of the roof. They should be installed over insulation. You need to check the structure first, because of the additional weight.

Turning things off
There is no better way to save energy than to switch things off! Don't be misled by urban myths that fluorescent lights (this includes energy-efficient bulbs) should not be turned off too often.

Under-floor heating
Useful in well insulated houses, a warm floor provides a more comfortable heat than radiators and can use lower temperature heat sources.

Ventilation
Fresh air is needed to control both moisture and smell. As a house becomes better insulated and air tight, proper provision must be made to provide the right amount of ventilation at the right times with the lowest energy costs, e.g. heat recovery extractor fans with humidistats or whole-house heat recovery systems.

Wind turbines

These come in all sizes. Off the coast, machines of 5 MW (5000 kW) have blades 50 metres long and feed the national grid. Local wind turbines of about 1.5 MW can supply 1,100 homes. You can buy small units about 2 metres across to install on your roof, like a satellite dish but we wouldn't recommend these. They are designed to produce 1 kW in ideal conditions and may produce up to 2500 kWh a year. However, they are not ideal in urban areas. They can be noisy, turbulence from other buildings lowers their efficiency, and planners may object.

Wood-burning stoves

Wood is sometimes seen as a sustainable fuel and a stove is much more efficient than an open fire. There is a great range of stoves including models that can heat hot water and run radiators. Wood is only a transitional solution however. See Biofuel heating.

Zero-carbon home

A zero-carbon home is one that meets Code 6 of the Code for Sustainable Homes. The term does not include embodied carbon in the fabric of the building but does include electricity used by lighting, cooking and appliances. A certain amount of off-setting or generation from off-site renewables is allowed.

CHAPTER 3

Travel and transport

"I have a love-hate relationship with my car. I know I'm contributing to congestion and pollution but it means freedom and security to me."

Transport policy has encouraged car dependency and congestion

Travel makes up about a quarter of the average UK footprint. It's quite easy to work out how big your travel footprint is but harder to know how to reduce it.

The main issue is the distances we travel. Most of this takes place by car, one of the least efficient means of transport. Cars are woven into every aspect of life, promising freedom but producing traffic jams and frustration. They encourage people to make longer journeys. Those without a car can be excluded from opportunities that others enjoy such as the choice of where to work, where to live and where their children go to school. In this chapter we explore:

- the meaning of travel;
- ways of reducing your CO_2 impact now;
- putting climate change at the heart of future travel decisions;
- options for low-carbon travel in the future.

carbonconversations.org

What's the problem with transport and travel?

The problems with transport and travel come from a difficult mix of corporate self-interest, failed government policy, and the dreams of freedom and fulfilment that car use and foreign travel represent. Oil companies, car manufacturers and governments have worked together since the Second World War to sell a dream that most people have been happy to embrace. Until recently, the downsides of congestion, road accidents and pollution may have seemed a reasonable price to pay. Changing the complex, inter-related systems that revolve around road transport will not be easy, but climate change means that it is essential that we do so.

How did we get here?

Over the last 50 years we have changed:

- the amount of time we spend travelling;
- the distances we travel;
- the balance between the different types of transport we use.

Older people will be able to remember these changes taking place. Younger people may be surprised to learn how different life is now from the way it was 20, 30 or 40 years ago.[1]

- The distances travelled have increased, almost doubling between 1971 and 2006. The average distance for a shopping trip in Britain is now 4.3 miles. The average journey to work is 9 miles.
- Car travel has become cheaper. Between 1998 and 2008 the cost of running a car fell (in real terms) by 13%.
- Car travel has become the norm. It has become hard to have an ordinary life without a car. People who have to use public transport are excluded from some of the things that others enjoy. Car ownership gives status.
- Car-based lifestyles have been encouraged. Patterns of work, housing and shopping have grown up around the convenience of the car.
- Public transport has declined and has become more expensive. Between 1998 and 2008 the cost of bus and coach fares rose (in real terms) by 17% and the cost of train fares (in real terms) by 6%.
- Walking and cycling have decreased. The numbers of journeys made on foot have dropped by about 27% since 1996.
- Cycling has changed from a means of transport to a leisure activity.
- Air travel has become cheaper and more popular. In 1980 UK residents made 18 million overseas visits. In 1998 they made 34 million and in 2012, 56.5 million.

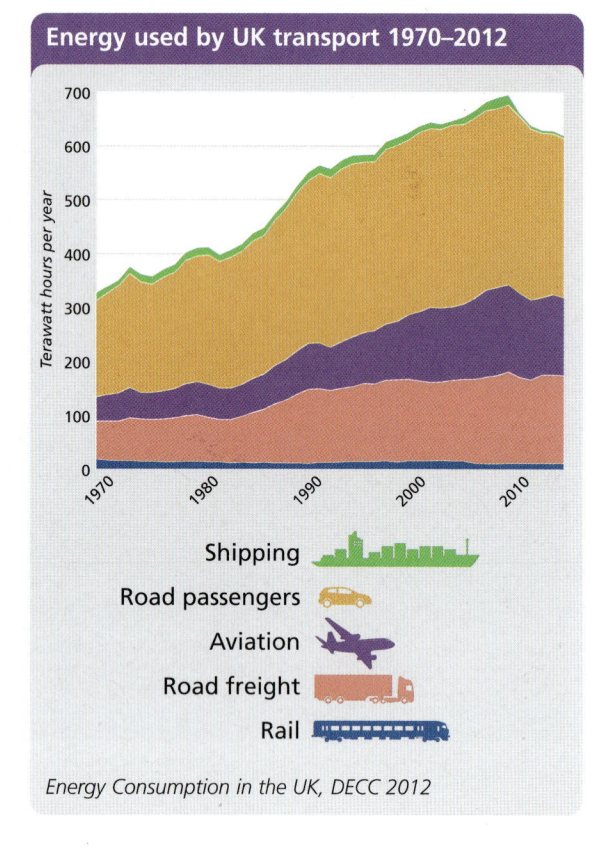

Energy used by UK transport 1970–2012

Shipping
Road passengers
Aviation
Road freight
Rail

Energy Consumption in the UK, DECC 2012

carbonconversations.org

- Governments have all operated a 'Predict and Provide' policy for road and air travel. Forecasts of increased use are made and new roads and airports are planned to meet the demand.

Travel patterns are not uniform. Some cities are less car-dependent than others. In Cambridge 75% of children walk or cycle to school. In London, with its congestion charge and reliable public transport, only 40% of trips are made by car, compared with 69% in the south-east as a whole.

The biggest differences come with income however. In 2012, people in the highest income bracket travelled, on average, nearly three times further than people in the lowest income bracket – 10,128 miles against 3,546 miles a year. Wealthier households are much more likely to own two or more cars and apart from rail travel they use public transport very little.

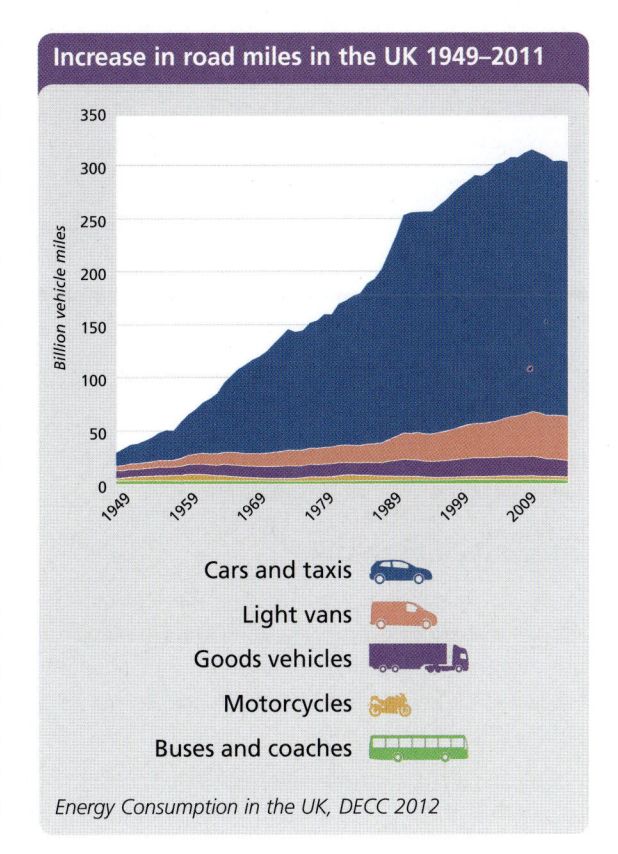

Increase in road miles in the UK 1949–2011

Cars and taxis
Light vans
Goods vehicles
Motorcycles
Buses and coaches

Energy Consumption in the UK, DECC 2012

Status, belonging and security

The way we travel is clearly associated with status. Car ownership is often associated with masculinity and success. The popularity of Jeremy Clarkson's high-octane celebration of petrol and bloke-ishness in the Top Gear TV programme offers a stereotype that many identify with and enjoy.

Conversations about travel are also important to social bonding, whether this happens at work or over a drink with friends. We show that we are part of the group by moaning about congestion, comparing notes on car mileage and insurance or swapping experiences of holiday destinations overseas. These are usually easy conversations that follow predictable patterns.

> **“** My first car was a new, electric-blue Volkswagen Polo. I think people often remember the particulars of their original car because, at the time, it's a cherished possession first, a means to travel second. My identity was augmented by the status of owner, a qualified one, and it marked my entry into adulthood.
>
> I disowned my car at university, and I started cycling. Living in London it was more convenient and, as I came to realise, more enjoyable. I now hire a car for travelling long distances (when rail isn't an option), and though I still like to drive I much prefer this way of getting around.
>
> Jonathan Baldwin

People who don't fly or don't own a car find themselves outside the friendly circle. It may be assumed they are poor. Worse still, it may be assumed that they are puritanical environmentalists who want to make others feel bad. One woman recounted how she had overheard a colleague say to others: "Pipe down about your holidays girls – here comes Jeannie!" She was treated with frosty politeness because it was known that she didn't fly.

Comfort and security can be equally important. Take for example a young woman whose car is her cocoon. She has chosen it for its colour and style. She fills it with personal comforts – her music, a favourite rug, a mascot, water-bottle and tissues within easy reach, radio tuned to her favourite station. Snug inside, she feels safe. At the start of the day, it helps her make the transition from sleepy, child-like dependence to independent, responsible, working woman. At the end of the day its privacy comforts her from the bruises of working life. Its outward gleam and shine speak of her success. Its inner warmth and comfort acknowledge her fragility. It both protects and expresses her identity. The suggestion that she might take the bus to work or lift-share with colleagues will not be appealing.

International families

Many UK residents are part of international families. 13% of the population (about 8 million people) were born overseas[2] and most have families in their home countries whom they want to visit. Another 5.5 million people who were born in the UK live abroad and they and their families also travel backwards and forwards on visits. 1.3 million of these people are in Australia, a long, carbon-heavy journey away.[3]

In the past, emigration meant separation. Families might not see an absent member for decades. Letters were the only connection. Cheap flights and social media have changed that. People with relatives in Europe expect to visit them several times a year. People with relatives in the US, India or Australia expect to visit at least once a year. The pain of separation is less acute for these families than for those who emigrated in the 1950s or '60s. Sadly, climate change means that being part of an international family may once again bring painful experiences of separation as flights are likely to become more expensive and harder to justify. Anyone who is concerned about climate change and is also part of an international family faces difficult decisions.

Need, freedom and choice

Many of us feel that our travel choices are not negotiable. It can be difficult to organise life without a car and hard to imagine not flying. Jumping in the car, whenever you wish, isn't just convenient. It's associated with freedom and choice. This state of affairs is full of paradoxes. One person's freedom to drive is another person's traffic jam. Busy streets have made it hard for chil-

> ❝I was 24. I was in love. There's an innocence when you're young. You don't think about what's down the line – logistically, financially or environmentally. You think about how you feel and that's that. We've been together 12 years now. I'm from the US, my husband is from Venezuela and we've been working in the UK for the last three years. I grew up thinking flying was normal. It didn't occur to me that this could or would have to change. We try to see each of our families every 12-18 months. The hardest thing is missing out on family.
>
> *Rebecca Miller*

dren to walk to school and play outside unsupervised. In many cities walking is a nightmare of dusty dual-carriageways and noisy lorries. Government research shows that a commute of over half an hour lowers people's life satisfaction and increases their sense of anxiety and unhappiness.[4] In reality much of the freedom that cars originally brought has vanished.

In the long term, social and policy change is needed. This can make it easy for us to shrug our shoulders and hope that someone else – government, bus companies or just a vague 'somebody' – will pick up the tab. Sometimes we dress up our desires and our personal convenience as need. It feels normal to put a good school, interesting work or a pleasant neighbourhood at the top of our wish list and disregard the implications for travel that may be involved.

Taking personal responsibility for the way we travel is not easy. It can:

- be practically difficult;
- put us at odds with colleagues, family or friends;
- involve painful choices.

If society as a whole were to make the shift towards sustainable transport there would be advantages however. We might see:

- quieter, safer streets;
- shorter journeys to work and shops;
- less congestion;
- a healthier population as people walked and cycled more;
- more interesting holidays offered in the UK.

It will take a mix of technical changes, policy changes and personal action to deliver a sustainable transport system.

Options for low-carbon travel

There are differences of opinion between experts about the mix of solutions needed for low-carbon travel. All agree that there will have to be some mix of:

- technical solutions;
- policy changes;
- reduction in travel.

Some are optimistic about the technical possibilities. Others emphasise the power of a shift to public transport or a rationing scheme. A third group see reducing everyone's travel as the safest and quickest option. It's the interaction between all three that is most likely to bring the answers we need.

> *But it doesn't make any difference because the plane will be flying anyway.' My nine year old daughter was about to fly on holiday with her (separated) Dad. Her statement wasn't a response to anything negative I'd said about flying, more like a pre-emptive, defensive statement, possibly copied from an adult. I remember feeling like crying. No anger or resentment, just an overwhelming sadness and loss of control. And feeling silly for making my own life so deliberately difficult.*
>
> **Tanya Hawkes**

Technical solutions

There are a number of technical approaches to low-carbon travel.

More efficient vehicles

Modern vehicles are much more efficient than those made 15 or 20 years ago, with further improvements expected. Efficiency alone can't solve the problem though. Firstly, there is a limit to how much more efficient vehicles can get and we are already quite a long way there. Secondly, as engines become more efficient and cheaper to run, people opt for larger cars and longer journeys – an example of the rebound effect. Taxes that encourage people to buy smaller, less powerful models may be needed to counteract this effect.

Biofuels

In principle biofuels, made from crops, can provide low-carbon travel. The Renewable Fuels Transport Obligation (RTFO) means that all petrol and diesel sold in the UK is currently 5% biofuel. Going further than this is problematic. Even the most optimistic estimates suggest that the UK could grow crops for only a small amount of its current fuel consumption. Worldwide, the demand for biodiesel is leading to the expansion of palm-oil plantations in Asia and the destruction of native forests and their wildlife. Food supplies are also threatened as land once used to grow food is given over to other biofuel crops. Processing some biofuels is also so energy intensive that it does not provide much net gain.[5] Algae are another possible source of biofuel but there are still technical challenges to be solved and it is likely to be 10 or 15 years before we see mass production.

Biofuels may have a small role to play but can't provide the whole answer.

Electric and hybrid vehicles

Electric cars and buses may be the vehicles of the future. They are about three times as efficient as diesel or petrol vehicles and further development could increase this advantage. At present electric cars are expensive and can only be used for journeys of under 100 miles. A good network of charging points or battery-swap points would allow them to be used for longer journeys. In principle there are no technical problems in creating this new infrastructure. The price of electric cars will fall as more are produced.

An electric car belonging to Oxford's E-Car Club

The electricity powering the cars needs to come from renewable sources. They are only a solution if the electricity grid is de-carbonised. As we also need renewable electricity for our homes and industries, some reduction in people's average mileage will also be necessary.

A hybrid car is a cross between a petrol car and an electric car. During part of the driving time, the petrol engine charges a battery. At other times, the car uses that stored electricity. This makes it very efficient in urban driving when you start and stop a lot. On the motorway, the efficiency is not much better than that of an ordinary car. Some hybrids with larger batteries can also be charged at home from the grid.

By 2050 most cars should be electric. HGVs and off-road vehicles such as tractors and diggers would still need to use some liquid fuels. As long as the numbers of these vehicles was reduced and their use minimised, biofuels could be used to power them.[6]

Hydrogen
Hydrogen could be a useful fuel for transport if it was made by electrolysis rather than from coal or gas, and if the electricity used in the electrolysis came from renewable sources. This technology is still being developed and may take several decades before making a significant contribution. Its best use will probably be powering buses.

Policy changes
Many of these solutions require legislation. Some need regulation. Some need incentives, like tax breaks or subsidies. Regulation is rarely popular. Politicians are often nervous about taking on vested interests like the supermarkets or the road-transport lobbies.

Patterns of living
Urban sprawl and out-of-town shopping both place increased demands on the transport network. The centralisation of services like hospitals, and the loss of local amenities like Post Offices add to this problem. Policies to press for include:

- more mixed development, with employment, shops and housing clustered together;
- urban expansion only allowed if it is linked to provision of public transport and good walking and cycling routes;
- health, education and other government services planned with sustainable transport higher up the agenda;
- more local sourcing, reducing the need for road freight;
- more home-working – already popular with some large employers, thanks to the internet;
- more electronic communication, such as Skype, to avoid the need for face-to-face meetings;
- harmonised working hours, so that car-sharing and bus travel are more practical.

Integrated low-carbon transport
A variety of forms of public transport (buses, trams, tubes, coaches and trains) plus good facilities for walking and cycling are the key ingredients of a low-carbon transport system. All the elements need to work together. Services need to be frequent, fast and reliable. Vehicles need to be comfortable and accessible. Timetables need to be harmonised so there are good connections. Car use needs to be discouraged and other ways of making the journey need to be made more attractive. Policies to press for could include:

- congestion charges, like the one in London, linked to better provision of buses and bus lanes;
- serious investment in public transport;
- provision of better cycle and pedestrian routes;
- city bike hire schemes, like those in London and Paris where you can pick up a bike for a very small fee, dropping it off somewhere else if you wish;
- encouragement of car clubs, where people can hire a car by the hour when they need one, rather than owning their own vehicle;
- real support for rural transport schemes like school buses, car-sharing schemes, dial-a-ride services, and off-road cycle routes;
- workplace transport plans, with car-sharing schemes, workplace bus services and encouragement of cycling all forming part of the mix.

Cities differ hugely in their dependence on car transport. Wigan and Colchester have high car dependency while London, Brighton and Nottingham have much better scores. But in a European survey even London ranks poorly, along with Edinburgh, Cardiff and Belfast. Stockholm, where 79% of peak hour trips are made by public transport, came top.[7]

Investment and taxation

Significant investment is needed to provide the infrastructure for low-carbon travel.

Taxes on fuel or carbon use are often suggested as they might also help to discourage excess travel. However when tax is put on essential items, like fuel, it can hit poorer people hard. Schemes which directly link tax with better public transport are likely to prove more acceptable. London's congestion charge is a good example. It has proved successful and popular though it was bitterly opposed at the start and still has its detractors. Road pricing, where people are charged for using particularly congested routes, could have similar effects.

One idea for a fairer scheme is that of personal carbon allowances. Personal carbon allowance schemes would give each person a yearly allowance of carbon dioxide. Everyone would have a carbon-allowance card, rather like a debit card. Whenever they purchased fuel or used public transport, units would be deducted from their card. People who used less than their allowance would be able to sell the units to others who wanted to use more. Research is being done into such systems.

Good public transport makes Stockholm one of the least car-dependent cities in Europe

Currently aviation fuel is not taxed. Taxing aviation emissions requires international agreement. A first step was made in 2012 when the EU brought aviation into its Emissions Trading System. It is hoped that this will save 176 million tonnes CO_2 in the period to 2015, but many think this is optimistic.

Reduction

It's important to help people:

- reduce the distance they travel;
- reduce their use of the most carbon-intensive modes of travel (cars and aviation);
- use their cars in the most carbon-efficient ways.

Lower speed limits

Enforcing the current 70 mph speed limit could reduce the UK's CO_2 emissions from transport by as much as 5%. A 60 or 50 mph limit would have a more dramatic effect. Slower speeds are also good for safety.[8]

Less car travel

Research by transport analyst Lynn Sloman found that 40% of current car journeys could easily be made by bike, on foot or by public transport.[9] A further 40% could be made this way if facilities were improved. Only 20% absolutely need a car.

Fewer empty seats

More people per car would mean fewer cars on the road. The same is true of buses, trains and planes. For car travel, lift sharing through social media may help.

Fewer, shorter journeys

Changes in patterns of work, home and shopping should help here. Tradable allowances would encourage people to look for the energy-efficient options.

More efficient driving

Avoiding harsh acceleration and braking can knock 30% off your fuel consumption. Keeping your tyres at the correct pressure, and removing unnecessary items such as the roof rack or work tools left in the boot will also help.

Less air travel

Sadly there is no easy solution to the problem of air travel. Despite improvements in aircraft efficiency and the use of biodiesel in the fuel mix, flying will remain unsustainable. We should expect the end of cheap air flights and to fly much less. Flying will not disappear but, within 30 years, it is likely to be restricted and expensive. Flights within the UK and to much of Europe will disappear. Europe will be accessible (as it used to be) by good train and coach links. Trips to the US, Asia or Australia will become rarer events and perhaps mainly the preserve of people visiting family overseas.[10]

One tonne travel

In a low-carbon future you might only have a one tonne or possibly just a half tonne CO_2 allowance for travel. For many people, life would be extremely difficult on a one tonne travel allowance. Although you can go quite a distance via bus, train or in a small fully occupied car, this is not how most people run their lives.

Each of the following represents one tonne:

- a return flight from London to Greece;
- 2,325 miles in a large car on your own;
- 5,500 miles in a medium-sized car with two people sharing;
- 5,882 miles travelled by local bus/underground;
- 10,000 miles travelled by train;
- 10,714 miles in a small car with three people sharing;
- 12,500 miles travelled by long-distance coach.

If you are taking part in a Carbon Conversations group, you will be encouraged to keep a travel diary and calculate the carbon costs of all your journeys over a year. If you are not part of a group, you can use the figures in the table overleaf to tot up your emissions. Alternatively you can sign up to the Carbon Account site, www.carbonaccount.com, which will do the sums for you and help you keep track of any changes you make.

Typical CO$_2$ emissions today[11]

CO$_2$ emissions per vehicle	Grams per kilometre	Grams per mile
Large car	270	430
Medium car	220	360
Small car	170	280

CO$_2$ emissions per passenger	Grams per kilometre	Grams per mile
Urban bus/underground	100	170
Train	60	100
Long-distance coach	50	80
Short haul flight	260	416
Long haul flight	227	363
Cruise liner	400	640
Car passenger on a car ferry	400	640
Foot passenger on a car ferry or cargo ship	20	32

In thinking about this table remember that there are 1000 grams in 1 kilogram, and 1000 kilograms in 1 tonne!

Imagining the future

In the imaginary future which we describe below it would be much easier to live on a one tonne allowance than it is today.

How life might change

Our imaginary future[12] is a world of quieter streets where people live closer to their work. An efficient public transport system takes most of the strain. Traffic density has decreased by 25% from 2014 levels. Cycling is usually a pleasure as most cities now have a good network of prioritised cycle lanes. Walking has become the norm for many short journeys, and safer streets mean that children can make their own way to and from school. The rising price of fuel has

“Having been asked to consider a travel limit of one tonne per year I was shocked to learn my trip to Japan was 6 tonnes. Shortly after there was a family wedding in New York and I said 'no' but my family insisted they were going, so I did too – these invitations are very tempting when there's family pressure. My position now is that I have not given up flying completely but I now need a really good reason to fly, and I've discovered the joys of travelling by train.

Belinda Ellis

made car travel a luxury for many. In the big urban centres, many people have given up owning their own car and hire cars by the hour or day when they really need them. Large-engine cars are now found only in museums. People who do own cars choose the smallest, most efficient model they can find. Most cars and all urban buses are electric.

A focus on local production has reduced some of the need for road freight and much of what remains has been transferred to the rail network. For long-distance journeys, coach travel is now an attractive option. Local buses take you to pick-up points on the motorway system, which has dedicated lanes for fast, efficient coaches. On the main motorway routes, you rarely have to wait more than five minutes for a coach.

The speed limit has been reduced to 50 mph on motorways, 20 mph in built-up areas and 40 mph on other roads. Thanks to the reduction in congestion, overall journey times are nonetheless shorter than at present.

All forms of transport have seen some modest efficiency gains. As both public transport and private cars are more often full, the emissions per passenger mile have reduced quite a lot.

Domestic air travel has disappeared and flights to Europe are a rarity, with most European journeys being made by train. Long-haul flights are expensive.

All this is managed through a scheme of tradable carbon allowances which allow each person one tonne per year for their transport needs.

Four altered lives

Try imagining how you would live in a world like this. What aspects of your current life would work easily? What would have to change? Two of the families featured below would face real challenges while two would not be strongly affected.

Edward, Sarah and family

Currently (2015) Edward, Sarah and their daughters are a successful high-income family, living in the prosperous South-East. Their house is in a country village, 12 miles from Cambridge where the children are at private schools. Both parents have full-time, stressful jobs and they feel that they deserve their foreign holidays. In 2014 the parents had a weekend in Prague; the whole family took a week's winter holiday in Thailand and a summer holiday in the USA.

Their daily routine is complex. Edward drives their medium-sized car to the nearest station to pick up the London train. Sarah has a round-trip drive to work of 50 miles a day in their old and inefficient 4x4. She drops the children at school, drives on to work, collects them from after-school clubs at the end of the day, and sometimes stops at the supermarket en route. Their combined annual car mileage for work is 13,760 miles, in addition to Edward's train commute of 23,000 miles. They also use their cars a lot to see friends, to take the children to out-of-school activities and to shop. Both parents often drive into Cambridge twice at the weekend. Their social and leisure car mileage adds another 16,100 miles.

Their overall travel footprint in tonnes of CO_2 is 45 tonnes, or 11.3 tonnes each, way beyond the one tonne each they would be allocated in our imaginary future. How would they manage? Moving into Cambridge would reduce their footprint hugely but this family would probably be unwilling to give up village life, would think twice about changing their high-powered jobs and would probably want to hang on to their foreign holidays as well.

In our imaginary future most people now choose to work close to home and companies prefer to recruit local people when they can. Although Edward continues to be based in London, he now works from home two days a week and Sarah has a job in Cambridge where the children are at school.

The family now own just one vehicle, a medium-sized electric car with a small engine and a range of about 100 miles. On three days a week Edward drives six miles to the nearest station to pick up the London train, while Sarah and the children take the bus into Cambridge for school and work. The congestion charge and improved public transport mean that this is now an easy 30 minute trip with no traffic jams. On the days that Edward works at home, they take the car, leaving it at the park-and-ride site and going shopping on the way home.

For local trips, the family now use the car only if at least two of them are travelling; otherwise they take the bus or cycle on the improved cycleways that connect the local villages. They also use their village-based lift-share scheme, which operates via the village website. For longer leisure and holiday trips within the UK they hire a petrol or diesel engine car but monitor their mileage carefully, as fuel is expensive. Their annual mileage is now 3,816 miles for commuting and 4,000 miles for leisure and other trips. For holidays, they take weekend breaks in the UK and a winter holiday in the Channel Islands by car and ferry.

If they left it at this, they would be living within their carbon allowance, but they still like to fly abroad once a year. A sailing holiday in Turkey would mean buying another six tonnes of carbon on the tradable carbon market. As a wealthy family, they are able to pay for this although they grumble about it from time to time.

Manju

At present, Manju lives in Glasgow but works in Irvine, an hour's drive away. Her parents moved to the UK from India before she was born. She is in her twenties, has a good job as an optician and lives with her sister in a house they are buying together. She goes to India regularly, usually to Ahmedabad where her mother's family live. Last year she went three times: once for a cousin's wedding, once for a family sightseeing holiday, and once with her mother and sister on a shopping trip. She drives a medium-sized car about 20,000 miles per year, almost 15,000 of which are commuting to work. She occasionally uses the train to go to Edinburgh to see old university friends. Her travel footprint is about 7 tonnes for her car, 9.5 tonnes for her flights and a mere 36 kg for her train journeys. Like Edward and Sarah she would face major challenges in a sustainable future.

In our imaginary future Manju, like many others, has found a job closer to home. She and her sister live in an energy-efficient house that uses less than the average carbon allowance. She has got rid of her car and now uses a bike for local trips and buses for leisure trips. She tries to save as much of her carbon allowance as she can for an annual flight, staying in India for four weeks. Her energy-efficient house provides half a tonne spare allowance, so she buys the extra 2 tonnes she needs on the carbon market. Like Edward and Sarah, she probably grumbles but accepts that there is no alternative.

Evan

Evan would find life in our imaginary future much easier than either Manju or Edward and Sarah. He lives in Cardiff and is a keen cyclist. He doesn't own a car and cycles five miles to work every day. He uses the train a lot, going to Bristol frequently and London occasionally. This year he enjoyed a weekend in Paris and a week's skiing in the Alps, all accessed by train. He uses local buses when it rains and sometimes takes a taxi. His travel footprint is currently just over half a tonne.

In our imaginary future the main change to Evan's life is that cycling has become easier and pleasanter as traffic volumes have decreased and good cycle paths have multiplied. 20% of

carbonconversations.org

Cardiff's population now cycle to work. He continues to use public transport for his other trips, though fast coach journeys have replaced some of the train trips. The system of personal carbon allowances means that he has half a tonne of carbon to sell on the carbon market. Overall he's very pleased with the changes.

Joe and June

Joe and June recently retired from jobs with the Yorkshire Dales National Park Authority. They live in the country about six miles from Skipton, their nearest town. The annual mileage in their medium-sized car is 12,000 miles. They are dependent on it for shopping, social activities and for visiting friends and relatives. They also make a few trips by train every year. Their current travel footprint is almost 2.5 tonnes each, most of which is due to their old, inefficient car. They used to cycle a lot but a recent knee operation means that this is no longer an option for Joe. Although there is an hourly bus service to Skipton, they prefer to use their car.

In our imaginary future, Joe and June's car use would cause them problems. As people with only modest pensions they would struggle to buy any extra carbon allowance. As most of their trips are local, a combination of buying an efficient, electric car, arranging for heavy shopping to be delivered and taking the bus for some trips would be the solution. These steps would have a surprisingly large effect. Their travel footprint would decrease to about 0.75 tonnes each, leaving them a small amount to sell on the carbon market. It would probably take them a little while to adjust to these changes, but as people with a love of the natural world and a strong community spirit, they would not find it a real hardship.

Making changes now

Although some of the changes which our fictional characters make depend on policy and technology, many of them don't. If we were to imagine what they could achieve today, it might look something like this.

Edward, Sarah and family

Their family travel footprint of 45 tonnes is an unsustainable 11.3 tonnes each but some straightforward changes could almost halve their footprint without affecting their quality of life. Sarah cannot bear the thought of giving up a winter holiday somewhere warm, and Edward and the children won't give up an overseas summer trip. But, they could:

- swap the parents' weekend in Prague for one in Paris by train (almost one tonne less);
- go to the Canaries, instead of Thailand, at Christmas (about 12 tonnes less);
- trade in Sarah's petrol-guzzling 4x4 for a large family diesel and swap Edward's old medium sized car for a small new car, efficient enough to avoid road tax (3 tonnes less);
- take their summer holiday in Europe instead of the US (8-10 tonnes less).

These changes are significant and show how better-off people with large footprints can make a real difference. The family might also consider keeping to the speed limit on motorways and explore working from home occasionally. Moving into Cambridge as the children become teenagers might also be something to think about.

Manju

Manju could also halve her travel footprint without affecting her quality of life. In conversation, she admits to finding the three regular trips to India a burden. They require her to be on her best behaviour with family which can be tiring and they take up all her annual leave which has stopped her exploring Europe as she would like. She also finds the drive to work stressful. Although there is a good train service between Glasgow and Irvine she hasn't considered this because her parents feel that as a young woman on her own she is safer in the car. She doesn't agree with her parents but she isn't used to train travel. For Manju, making some changes involves challenging some of her family's and her own assumptions but she could:

- make one longer trip of three weeks to India which would allow time to see the extended family, without taking up all her annual leave (about 6 tonnes less or 5 tonnes less if she substituted one of the flights to India with a holiday flight to Europe);
- take the train to work (4 tonnes less) or
- find a driving partner through Liftshare, alternating use of her car with her partner's and so halving her petrol consumption (nearly 3 tonnes less);
- drive more efficiently saving 10% of her petrol consumption (half a tonne less).

If she found she liked commuting by train and wanted to be more adventurous, Manju could consider getting rid of her car and using one of the Glasgow City car clubs where you can hire cars by the hour. She might also like to take up cycling for local trips in the city. Glasgow has an ambitious plan to improve cycling facilities in the city and using a bike should become easier and more pleasant over the next few years.[13]

Joe and June

Joe and June's carbon emissions aren't much above the average but they could still halve them without much difficulty. They are higher than they need to be, mainly because of their inefficient car and because of the distances they drive. Joe also likes to put his foot down the moment they hit the motorway and regularly exceeds the speed limit. They are reluctant to buy a very small car because they like to be able to take their grandchildren on day trips. Nonetheless they are concerned. They have always been passionate about conservation and were troubled to discover how large their footprint was. They could try:

- trading in their old car for a slightly smaller, second-hand diesel, for example a 2012 VW Golf (1.5 tonnes less);
- observing the speed limit on motorways and driving more efficiently (about 400 kg less);
- combining some trips together and taking the bus occasionally so that they reduce their overall mileage by 1,000 miles (about 240 kg).

These measures would roughly halve their current footprint. They need to draw on savings to pay for the replacement car but their current car has 180,000 miles on the clock. It is costing them more and more in maintenance and they are beginning to worry about its reliability. Road tax on the smaller, more efficient vehicle will be less and they will save on fuel so the financial disadvantages may not be as great as they fear. Observing the speed limit means changing the habits of a lifetime for Joe, but June and their daughter-in-law would prefer him to slow down when he has the grandchildren in the car. Joe could also consider buying an electric bike so that he and June could continue to cycle together sometimes.

Evan

With a travel footprint of only half a tonne, Evan has no need to make reductions. He does need to think about the future however. He is 29 and getting married in six months' time. He and his wife hope to start a family soon. With small children the pressure to buy a car will be strong, particularly as his wife is not a keen cyclist. Car use peaks in people's 30s and 40s, with 40% more trips in your thirties than in your twenties and 65% more trips in your 40s than in your 20s.[14] Evan could think about joining the Cardiff City car club as a compromise.

Change and complex systems

The transport system is complex and slow to change. Some of the decisions that affect us were made long before we were born. Some are the result of forces beyond our control. We didn't decide to close railways 50 years ago or plan the road expansion of the 1980s.[15] We didn't invent a society where status depends on the size of your car and your holiday destination. More personally perhaps, we didn't choose to fall in love with someone from another continent, have our jobs relocated or vote for out-of-town sprawl. Your life may be woven into the transport system in ways that give you little room for manoeuvre. If you're faced with a difficult balancing act, like those faced by Joe, June, Manju, Edward and Sarah, it can be hard to keep everything in mind and reach a good decision. Reducing your travel footprint:

- requires planning;
- needs the involvement of family and/or close friends;
- may challenge your sense of self or your expectations;
- is likely to be a gradual process.

Force-field analysis

Force-field analysis is a technique that can help you make changes in complex situations.[16] It helps you see your place in the 'field' of interacting forces and decide on some realistic actions. In any system, some forces are pushing for change and others are preventing it from happening. The status quo is maintained when these forces are evenly balanced, keeping the system in equilibrium. If you want to see change, you have to decide how you will affect these forces. The system in question could be your own inner world, your workplace, your family, a wider social system (such as transport) or some combination of all these.

In the transport system as a whole many forces are in play, for example: the infrastructure of roads, railways and airports; the price of oil, the demands of business, the policy decisions taken by government, the extent of privatisation, the pressure of climate change, the profitability of transport companies, people's social aspirations and so on. At a personal level, more forces are added such as your own desires and attitudes, the facilities in your area, your family's expectations or your sensitivity to other people's opinions.

Force-field analysis helps you build a picture of all the forces influencing a change that you have in mind. In the diagram overleaf, we have imagined Manju thinking about taking the train to work, instead of driving. The change she is considering is in the centre. On either side are brainstormed lists of the driving forces (which are pushing for the change to happen) and the restraining forces (which are preventing it from happening). Brainstorming means listing all the ideas you can come up with, without stopping to analyse or argue about them. Brainstorming with someone else usually helps you come up with a more creative list. With your brainstorm complete, you then score each force for its strength on a scale from one to five, where one is weak and five is very strong. This will give you a picture of how strong you think the relative forces are.

Commuting by train can be more relaxing than driving

carbonconversations.org

Manju's force-field analysis

Driving forces

3 I want to lower my impact

2 I'm concerned about climate change

4 It's a stressful drive, particularly in winter

1 I'd contribute to reducing air pollution

3 I could read on the train

4 I could catch up with Facebook and email on the train

4 Fuel prices are really high

3 It doesn't take any longer by train

Restraining forces

4 Mum and Dad prefer that I drive

5 An annual season ticket is really expensive

4 I'm not sure the train's reliable

4 The train might be crowded

3 I wouldn't be able to leave work exactly when I want

2 My friends will think I'm daft

1 I'll feel like a loser

2 I sometimes have to go to our other branch in Kilmarnock

Commute to work by train instead of by car

It is always more effective to remove or weaken the restraining forces rather than increase the strength of driving forces. Think of it as the difference between trying to open a locked door by pushing hard on it and simply sliding the bolt to let it swing open.

> *As a wheelchair user I need my car for everything – so I'm very attached to it! I even have to use it for some short distances in the winter as I get a lot of pain if I get really cold. I think buses and so on are a grand plan. I use the accessible park and ride buses in the summer but coaches and trains can't take my powered chair. I've replaced my car with one with a small engine, I try to have one car-free day a week and car share with my husband and neighbours when I can. It isn't enough, but you have to start somewhere. Feeling guilty achieves nothing.*

Kirsty Wayland

On the restraining side Manju's issues cluster round her uncertainty of what the train commute might involve, her feelings about what other people will think and how she thinks she will view herself if she becomes a train commuter. Reducing the strength of the restraining forces would involve Manju opening conversations with her parents and friends and finding out more about rail travel. If she looked up the price of an annual season ticket she would discover that it is roughly the same as the cost of the petrol for commuting. As the wear and tear on her car would reduce with the reduced mileage there might be a financial advantage to Manju in taking the train. She could buy a weekly season ticket to find out whether she liked it and she could check out Scotrail's reliability by looking at online reports.

On the side of the driving forces, Manju's feelings about climate change and sustainability are weak, but if the power of the restraining forces could be reduced, then the combination of all the driving forces together might persuade her to give the train a try. The fact that she finds driving stressful and that the train journey would not cost any more might be the clincher.

The support of a sympathetic friend might help Manju talk through the issues. Chapter Six has some pointers on how to hold constructive conversations with friends, and this is the kind of support that someone like Manju might find useful.

Practical steps

Some changes are easily adopted but many require you to plan ahead.

In the table overleaf are a list of changes that anyone might consider making. You may already be doing some of them. Others may be straightforward to adopt. For any that sound more difficult, try using force-field analysis to explore which ones are most likely to work for you.

Each one has a star rating against it. As before, the greater the number of stars, the greater the impact the action is likely to have. It's difficult to give an exact figure in CO_2 for each action because we don't know your exact starting point, the distances you go and the efficiency of your car, if you have one. Keeping a travel diary and monitoring your use more precisely will give you those answers.

> ❝ I cycle the 4.5 miles from my home in Joppa to work in Edinburgh. Most of the route is on cycleways and I do the first three miles with my daughter which gives us time together. I cycled as a child round the country lanes in Northern Ireland but I was nervous about getting on a bike in city traffic. An hour's cycle training helped. I started by just cycling in the summer months but now I do it every day, whatever the weather. You don't need special gear. You don't need to rush and it's great for your health.
>
> **Elaine Wilson**

> ❝ Driving is about being lied to: all those promises of higher MPG and technological transcendence burst open to reveal a bitter cinder of ridiculousness in the middle. Cycling knits things back together. Riding a bike reunites efficiency with aesthetics, but also with glorious waste. It brings an echo of the joy once felt riding a Chopper or Grifter on the edge of control over too-high hillocks and makeshift ramps.
>
> **Chris Groves**

Smarter travel

		I'm already doing this	I would consider this	This would be really hard
Keep to the speed limit	**	☐	☐	☐
Drive at a maximum of 60 mph on motorways and at no more than 50 mph on other roads	***	☐	☐	☐
Check tyre pressures regularly	*	☐	☐	☐
Remove heavy items/roof rack from the car when not in use	*	☐	☐	☐
Drive smoothly, avoiding unnecessary changes of speed	**	☐	☐	☐
Take the bus, tube or train to work instead of the car	****	☐	☐	☐
Walk or cycle to work in summer	**	☐	☐	☐
Walk or cycle to work every day	***	☐	☐	☐
Join a lift-sharing scheme & share your commuting	***	☐	☐	☐
Trade the car in for a smaller, more efficient model	****	☐	☐	☐
Walk or cycle for short trips	**	☐	☐	☐
Combine more trips together	**	☐	☐	☐
Share the school run with other families	**	☐	☐	☐

Collective action

Sometimes collective action feels more appropriate than concentrating on your personal footprint. Try to do both. Most local areas have organisations and campaigns that would welcome your support, protecting bus services, planning cycle routes, or protesting about road building and developments that increase car use. Nationally there are organisations campaigning for policy change. See More Information for details.

Parents and children in Swansea protest about cuts to bus services

> **❝** I have a long commute to work but I use public transport. I avoid the hassle of roadworks and the stress of driving. I can sit back and admire the views of the mountains and hills.
>
> **Ammar Waqar**

92   carbonconversations.org

Lifestyle changes

		I'm already doing this	I would consider this	This would be really hard
Negotiate working from home one or two days a week	***	☐	☐	☐
Shorten your car commute by 20 miles a day by changing your job or moving house	*****	☐	☐	☐
Shorten your train commute by 50 miles a day by changing your job or moving house	*****	☐	☐	☐
Halve your car mileage	*****	☐	☐	☐
Get rid of the car	****	☐	☐	☐
Holiday in the UK, instead of abroad	****	☐	☐	☐
Take the train if you're going to Europe	****	☐	☐	☐
Reduce your flights by 75%	***	☐	☐	☐
Reduce your flights by 50%	****	☐	☐	☐
Stop flying altogether	*****	☐	☐	☐

Getting stuck

There are many reasons why people struggle to reduce their transport emissions. Here are some of the common ones we've found.

Planning ahead

More than with any other aspect of your footprint, transport requires you to plan ahead. For the big changes, you will need to acquire information, talk with family and friends and possibly take difficult decisions. Allowing yourself time to do this is essential. Without advance planning you will find that decisions overtake you. If you are under pressure to sort out a holiday you will book a flight. If you are desperate for work you will accept a job with a long commute. If you are faced with a written-off car you will go for the first one within your budget. Try to make time for conversations with those you love, about:

- including your travel footprint as a factor in decisions about jobs, housing or schooling;
- how and why you use your car;
- taking days out by public transport;
- holidaying closer to home;
- train and ferry alternatives to air flights.

You might want to gather information about car clubs (where you hire a car by the hour as you need), lift-sharing schemes, bus and train timetables. Online you could explore the 'Man in Seat 61' website which will give you a route to any European destination without flying. The government's Car Fuel Data site will give you information about the environmental impact of both new and used cars. Look in the More Information section for details on all these.

Underestimating the difficulties

It can take a while to establish a new routine. If you don't realise this, the first rainy day, late train or overcrowded bus will find you back in the car.

Skills and knowledge

Sometimes it's a question of developing new skills and knowledge. Using public transport, cycling and even walking require different sets of skills from driving. Listening to the weather forecast, having suitable shoes for walking, keeping a set of smart clothes at the office, knowing how to decide that it's too wet to cycle and keeping abreast of timetable changes are just a few of the skills that separate car drivers from low-carbon transport users.

Change takes time

Sometimes it's a question of time. Research suggests that it takes about two months for a simple change in habit to become automatic.[17] This is likely to apply to a number of the Smarter Travel actions. If you decide to change a habit of harsh braking or reduce the speed you drive at, don't expect to manage it consistently. Look for ways of reminding yourself of your intention and don't beat yourself up if you sometimes forget.

All or nothing

People sometimes develop an all or nothing attitude that leads to inaction. Believing that something is only worth doing if it's done perfectly becomes the justification for doing nothing at all. "I can't cycle every day," quickly becomes "It's not worth cycling at all". "I keep forgetting that I was going to observe the speed limit" becomes "I'm not making much difference, so I'll stop bothering." A lot of things may be in play here. You may dislike failing or falling short of an ideal you have set up for yourself. You may be finding a change more difficult than you imagined and this affects your self-esteem. You may feel that the change brings a loss of status, comfort or convenience. The trick here is to try to understand yourself better, to have more sympathy for your own shortcomings and to plan for change to take place gradually, rather than all at once.

Support is important

It is often easier to make changes with the support of others. If your family, friends or colleagues are not on board you will find it much harder. Talk about what you are doing and why you are doing it. Look for people who are sympathetic. If you are part of a Carbon Conversations group plan for some reunions where you can compare notes and plans.

I will if you will (and if you won't, I won't)

It can be a downer to realise that other people are hopping in the car to buy a pint of milk, jumping on a plane several times a year or commuting thousands of miles to work without a

> **❝** One year I managed to persuade my partner and our teenage children that we should travel by train for our European holiday but the following year, when we were planning to do the same again, the teenagers argued. They said they hadn't liked the long train journey and they wanted to fly. I remember feeling very tearful and conflicted. Eventually we did agree that we would take the train but it made me see how much grief there is in giving up flying.
>
> Rebecca Nestor

thought. Research suggests that people are much more likely to agree to reduce their own emissions when this feels fair.[18] If we are going to give something up or be inconvenienced then we want the burden to be shared. The majority of the population would also like laws passed to make this happen. The absence of such laws can sometimes leave those of us who are already acting feeling like mugs. If you are angry it can help to recognise that this is justified. It may help to get involved in collective action that could change policy. Don't give up what you are doing. Think of yourself as part of the vanguard that will eventually bring change across society.

Convenience, time and infrastructure

Sometimes it just isn't possible to make all the changes we wish to. Sometimes the infrastructure of bus routes, cycle routes or low-priced trains isn't there. The inconvenience of public transport or the time a journey takes proves to be a stumbling block.

Our daily actions depend on what is available, what is convenient and what is usual amongst the people we know. If there isn't a bus you can't get on it. If the roads are dangerous you can't cycle. The problem is that it's common to assume, without knowing much about it, that public transport takes longer than going by car, is inconvenient and costly. If you are usually a car user, make sure you have done your research. Look up bus and train timetables. Find out about cycle paths and pleasant walking routes. The trick here is to identify those routes and journeys where cycling, walking or public transport does make sense and to stop worrying about the rest.

Rebound

Rebound is the hidden factor in all our attempts to save energy. A more efficient car can encourage you to drive further. If you save money by walking, cycling or making fewer journeys you will probably spend it elsewhere. These purchases will also be responsible for carbon emissions, though they are likely to be lower than the emissions from transport. If you're careful to keep your mileage down and try to spend your money in the low-carbon sectors of the economy or save it in low-carbon investments, you can keep the rebound factor to about 12%.[19] See Chapter Five for more information about which sectors of the economy are the low-carbon ones.

What about at work?

Many of the barriers to low-carbon travel in our personal lives also apply in the workplace, with the additional challenge of fitting low-carbon choices into a work system that assumes high-carbon choices. Using public transport, or surface travel instead of flying, may mean journeys take longer. To what extent will that be allowed? Will colleagues think we're strange for suggesting it; will managers mark us down as difficult? And what about the cost? Will employers be comfortable with a £150 train journey on a UK or European route for which the flight costs £30?

> " I find it very difficult to think that we shouldn't ever fly anywhere. I do subscribe to the notion that we should all only use a one tonne allocation, but if that conflicts with speed, or convenience or cost, then a whole load of brainwork needs to take place to enable me to decide to go on the train to see my daughter in the Languedoc.
>
> **Barbara Nestor**

carbonconversations.org

Ideas to try

A good first step is to find out what your employer's policy is on workplace travel. Most large companies and public sector organisations set targets for reducing their own carbon emissions from transport and also try to reduce the impact of employees' commuting. Your commute to work forms part of your personal carbon footprint but many employers have schemes to help employees leave the car at home.

You may find that there are options you weren't aware of, or encouragement to make low-carbon choices. For example, the University of Southampton has a useful checklist encouraging staff and students who are planning meetings to decide first if a meeting is necessary, then whether video-conferencing would work, then whether it's possible to walk or cycle to the meeting.[20] Many big organisations have travel-to-work policies which provide both sticks and carrots that encourage lower-carbon forms of commuting. Buckinghamshire County Council's policy includes discounted public transport fares for staff alongside removing the traditional staff discounts on car parking at Council car parks. If you find a policy that your colleagues don't seem to be aware of it, perhaps you could pass the information on to others and start a conversation.

Travel in the course of the job is usually closely monitored by employers, whether it is deliveries or trips to meetings. Company vehicles may be involved, and the time the journey takes is generally part of the working day. The rising cost of fuel and the demands of sustainability policies, mean that many employers with vehicle fleets are working actively to reduce travel emissions. For example, Oxford City Council:

- trained 330 of their drivers in Smarter Driving techniques;
- fitted 240 of their vehicles with telematics systems which can reroute vehicles to save mileage and report on emissions;
- uses route optimisation software to plan recycling and refuse collection rounds to be as fuel-efficient as possible;
- provides pool bikes (including electric bikes) to encourage staff to cycle for work journeys.[21]

If your employer has a policy like this, are you taking advantage of it? Have you been to look at the bikes or asked about Smarter Driving training? If your employer doesn't have a policy could you start talking about the Oxford example within your work team and see what happens?

You may have more say in how you travel to training events, conferences and other one-off activities as the travel may be planned further in advance and may start from home. If your employer has no stated travel policy you could:

> *Time is the big issue if you use public transport for travelling at work. You don't want to be late for a meeting – it's not very professional – so you do have to get your timing right. But then I also find that being on public transport is quite a nice way to close a meeting – you can't let it run over because actually you've got a bus to catch. So from my point of view it's quite time-efficient, because I can explain to whoever I've got the meeting with that I have to leave at such-and-such a time in order to catch my bus.*
>
> Julie Pickard

- look for cheap train tickets a few months ahead, instead of booking a short-haul flight;
- offer to use a bit of your own time alongside a bit extra of your employer's time in order to use a lower-carbon but slightly longer form of transport ('if you will, I will');
- combine a longer trip with a few days' holiday to make better use of the travelling;
- ask a colleague to join you in trying out a public transport route to a meeting you are both attending;
- experiment with video-conferencing as a substitute for face-to-face meetings.

You may be able to start the conversations with colleagues and managers that lead to your organisation taking some of the larger steps that all workplaces need to take, but it is just as important to be part of a growing group of people who make it normal to think about the impact of company travel. Once it feels normal to think about efficient driving, video-conferencing and minimising travel, everyone will do it. Don't underestimate the importance of this contribution.

Rules of thumb

Distance matters
Long journeys, whether for commuting or overseas holidays, cause the greatest emissions. Reduce them as much as you can.

Slow is good
Choose a slower means of transport: walk or cycle instead of driving; take the train rather than flying; if you drive, reduce your speed. Enjoy the journey.

The more the merrier
Full cars and buses are more efficient per passenger. Offer and accept lifts as often as you can.

Is your journey really necessary?
Consider the alternatives, before reaching for the car keys.

Look at your lifestyle choices
Keep the effect on your CO_2 output in mind.

Air travel is always worse than you think
Avoid using the plane whenever possible.

Frequently asked questions

Can't I offset my air travel?
Carbon-offsetting schemes offer to compensate for the carbon you have emitted by offsetting it against carbon that is saved elsewhere. When you take a flight, you pay for a tree to be planted or for more efficient cooking stoves in one of the poorer countries in the world. The projects themselves may be worthwhile but there is little to suggest that they compensate in any meaningful way for your emissions.

For an offset scheme to be effective, it must fund activities that would not otherwise have taken place– they must be additional. It is particularly difficult to prove additionality and few schemes meet this standard satisfactorily. Carbon-offsetting schemes are also ethically questionable: they shift the burden of reducing CO_2 emissions to other people, other places or other times. If you fly to New York today, your trail of gas starts warming the planet immediately. A tree planted today will take 50–100 years to absorb enough CO_2 to offset the fuel your flight burned.[22]

Isn't the growth in air-travel all to do with business travellers?
No. The biggest increase in air travel is in leisure journeys. In 2012, 43% of trips made by UK residents were for holidays, 35.4% were to visit relatives or friends and a mere 19% were business trips.[23]

Won't reducing air travel damage the economy?
No. Tourism causes a net loss to the UK economy, taking more trips and money away than it brings in.[24] Air travel is heavily subsidised in the form of untaxed fuel, by the provision of infrastructure (motorways to airports), and by everyone having to pay the costs of the pollution it causes.

Surely my holidays abroad support poorer countries?
Tourism brings very limited benefits. Most of your money goes to the airline and travel company, very little helps the local population at your destination. Tourism frequently brings environmental degradation in its wake, stressing water systems and natural habitats.[25]

Won't putting up the cost of air travel discriminate against poorer people?
Poorer people – those in social classes D and E – hardly fly at all. The recent expansion in flying has occurred because better-off people are flying more. 75% of budget flights are taken by people in social classes A, B and C.[26]

What should I do about my business flights?
Your business flights don't count as part of your personal footprint. The emissions from them become part of the embodied carbon in the products or services that your company produces. This doesn't mean that you should ignore these flights however. Look at ways of influencing your workplace to use video-conferencing whenever possible and question it when you are asked to fly abroad.

I've seen different figures for transport CO_2. Whose are right?
For air travel, some figures give the emissions from the fuel per mile only, others take account of the greater fuel consumption at take-off and landing, and still others include the particularly damaging effect of emissions at high altitude. For coach and train travel, researchers account

differently for factors such as occupancy, urban versus long-distance travel, age of rolling stock, type and size of vehicle. For car travel, results will differ between test conditions and real life driving. The figures on the VCA Car Fuel Data website relate to ideal conditions. In practice a car's emissions vary hugely depending on speed, driver behaviour and car maintenance, as you will discover if you monitor your fuel use. Our figures mostly come from government data. See the notes to this chapter for details.

Is it true that driving more slowly creates less CO_2?
Yes. Slowing from 80 mph to 70 mph might save over 15% of your fuel consumption.[27]

Is it true that driving more slowly leads to less congestion?
Yes. At slower speeds drivers have more time to react and so shock waves and flow breakdowns are less likely. On a busy motorway the best flow rate can be as low as 40 mph. Variable speed limits, which you see displayed on busy stretches of motorway, use complex monitoring and modelling to identify the best speed.[28]

What's a good efficiency for a car?
The figures for car efficiency are usually published in grams of CO_2 per kilometre. If you are buying a new car, look for 100 g/km or less. The performance of a car is usually a little worse than the published figures because the tests are done under ideal conditions.

Should I scrap my old car for a new efficient model now?
The embodied CO_2 in a new, small car is about 6 tonnes, so the answer depends on your mileage. If your mileage is high, it makes sense to get a more efficient model. If your mileage is low, it may be better to hang on to your old one.

How much of the problem is caused by road freight?
Road freight increased hugely, particularly during the 1980s. It is now responsible for about 35% of the fuel used in all road transport.[29]

Should I buy an electric car?
Electric cars may be the vehicles of the future. At present they are expensive and the network of charging points or battery-swap points that would allow them to be used for longer journeys is in its infancy. Buy one if you can afford to and like experimenting with new technology. The price will fall as more are produced. If a way of swapping batteries in much the same way as we fill up with petrol can be introduced, they could make a real contribution. To be really effective they need to be powered by electricity produced from renewable sources. As we also need this electricity in our homes and in industry, electric cars are also only viable if everyone reduces their mileage.

Do home deliveries save CO_2?
A study of internet shopping found that home deliveries of the goods ordered used less CO_2 than a trip to the shops for the same items.[30] We don't have figures for supermarket deliveries of food shopping but the same logic should apply.

Why are passenger ships such a problem?
Ships vary from dreadful to not-so-bad. The worst, such as cruise ships, travel great distances, carrying few passengers at great speed. If they slowed down and stuffed in the passengers like sardines (like troop ships in the 1940s) they would do better. A cruise liner propels a huge

amount of steel per passenger against water resistance, so the energy used is very high. Ferries and freight ships usually do better. Most ferries only travel short distances, so if you take a slow one, don't worry about its emissions. Freight ships dawdle along while carrying huge amounts of cargo so are a good option for transporting goods.

I'd like to cycle but is it really safe?

It is true that cycling is more dangerous per mile than driving a car but statistically it is no more dangerous than walking.[31] You can do a lot to increase the safety of your journeys by picking quiet routes, avoiding busy junctions and roads used by HGVs, and making sure you are properly equipped with lights, reflective gear and a helmet. Cycling is also good for your health and on quiet routes and in daylight carries little risk. It is also safer in cities where more people cycle.

More information

This section lists a small number of books and websites with good, accessible information that will help you fill in the background and follow up facts you are not clear on. You will find more detailed sources and a wider selection of reading in the Notes.

I'd like to know more about…

…campaigning

The Campaign for Better Transport works to "create transport policies and programmes that give people better lives", www.bettertransport.org.uk.

Sustrans promotes sustainable transport and created the National Cycle Network, www.sustrans.org.uk.

HACAN Clear Skies, http://hacan.org.uk/, the *Aviation Environment Federation*, http://www.aef.org.uk/, and *Plane Stupid*, http://www.planestupid.com/, all campaign on aviation issues from different standpoints.

…car clubs

City Car Club, http://www.citycarclub.co.uk/, *Zipcar*, http://www.zipcar.co.uk/, *Moorcar*, http://www.moorcar.co.uk/, and *Co-Wheels*, http://www.co-wheels.org.uk/, let you hire cars by the hour. You book online or via your phone and access to the car with a swipe-card.

Carplus supports communities who want to set up their own car club or car-share scheme, http://www.carplus.org.uk/.

…cycle and walking routes

The National Cycle Network has a map of routes across the UK, http://bit.ly/sustrans-cycle. Most local authorities publish maps of cycle routes in their areas.

Cycling to Work: a Beginner's Guide, by Rory McMullan, Green Books, 2007 will help you get started.

Google Maps offers cycling directions.

Walkit will find you a walking route across most of our big cities, http://walkit.com/.

...driving more efficiently
Changeworks offers impartial advice, http://bit.ly/changeworks-ecodriving.

...engine efficiencies
The *VCA Car Fuel Data* website lists the efficiency of both new and used cars. The CO_2 emissions given relate to ideal conditions, so expect to do a bit worse in real life, http://carfueldata.direct.gov.uk/.

...finding good routes by public transport
Traveline will plan a journey from any point in the UK to another, http://www.traveline.info/.

National Rail provides information on train journeys, 08457 484950, http://nationalrail.co.uk.

Your local bus company, and often your local authority, publish bus timetables.

...lift sharing
Liftshare will help you find a lift or a passenger, https://www.liftshare.com/uk/.

...managing without a car
Cutting Your Car Use: Save Money, Be Healthy, Be Green, Anna Semlyen, Green Books, 2007, is short and practical.

50 Ways to Greener Travel, Sian Berry, Kyle Cathie Ltd, 2008, is another book of tips with short explanations.

...taking the train to Europe
The Man in Seat 61 will find you cheap train and ferry alternatives to air travel, http://www.seat61.com.

Lo CO_2 and *Rail Europe* will find you the route and also book the tickets, https://lo CO_2.com/, http://www.raileurope.com.

...tourism
The Final Call: Investigating Who Really Pays for Our Holidays, Leo Hickman, Guardian Books, 2008, made us reluctant to ever step on a plane again.

The No-Nonsense Guide to Tourism, Pamela Nowick, New Internationalist Publications Ltd, 2007, explains succinctly why so much overseas tourism is damaging.

...transport policy
The *Campaign for Better Transport* produce numerous policy reports on how to plan for an integrated transport system. Look at the research pages of their website for reports like *Reducing the Need to Travel* (2011) and *Door to Door Journeys* (2011), http://www.bettertransport.org.uk/research.

ZeroCarbonBritain: Rethinking the Future, the Centre for Alternative Technology, CAT Publications, 2013, discusses policy and technology options for the future, http://bit.ly/zerocarbon-2013.

Car Sick: Solutions for Our Car-Addicted Culture, by Lynn Sloman, Green Books, 2006, discusses car culture and national policy in the context of personal action.

...travel to work

Act-Travelwise helps workplaces set up travel plans to help employees get to work without cars, www.acttravelwise.org.

...what's happening in Scotland

Greener Scotland has good information, http://bit.ly/greenerscot-travel.

CHAPTER 4

Food and water

"I love my food. I don't like thinking about what has happened to it before it gets to my table. I'm surprised it has such a big impact on my carbon footprint."

Supermarkets are the end point of a global food supply chain with high emissions

Food and water are two of the essentials of life. Both are threatened by climate change. The natural water systems in many parts of the world are likely to alter, producing droughts in some places and floods in others.[1] World food production will be affected and substantial drops in world crop yields are likely.[2] Meanwhile the global food system and the typical Western diet are responsible for large amounts of greenhouse gas emissions. Our eating patterns themselves need to change. In this chapter we explore:

- the place of food in our lives;
- how to limit the impact of our food choices;
- how to minimise the stress we put on the world's water systems.

carbonconversations.org

What's the problem with food?

The food system has a surprisingly large impact on greenhouse gas emissions and is also responsible for deforestation, water stress and loss of biodiversity. It's not just that fossil fuels are used in growing, processing, packaging and transporting our food. Deforestation, caused when land is cleared for food production, leads to an increase in emissions as the forests no longer absorb CO_2 and create more CO_2 as their wood is burned or left to rot. Food production is also responsible for other greenhouse gases, methane and nitrous oxide. Methane is produced when livestock belch (something which ruminants like sheep and cows do a lot). Nitrous oxide results from the use of nitrogen fertiliser and from cultivation of the land. For simplicity's sake, we talk about CO_2 equivalents or CO_2e.

Food choices can feel purely personal or cultural. But since the 1960s there have been huge changes in the kinds of foods that are available, where they come from, how they are produced and how they are prepared. Older people may be able to remember these changes taking place. The impact of food is not obvious. It is hidden, caught up in all the processes that bring your dinner to your plate – growing the crops and rearing the animals, processing and packaging the food, transporting it from the farm to processing plants, shops and homes. Many of the changes of the last 30 – 40 years

Changes in our food during the post-war period[5]

From:	To:
Most fruit and vegetables eaten in season	Most fruit and vegetables available all year
Most fruit and vegetables sourced in the UK	Most fruit and vegetables sourced internationally
Limited variety of products	Huge variety of products
Most food unprocessed	Most food processed (tinned, frozen, freeze-dried, cooked, bottled, chilled, heat-treated, washed – even peeled and chopped!)
Minimal packaging	Heavy packaging
Most meals made at home	Many meals bought ready-prepared or eaten out
Few homes with fridges or freezers	Most homes have fridges and freezers
Food shops within walking distance for most people	Food shops a car trip away for most people
A mix of medium-scale and large-scale farming	Mostly large-scale farming
Lots of mixed farming	Lots of monoculture farming
A mix of non-intensive and intensive meat production	Meat production largely intensive

have added to the carbon emissions of our diets. Your food choices can make a difference. For example the difference between a high meat and a low meat diet is about 1.2 tonnes a year and the difference between a high meat diet and a vegan diet is about 2.6 tonnes a year.[3]

It can be hard to work out exactly how much CO_2e a particular item embodies. There is research into how to label food to show this, but it is still in its early stages.[4] In the pages that follow, we look in detail at where the embodied CO_2e in food comes from and give you a rough guide to reducing it in your diet.

The meaning of food

Food evokes strong feelings. It's part of relationships and embedded in culture. From the very start of life, when a baby first sucks from breast or bottle, it means more than just nutrition. People show love by giving food and rejection by refusing it. It's common to make a special cake for a child's birthday or to celebrate an anniversary with a meal. Parents feel pleased when their children eat well and fret if they don't. Sometimes food is used to provide comfort or is given as a reward. A sweet is offered to a child with a grazed knee. A trip to a fast-food restaurant is seen as a reward for good behaviour. An adult who is feeling miserable settles down with some pints of beer or treats themselves with a cake.

Battles for control are often played out over the dinner table. Emotions that are hard to express are hidden in subtle – and not so subtle – actions around food. A toddler becomes picky, a teenager refuses breakfast, a partner is late for a carefully prepared supper. Anger, resentment and protest can all be concealed in the way food is prepared, eaten, offered or refused.

On the positive side food is associated with love and kindness, affection and celebration. No special occasion is complete without an appropriate meal. Food is also strongly cultural. Although we might appear to have embraced an international cuisine each sub-group has its own 'good' and 'bad' foods, its dishes for feasts and special occasions and its food rules and taboos. Understanding the place food plays in your life and that of your family can be important in tackling its carbon emissions.

- What has influenced your food choices? Think about childhood patterns, religious rules, family attitudes.
- Who decides what you eat? Think about who shops, who cooks, who has special food needs or who makes a fuss in your family or household group.
- How do you use food to express or cope with feelings? Think about rewards, comfort, approval and celebrations.

> **❝** Food was very important in my family. Even though we were poor and lived in a house with no bathroom, no electricity upstairs and an outside loo, our diet was top quality fish, meat and vegetables. Food was the way my mother showed love. I was a fussy eater and I now realise I used food as a form of control in order to receive more attention. When I became pregnant I started eating all the things I had previously rejected - and continue to do so. Cooking is showing self-care and care and love to my family. I have reached this point after a journey of fad dieting and denial.
>
> **Mary Evans Young**

Food worries

Food is also a source of anxiety. It can seem that scarcely a day goes by without another food scare. It can be difficult to know what is really good to eat – whether we are talking about a healthy diet, farming or Fairtrade. The list of food worries below was created from discussions with people in Carbon Conversations groups. Which would feature on your list of food worries? Are there others that you would add?

- Junk food – people eating too much fat and sugar and not enough fresh fruit and vegetables.
- Poor quality food in schools, prisons and hospitals.
- Eating disorders – anorexia and bulimia.
- Health risks from the typical western diet – obesity, diabetes, heart disease and cancer.
- Livestock-farming methods – battery chickens, intensive pig farming.
- The spread of major animal diseases like BSE, foot-and-mouth and bird 'flu.
- Food safety – problems like *Salmonella*, *Listeria* and *E. coli*.
- Chemical additives in food.
- Residual pesticides and herbicides on food.
- Unhealthy chemicals – like dioxin or growth hormones – getting into the food chain.
- Genetically modified foods.
- The dominance of big supermarkets and the loss of small, local shops.
- The destruction of the marine environment through overfishing.
- Treatment of small farmers in the UK and overseas.[6]

Connected problems

Many of the items on this list are connected. They are linked to intensive farming practices, the influence of large corporations and the global supply system. We may be grateful for our reliable, cheap food but it comes with hidden costs.

- The **environment** suffers from the use of pesticides, fertilisers and other chemicals; from the high demand for water of some crops; from forest clearance for soy and livestock production; and from the loss of bio-diversity.

> *Food is a real bonding thing – it brings families, communities and cultures together. My cakes and patties are made from real Jamaican recipes, fresh and home-made with natural ingredients.*
> **Thomas**

> *I love food – I live, breathe and sleep food. When I was a child my mum wasn't well a lot of the time and as the eldest of five children I cooked for the family. I learned to produce a meal out of not very much. I love to put a whole variety of properly cooked food on the table and I love finding new recipes. It's the day-to-day cooking that I like the best. It's one of the things that makes me feel good about myself but it's also connected with showing love, with caring and giving.*
> **Claire Melling**

- Our **health** suffers because many of the more profitable foods are also high in fats and sugars and low in fibre and fresh ingredients.
- **Small farmers** across the world suffer, as they are driven out of business by large corporations and the demands of supermarkets.
- **Control** over the system is lost as supply chains become longer and it becomes hard to maintain responsibility for standards.
- It is a **greenhouse gas-intensive** system and a key cause of climate change.

Recent years have seen increasing demands for an alternative to the current globalised, industrial system, not just because of climate change but because of many of these inter-related issues.[7] Protests across the world have given rise to a movement for food sovereignty – a system that would be ecologically sound and which would put the people who produce, distribute and consume food at the heart of decisions about food rather than the corporations and market institutions. Exactly what the changes should be is a matter for debate. Understanding how the food on your plate relates to climate change and to the current food system may help you make up your mind.

Across the world, small producers are protesting against a global system that is ecologically unsound, socially unfair and leaves over 1 billion people hungry

Where's the CO_2e in food?

We can look at the CO_2e in food in four stages that bring it from the farm to our kitchens.

- **Production** – everything that happens on the farm.
- **Processing** – everything that happens to turn raw ingredients into the products we buy in the shops, including chilling and freezing them.
- **Packaging** – the tins, bottles, plastic and cardboard that keep food fresh and allow it to be transported.
- **Transport** – the journeys that food takes, from the farm, to the processing plant, to the shops and to our homes.

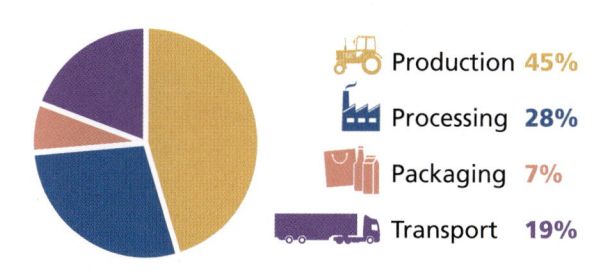

Production 45%
Processing 28%
Packaging 7%
Transport 19%

Carbon emissions of food

Adapted from information in *Cooking up a Storm*, Tara Garnett, FCRN, 2008

There are also CO_2e emissions associated with food waste but we discuss those in Chapter Five.

carbonconversations.org

Production

Growing crops and rearing animals is responsible for about 45% of your food footprint.[9] It takes energy to produce food and, when energy is used, CO_2 is emitted. Energy may be used in:

- manufacturing and using farm equipment (tractors, combine harvesters, slurry-management facilities etc.);
- manufacturing fertilisers and pesticides – roughly 1% of the world's energy production is used in creating nitrogen fertiliser;[10]
- protecting crops to extend the growing season by using heated greenhouses and polytunnels;
- growing crops to feed animals;
- heating or cooling cowsheds, battery henhouses and other animal housing.

Some types of food production are more energy-intensive and environmentally damaging than others. Modern, conventional agriculture is more energy-intensive than older, mixed farming methods where animals tended to be kept out of doors and fed on grass as part of a crop rotation. Meat and dairy production are both more energy-intensive than growing grains, fruit or vegetables. This is because, under modern methods, the animals have to be housed, kept warm and fed grain while they grow big enough to eat. This direct use of energy is not the biggest problem however. Simply bringing land into cultivation, fertilising the soil and keeping animals causes greenhouse gases to be released.

- Forests, savannah and pasture land are carbon sinks – absorbing more CO_2 than they release. When this land is converted to grow crops, ploughing releases the stored carbon back into the atmosphere as CO_2 and it stops acting as a carbon sink.
- The use of nitrogen fertiliser leads to the release of nitrous oxides.[11]
- Methane is released when cattle and sheep burp, is produced in the manure of all farm animals and is released when rice is grown in paddy fields.

Nitrous oxide and methane are particularly powerful greenhouse gases. Although methane is relatively short-lived, a tonne of methane causes far more damage than a tonne of carbon dioxide.[12] In the UK, about 31% of agriculture's GHG emissions come from methane and about 42% from nitrous oxides. Globally, the clearing of land is more significant, producing about 47% of agriculture's emissions.[13] Livestock production is responsible for a large share of these emissions. In general, beef, sheep and dairy products are the most carbon intensive foods you can eat. Meanwhile, (in case you thought fish was the answer) fishing is now a large-scale industrial activity and there are anxieties about its sustainability.[14]

> *Cultivate is a co-operative social enterprise owned by the community and dedicated to local food. We grow fruit and vegetables ten miles outside Oxford, and sell them in Oxford at community markets and via the VegVan, our mobile greengrocery. Cultivate aims to get local produce directly from growers to consumers – both from our own farm, and from other local growers and producers.*[8]
>
> Emma Burnett

Some uncomfortable facts

- Overall, livestock production may be responsible for about 14.5% of all human-made greenhouse gases.[15]
- It takes six to eight kg of grain to produce one kg of beef.[16]

So does this mean we should all give up meat, fish and dairy produce and become vegans? No. Climate-friendly food production needn't exclude meat and dairy altogether. Some land, like the Welsh hills where sheep have been reared for centuries, isn't suitable for growing crops but will support animals. Other animals are good processors of food waste and scraps, such as chickens and pigs on traditional mixed farms. Rational, climate-friendly food-production would probably mean:

- less reliance on meat, fish and dairy produce;
- a return to less intensive forms of farming;
- greater diversity in farming – less monoculture and more mixed farms;
- more support for smaller, less mechanised farms;

Processing

Processing is responsible for about 28% of your food footprint. Once the crops have been grown and harvested, or the animals are mature, a lot of food is processed. A few foods reach us without any processing: some fruit and vegetables and some fish. Almost everything else has been processed in some way, however small: for example, celery is often cleaned and trimmed, and it needs to be kept cool on the journey from farm to supermarket. Food needs to be processed to make it edible, to keep it safe, or to make it last longer. But not all processing is done for these essential reasons. It is also done to meet demand from consumers for convenience and because it is extremely profitable. All processing requires energy and produces CO_2.

- Animals have to be slaughtered, butchered and finished.
- Crops may be dried, ground, pulped, pressed, fermented, pasteurised, bottled or tinned in order to extract the part we use, to store them or to extend their use.
- Many foods are refrigerated or frozen.
- Foods may be cooked or combined to make some of the things we think of as basics such as bread, cornflakes, cheese, or margarine.
- Items that would once have been made at home are now usually bought ready-made, for example jams, pickles, ketchup, mayonnaise, yoghurt, biscuits, cakes, pastries, and oven chips.
- Even some processes that are still usually done at home, such as washing and chopping vegetables, can now be done for you: you can buy your carrots sliced, your lettuce washed and your beans trimmed.
- Finally, you can buy entire meals, ready-made, requiring nothing more than to be put into the microwave or oven – pizzas, lasagnes, curries and roast beef dinners.

> *My early memories are of quite good, healthy food. It's only since I got into adolescence that I've really enjoyed fast food. I tend not to eat it when I'm sober. Most of the fast food that I have is at three in the morning. Any food then is fantastic.*
>
> Robbie Nestor

Some food manufacturers have argued that less CO_2 will be used if food is processed and cooked in factory units. Huge factory ovens are more efficient than domestic ones; there is less wastage in a factory unit; even the packaging may be less, once you have taken into account the individual wrapping on all the items that make up a home-cooked meal. Other research shows that if you do a proper life-cycle analysis which looks at all the CO_2 in all the stages – from production, through processing, packaging and distribution – then, highly processed food has a higher carbon footprint.[17]

A good rule of thumb is that the more ingredients in a processed item, the higher its CO_2 impact. Much of this will come from the travel involved in assembling all the ingredients. There are also good health reasons for eating less processed foods as they tend to be high in sugars and fats.

Freezing and refrigeration are particular problems. Refrigeration features at almost every point in the chain which brings food from the farm to our plates. We eat more perishable foods, like salads, which need to be kept cool. Changes in patterns of work mean that people shop less frequently and need to store more food at home. Meanwhile, the homes themselves are warmer and so a fridge is a necessity. Food refrigeration is responsible for about 3-3.5% of the UK's greenhouse gas emissions.[18] Freezing is extremely energy-intensive. Freezing vegetables adds around 2 kg CO_2 per kilogram of food. The carbon emissions from a 1 kg pack of frozen peas are the same as the carbon emissions from leaving a 20 W lightbulb on continuously for 30 days.[19]

Packaging

Packaging is responsible for about 7% of your food footprint. Most of the food we buy is packaged in some way. Some packaging is necessary in order to keep food fresh and prevent damage, but some is not. Manufacturers and supermarkets like packaging. It does wonders for profitability by:

- controlling portion sizes, selling you the amounts they think you want, rather than the amounts you might choose;
- targeting particular audiences with essentially the same product (healthy yoghurts, children's yoghurts, luxury yoghurts; 'country-style', 'economy' 'traditional' and 'healthy' sausages);
- extending shelf-life, for example, salad in 'modified-atmosphere-packaging' – those plump bags of washed leaves that look fresh for up to 10 days after being picked;
- aiding handling and shelf-stacking;
- providing advertising space, helping each manufacturer compete for your business;

> *A lot of my business is filling (and refilling) bottles from kegs of wine I import from small growers in France who I know personally. The main reason I do this is to save glass. Even the kegs are recycled. Nothing is thrown away. It's very satisfying to see customers bringing back bottles to be refilled. Even the corks will do three to five trips. Over 50% of the wine in the shop is from growers I've visited. I try to keep it as local as possible and I love travelling by train. I don't like buying wines from the other side of the world. They are mostly imported in big tankers. It's a system that's hard for small growers to work with and it wrecks family businesses.*

Nicholas Hall, Cambridge Vinopolis

- encouraging customers to spend more time looking at the goods on display;
- reducing staff costs as goods don't have to be weighed and wrapped for each customer.

Packaging takes energy to produce, it adds to the weight of the goods being transported and it needs to be disposed of. All these factors add to the CO_2 burden of food. In terms of CO_2, aluminium cans are the worst offenders because of the huge amount of electricity used in smelting. Steel cans and glass come next, followed by paper, card and plastic.[20] Disposal of plastic is a problem. Much of it is hard to recycle and consumers are often confused about which types can be put in the recycling bin. Bottled water – almost unheard of in the UK till the 1990s – is an example of the way packaging has transformed a need that used to be met more cheaply and with a lower CO_2 burden. There is no evidence that bottled water is superior to tap water and both the packaging and the transport have serious CO_2 impacts.

Progress with packaging has been made however. Using lighter bottles or redesigning the shape of a box can cut the amount of packaging significantly. Since 2005 manufacturers who have signed up to the Courtauld agreement, a government sponsored scheme, have made big reductions in the weight and amount of packaging they use.[21] Recycling rates by the public are also increasing year on year. 61% of packaging was recycled in 2008.[22]

Transport

Transport is responsible for about 19% of your food footprint. 'Food miles' is a phrase many people are familiar with now. It refers to the distance food has travelled to get to your plate. Every mile your dinner travels adds to the CO_2 emitted on your behalf. About half of UK food is imported[23] and has travelled a long way before we buy it. The supermarkets' distribution systems mean that even food produced in the UK may have travelled round the country several times before finding its way onto a supermarket shelf.

- The food system accounts for about 25% of all European road freight.[24]
- Shops are farther away than they used to be and most people drive to get there.[25]
- Supermarkets stock very little food that has been sourced locally (within 30 miles). Only 1–2% of their turnover comes from local produce.[26]
- Some food is just swapped: in 2004, the UK imported 15.5 million litres of milk and cream from Germany and exported 17.2 million litres right back (there are similar figures for trade with France).[27]

A traditional Christmas lunch made with food imported from around the world, could clock up 30,000 miles. A similar Christmas lunch, sourced from the UK and Europe could come a mere 2000 miles, including the wine.[28] So, reducing food miles is important. Try to find out where your food comes from and how much CO_2 was used in getting it to you.

> *We eat a lot more vegetables than meat but Carbon Conversations showed me that where those vegetables comes from makes a difference. Being vegetarian is not important, food selection is important. I came to realize that opting for locally produced vegetables and meat, as opposed to those taking a flight to our market shelves, would make a significant difference.*
>
> **Gomathy Sethuraman**

carbonconversations.org

How did it get here?

It is important to take account of the mode of transport used. Some foods that have travelled a long way have come slowly, on a bulk carrier ship, and their transport emissions can be surprisingly low. For example 1 kg of lentils, shipped by bulk carrier from India have travelled 11,657 km. Their transport emissions are 46 grams of CO_2. In contrast, 1 kg of strawberries flown 8,774 km from California have transport emissions of 6 kg. The table below shows the amount of CO_2 each form of transport uses to carry one tonne of goods for one km.

CO_2 emissions by mode of transport	
Mode of transport	*CO_2 emissions (grams CO_2 / tonne-km)**
Air: short-haul	1360
Air: long-haul	692
Road: transit van	532
Road: medium truck	248
Road: large truck	88
Ship: roll-on/roll-off	51
Container ship	16
Ship: bulk carrier	4

Carbon Smart[29]
*CO_2 emissions arising from transporting 1 tonne of goods for 1 kilometre.

Here are some useful rules of thumb for guessing how your food was transported.

- Perishable items from outside Europe (green beans, grapes, blueberries for example) usually come by air.
- Perishable items from within Europe usually come via refrigerated truck and roll-on/roll-off ferry.
- Non-perishable items and items with a long storage life (for example, dried lentils, wine, bananas, apples) from outside Europe usually come by bulk sea carrier and then by truck.
- Non-perishable items from Europe usually come by truck and ferry.

Food diary

It can be difficult to know exactly how much CO_2e the food you buy is responsible for, particularly when an item has many ingredients. But it is worth taking a look at your fridge, freezer and food cupboards and thinking about how the food you buy affects climate change. Try keeping a food diary for a week, or simply check your receipts when you come back from your weekly shop. Look at what impact it is likely to have had. People are often surprised at what they find. Sometimes they discover that they buy more processed food than they thought. Sometimes they realise that there is more food from overseas than they imagined.

If you are taking part in a Carbon Conversations group you will find a Food Diary form to complete in your *Workbook*. This helps you rate each item for how 'Climate-friendly' or 'Climate-hostile' it is according to the four categories of production, processing, packaging and transport. One item such as grapes flown in from South America for example can have a high travel footprint but a low production one. Another item such as a joint of British beef would have a high production footprint but a low travel one. Meanwhile with a can of flavoured water it would be the aluminium packaging that gives it a high footprint and with a bottle of tomato ketchup it would be the processing.

Easy steps to a healthy, low-CO_2 diet

Remember that food is a complex, emotional matter. Changing your diet to reduce your carbon footprint is no easier than changing your diet to lose weight:

- crash diets don't work;
- faddy diets don't work;
- diets that make you miserable don't work;
- a pattern of bingeing and dieting gives you the worst of all worlds.

The changes that are most likely to work are the ones that:

- you choose yourself;
- fit your daily routine;
- make you feel good about yourself;
- you adopt gradually and steadily.

If you are going to alter your diet to make it CO_2 friendly, it is important to be sure that it is also healthy. The pyramid diagram[30] is a guide to a healthy, sustainable diet. The foods which you should eat plentifully for

A Sustainable Healthy Diet

the sake of your health – fruit, vegetables, bread, rice, pasta and other starchy foods – also have a low CO_2e impact. Increasing the amount of these foods and reducing the amount of high-fat and sugary foods in your diet will make you healthier and more climate-friendly. Reducing the amount of meat and dairy produce by substituting beans, pulses, nuts and seeds will make an even bigger difference. If you also try to eat as much local and seasonal food as you can and avoid heavily processed food you should reduce the carbon impact of your diet considerably.

What counts as local?

There is no legal definition of local food. One popular definition, used by campaigners, is that local food is "Raw food, or lightly processed food (such as cheese, sausages, pies and baked goods) and its main ingredients, grown or produced within 30 miles of where it was bought."[31] You will find some food, labeled as local, that doesn't stand up to investigation. In 2011 local government regulators found that 18% of local food claims were clearly false.[32] The best advice is to be a savvy shopper. Ask questions. Look for food that is grown or reared as close to home as possible. If you can't find local produce, look for regional. If you can't find regional produce look for food that comes from the UK.

carbonconversations.org 113

The table gives the carbon footprints for some common foods. Note the big difference between locally grown, seasonal fruit and vegetables and the ones that have been flown in or grown in a heated greenhouse. Note also the high numbers for meat and dairy produce and the enormous difference between tap water and bottled water.

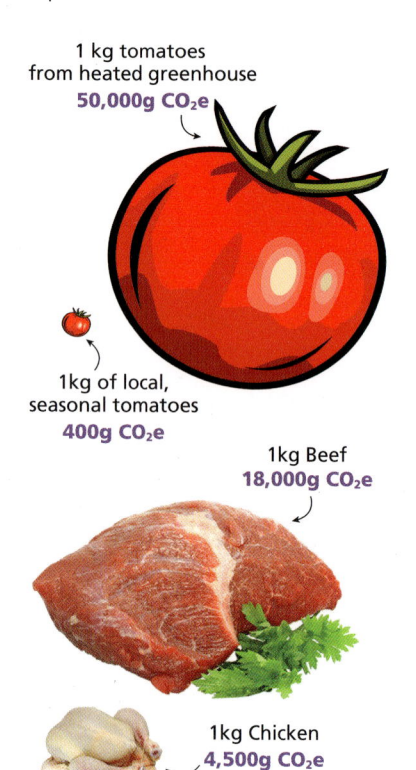

1 kg tomatoes from heated greenhouse
50,000g CO_2e

1kg of local, seasonal tomatoes
400g CO_2e

1kg Beef
18,000g CO_2e

1kg Chicken
4,500g CO_2e

What counts as seasonal?

Many people are confused about when different fruits and vegetables are in season in the UK. Many of our favourite fruits and vegetables, such as avocados and bananas, don't grow here at all. Some – like tomatoes, peppers and cucumbers – have very short growing seasons which can be extended by the use of heated greenhouses, a practice which produces a very high carbon footprint. The chart opposite shows you when fruits are in season in the UK and

Carbon footprints of some common foods[34]

Grammes of CO_2e per kilo of food

Fruit and veg
Apples, local and seasonal	70g
Apples (average)	550g
Bananas	480g
Oranges	500g
Strawberries, local, in season	600g
Strawberries, out of season, flown in	7,200g
Carrots	300g
Potatoes	370g
Asparagus, local, in season	500g
Asparagus, out of season, flown in	14,000g
Tomatoes, local, seasonal (July) organic	400g
Tomatoes from heated greenhouse in UK, in March	50,000g

Grains
Oats	800g
Wheat	800g
Rice	4,000g

Meat, fish and dairy
Beef		18,000g
Lamb		19,000g
Chicken		4,500g
Eggs	for six eggs	1,800g
Milk	per litre	1,300g
Cheese		12,000g
Fish – tinned		5,900g
Fish – fresh or frozen		6,900g

Fats
Vegetable oil	3,500g
Butter	9,500g

Drinks
Bottle wine	per bottle	1,040g
Beer	per pint	300-900g
Orange juice	per litre	1,440
Bottled water	per litre	320g
Tap water	per litre	0.24g

(note where the decimal point is!)

114 carbonconversations.org

Eat Seasonably[33]

Month	Seasonal UK	Seasonal Europe
January	Apples, pears,	Oranges, lemons, grapefruit kiwi fruit, pomegranate
February	Rhubarb, apples, pears	Oranges, lemons, grapefruit, kiwi fruit, pomegranate
March	Rhubarb	Oranges, lemons, grapefruit, kiwi fruit, pomegranate
April	Rhubarb	Oranges, lemons, grapefruit, kiwi fruit
May	Rhubarb, strawberries	Oranges, lemons, grapefruit, kiwi fruit
June	Rhubarb, gooseberries, strawberries, raspberries, blueberries	Peaches, nectarines, cherries, melons
July	Rhubarb, cherries, blueberries, gooseberries, strawberries, raspberries, blackcurrants	Peaches, nectarines, melons, apricots
August	Apples, plums, greengages, damsons, cherries, raspberries, gooseberries, strawberries, blackcurrants, blueberries, blackberries	Peaches, nectarines, melons, apricots
September	Apples, pears, plums, damsons, greengages, elderberries, strawberries, raspberries, blackberries, blueberries	Peaches, nectarines, grapes, figs
October	Apples, pears, raspberries, blackberries	Peaches, nectarines, grapes, figs
November	Apples, pears	Grapes, oranges, lemons, grapefruit, pomegranate
December	Apples, pears	Oranges, lemons, grapefruit, pomegranate

carbonconversations.org

Europe. Unseasonal fruits have often been flown in. The exception is the UK's favourite fruit – bananas – which comes by boat and so has a relatively low footprint. You will find information about seasonal vegetables on websites listed in More Information.

CASE STUDIES

Approaches to change

Exactly what you do and how you do it will depend on your particular circumstances. Think about how to make permanent changes over a longish period of time. You might start by cutting out meat a few times a week. Once you were comfortable with this you might increase the number of vegetarian meals you eat. Another possibility might be to make sure that at least half your fruit and vegetables are seasonal. As you get used to cooking with them, you could build up to three-quarters. Perhaps you could decide to buy less air-flown fruit and vegetables or reduce the amount of frozen food you buy, eventually doing so only on special occasions. Here are some examples from people who took part in Carbon Conversations groups.

❝ As a result of Carbon Conversations we have reduced our meat and fish intake and been inspired to buy more local and organic food. We could feed the world easily if we didn't feed so much grain to animals – that was my strongest motivation. I like vegetables a lot – they're more interesting to cook than meat. Yottam Ottolenghi's 'New Vegetarian' column introduced me to ingredients I'd never come across before and we've now joined a gardening group and are growing more vegetables of our own.

Sometimes your feelings can take you by surprise. When my mother and mother-in-law both died within ten weeks of each other I found I wanted to eat meat all the time – I craved the dishes they'd cooked – the steak and kidney pies and roast beef and Yorkshire puddings. For about six months I just needed to eat meat. It was part of grieving for them. Then I was ready to go back to a more vegetable based diet."

Mary Evans Young

❝ I discovered things I would have realized if I'd stopped and thought. The diary showed up that I eat a lot of processed food – ready-made soups, pizzas and pies. This really surprised me and it hit me from a health point of view as well as the carbon. These foods are full of salt, sugar and fat. The reason is I'm always too busy. I'm tired. I never have enough time so I grab something easy. It's comfort too – I think that's more important when you're living abroad. When I first came here I felt as if everything apart from work had to be on hold. I was on a visa, I was dependent on the job to stay here, I felt obliged to give it everything. Doing the diary made me realize how much my life has changed. In Venezuela we bought everything from the market. It was locally grown and we cooked from scratch, from the basics of rice, vegetables, legumes. I miss the lifestyle I had before. I felt more in contact. Now I'm like a hamster on a wheel. Here people work 12 hours a day.

I'm eating less processed food since doing the diary but it's taken an internal shift and some external factors to be able to do so. I've realized I have to create space for myself and work less, allowing time to cook. It's about the way I'm approaching everything in my life, not just carbon. The external factor is that we now live in a warmer house. The old kitchen was so cold you wouldn't stop longer than it took to put something in the microwave. Now it's possible to stay there long enough to cook a proper meal."

Rebecca Miller

❝ I haven't eaten meat or dairy produce for a long time now. It was the McLibel trial that opened my eyes to the destructiveness of the meat and dairy industry. It just seemed an overwhelmingly good idea to try being vegan and see what happened. Before I started, I thought it would be difficult but actually it's a lot easier and less daunting once you start and I think that's the same with anything to do with diet, whether it's stopping eating meat and dairy or eating more local and seasonal food. It's a question of getting into the habit of it, then realizing that there are lots of really lovely foods out there that you can eat.

Often the most difficult thing is actually the social aspect. Although you're not making a comment on what other people are doing – it's about the damage caused by the food industry – when people see that you're not eating meat they often react as if you are criticizing them. It took me a while to realize that this is an issue that brings up a lot of stuff for a lot of people. Although most people are supportive, people sometimes take the mickey or trivialize your choice because they're not feeling comfortable themselves. Over the years I've got better at recognising this and responding more empathically and in a non-judgemental manner, whilst at the same time refusing to play down the importance of the reasons behind this choice."

Katherine Simpson

Eating the recommended '5 a day' amount of vegetables and fruit will be good for you and good for your carbon footprint

❝ I'd like to go back to the seasonality of food. Nowadays you can get pretty much anything, anytime, like strawberries at Christmas. We're so indulged – we can have whatever we want whenever we want it. I miss the feeling that these things are treats to be anticipated at certain times of year.

Jane Orton

carbonconversations.org

117

In the table below are a list of changes you could consider making. You may already be doing some of them. Others may be straightforward to adopt. Each one has a star rating against it. As before, the greater the number of stars, the greater the impact the action is likely to have.

Practical steps

		I'm already doing this	I would consider this	This would be really hard
Reduce meat consumption by 50%	***	☐	☐	☐
Stop eating meat	*****	☐	☐	☐
Reduce cheese and butter consumption by 50%	**	☐	☐	☐
Stop eating cheese and butter	***	☐	☐	☐
Reduce milk and yoghourt consumption by 50%	*	☐	☐	☐
Stop drinking milk and yoghourt	**	☐	☐	☐
Cook vegetarian meals twice a week	*	☐	☐	☐
Cook vegetarian meals four times a week	**	☐	☐	☐
Eat only seasonal fruit and vegetables	**	☐	☐	☐
Join a local organic box scheme	*	☐	☐	☐
Grow some of my own vegetables, salads or fruit	*	☐	☐	☐
Buy air-freighted food only on special occasions	*	☐	☐	☐
Stop buying all air-freighted food	**	☐	☐	☐
Buy 75% of food produced locally or in the UK	**	☐	☐	☐
Eat frozen food only on special occasions	*	☐	☐	☐
Reject all frozen food except that stored from the garden/allotment	**	☐	☐	☐
Reject all frozen food and ready meals and get rid of the freezer	***	☐	☐	☐
Reduce amount of processed food by 50%	**	☐	☐	☐
Reduce amount of ready-meals and fast food by 50%	**	☐	☐	☐
Reject all aluminium cans	*	☐	☐	☐
Reduce food waste by 50%	**	☐	☐	☐
Give up drinking bottled water and soft drinks	*	☐	☐	☐

Water and climate change

Water is already a problem in many parts of the world. Rivers have dried up, inland lakes have shrunk, and underwater reserves have been emptied and will not refill.[35] Over 750 million people have no reliable access to clean drinking water.[36] Climate change is likely to make matters worse. It will bring changes in patterns of rainfall, causing droughts and floods in different parts of the world. The places that will suffer most include some of the poorest, such as sub-Saharan Africa and Bangladesh, where water problems are already severe.

Virtual water

People often concentrate on the wasteful use of water in British homes. But this use is tiny compared to virtual water – the water embodied in anything that has been grown or manufactured.[37] In the UK, the average person uses between 44 and 88 tonnes of water per year in their home. (Between 120 and 240 litres per day.) But the water needed to grow the crops which feed and clothe that person amount to a staggering 1,500 – 2,000 tonnes a year, or about 5,000 litres per day. Most of this is used producing meat. Eating a vegetarian diet reduces your water footprint to a mere 2,700 litres per day. Still more water is used by industry, bringing us goods we sometimes take for granted. Some of the water is used in growing crops used to make clothes. Some of it is used in industrial processes such as steel-making.

How much water does it take to make…[38]

Item	Quantity	Water required for production (litres)
Petrol	1 litre	70
Biodiesel from Soy	1 litre	11,400
Coffee	1 cup	140
Potatoes	1 kg	280
Bread	1 kg	1,608
Milk	1 litre	1,000
Rice	1 kg	2,500
Cheese	1 kg	3,178
Beef	1 kg	15,000
Cotton for one T-shirt	250 g	2,500
Bicycle	One	130
Car	One	80,000

Poorer countries often export their precious water in the form of goods sold to wealthier nations: wheat and soy for animal feed; cotton; rice and coffee. Sometimes these crops take precedence over growing essential supplies for local people. The relationships are complex but water problems are yet another reason for thinking about our heavy use of meat and dairy produce, our reliance on imported food and our throwaway attitude to clothes and other goods. They also suggest that water-hungry bio-fuel crops may not be the answer to our transport problems.

carbonconversations.org

Water in the UK

The UK used to be seen as a wet, rainy country with no problems of water supply. Population pressure in the drier South East, combined with increased demand from industry and consumers, has changed this. Water use in the UK is 70% higher than it was 30 years ago, while climate change means that, despite serious floods from time to time, we are likely to have more summer droughts and lower annual rainfall. The response from water companies has been to try to meet this increased demand by supplying more. It would be better for the environment, and better for climate change, if demand could be reduced.

Water use makes up a small part of your direct carbon footprint. Energy is involved in extracting, purifying and pumping water to your home and then in treating the waste water that is flushed down toilets and drained from sinks, baths and washing machines.

What can you do?

A diet of local foods with less meat and dairy will help both your carbon footprint and your consumption of virtual water. You can try to reduce your consumption of other goods that come from water-stressed parts of the world. You might like to support charities and campaigns like Action Water and WaterAid who work to provide clean water worldwide. See More Information for details.

At home, a sustainable target for water use is about 60 litres a day. If you have a water meter, you can monitor your use and see how close to this you can get. If you don't have a meter, consider getting one installed. Households with meters use 10-15% less water than people without. Most of the advice is common sense. Take short showers rather than baths, don't leave the tap running, clean the car with a bucket of water not the hose, only run the dishwasher on a full load and fix your dripping taps. Longer term it is a good idea to install water butts in the garden so as to avoid using the hose, to choose a low-use toilet if you are re-fitting the bathroom and to seek out dishwashers and washing machines with the lowest water use when the time comes to replace them.

> ❝ Drought is a big problem in Mexico. The rich people have big water tanks to store up the water, the poor suffer. I worry it will get worse.
>
> Jacqueline Gonzalez

Getting Stuck

People generally approach the food section of their footprint with enthusiasm. It's a topic where everyone has a view and people enjoy sharing stories and sometimes recipes too. Change is not necessarily easy however. People find that their good intentions don't always translate into day-to-day changes. For someone living in poverty, shifting your diet is hard. You have to buy what is cheap and can't afford to take risks with new foods that may not appeal to your family. For other people it is not money that is the problem. A climate-friendly diet doesn't have to be more expensive and there is enough slack in people's budgets to experiment. What goes wrong?

The power of the food system

The food system is powerful. Faced with twenty supermarket aisles you find yourself pushing your trolley round the familiar route. Faced with thousands of different products you pick the same ones as usual. Everyone else is doing the same. It feels normal. Standing in front of the fruit you start questioning yourself. Will the children really eat English apples instead of Chilean grapes? Grabbing sausages from the meat counter you wonder whether you've time to make a vegetarian meal and you reach for the familiar minced beef as well. Where are the lentils anyway? You revert to your familiar pattern and exit with relief.

Our routines, sense of identity and cooking skills lock together with the location of the shops, the convenience of what is on offer and the comfort of what is familiar. It's not just a question of buying a packet of lentils but of changing your place in a system that involves many elements. Most of us have a pattern of shopping, cooking and eating that works well for us. Changing one aspect can bring complications elsewhere. You may not know how to cook a vegetarian meal. Your family may think it's funny food. You may not have storage space for new ingredients. And so on.

Feeling insignificant

The size and power of the food system can also make your efforts feel futile. You may wonder what difference you are making. Is it worth scanning the small print to see where an item came from? Will a couple of vegetarian meals make a difference? How much does the Fairtrade farmer benefit? Rationally there are several good answers to these questions. For example:

- consumer pressure is one factor in bringing change to big systems;
- it's good to be part of the vanguard and adapt by choice;
- it's important to live by your values and principles.

These rational answers are important but they may cut little ice when you are feeling harassed or upset. Trying to do something, however small, about a big global problem is distressing. It brings to mind the damage to ecosystems or exploitation of other people involved in your dinner. Anxiety and guilt are never far away. The trick is to get these feelings in proportion as we describe below.

Rebound

Another systemic effect is rebound and an awareness of this sometimes contributes to people feeling that it is all too difficult. If you save money by changing to a more climate-friendly diet, rebound will have an effect on the carbon savings you make. The reason is that the money you save is likely to be spent somewhere else and may be spent on something that has a higher carbon impact than food. If you decide to substitute two or three meat meals with vegetarian ones made from lentils or other pulses, this is likely to save you money. If you then allow yourself to drive a little further each week your carbon emissions may actually rise as the extra petrol has a higher carbon impact than the meat. Households who waste less food face the same dilemma. Research by WRAP suggests that about half of the money saved when people stop wasting food is spent trading up to buy more expensive food and drink but the other half is saved or spent on other things.[44]

This means that it is important to think about the whole of your carbon footprint when you are making changes and to think carefully about what happens to any money you save. Although rebound has an effect on the carbon savings you make, it doesn't eliminate them and doesn't mean that they are not worth making. We discuss this further in Chapter Five where we explain which sectors of the economy are high carbon and which are low carbon.

Family and culture

Although we often think of our food choices as individual they are strongly influenced by family and cultural norms. There are often strong norms about which foods are seen as healthy, what makes a good breakfast, what you should eat on a night out, what's appropriate for a family party and so on. If a change you want to make runs counter to these patterns you may find yourself in trouble. One woman found herself cooking three separate evening meals in order to cope with her own concerns, her gluten-intolerant daughter and her meat-loving husband. Here are some examples of strong cultural and family norms taken from participants in Carbon Conversations groups:

- "A good night out for my friends means several pints of lager followed by a vindaloo."
- "Our favourite Friday night supper is pizza on the sofa with a bottle of wine."
- "In our family, Christmas dinner has to be exactly the same every year – no deviations allowed!"
- "I used to do manual work and I don't feel prepared for the day without eating a 'Full English' even though I'm retired."

None of these examples felt easy to change. Other people's feelings, the pleasure of shared experiences, your own expectations and your sense of identity may all be at stake.

Pleasure and comfort

Some of our food habits are not social but very personal. Most people take comfort and pleasure from food and it can be a shock to realise that despite your good intentions you don't really want to change. One part of you thinks that a climate-friendly diet is a good idea. Another part wants to keep things the way they are. This may be to do with your delight in particular tastes or cuisines or it may be to do with the way you use food to reward yourself or cheer yourself up. Many people use food as a treat. Others use it to squash down angry feelings, dull a sense of depression or take the edge off anxiety. You may need to take these feelings into account as you work out

> *I do care about how animals are treated. They should be able to live well while they're alive. When we had a barbecue last week me and my friend James had a little argument over what to buy. There were sausages for 60p for a pack of twelve, and apart from not being very nice to eat the pigs probably weren't treated very well. So I looked for ones that were treated a bit better. I maybe don't care as much as I should, but it matters.*
>
> Robbie Nestor

what to do. If you feel that you've failed because you can't resist cheese or need a fix of fast food to cope with a bad day, you are unlikely to look at other changes that feel easier for you.

Preoccupation

In a slightly different twist some people find themselves pre-occupied with the carbon impact of food in an unhealthy way. Just as you can become over-concerned with the health impact of your diet, you can also become over-concerned with its climate impact. Food becomes threatening instead of enjoyable. You feel you have to take precautions at every turn. Where is this food from? How was that food made? Is this good or bad? Better or worse? You start to punish yourself for mistakes. You deny yourself any pleasure in food. You become an irritant to your family and friends who regard you as faddy and difficult.

Feelings of insecurity are usually at the heart of this. You don't feel safe and don't trust anyone to protect you, least of all an out-of-control global food system. You feel anxious and miserable but often come across as irritable and selfish. Proportion is important here. If you have a tendency to worry about food, be cautious about adding climate change to your list of worries. Concentrate on eating an ordinary healthy diet or limit yourself to one or two changes that feel easily doable.

Things that may help

It may help to:

- explore how other changes happened to your diet;
- talk with family and friends;
- take it slowly and plan;
- keep a sense of proportion.

Explore other changes

Try looking back at how other changes to your diet happened. Unless you deliberately go on a diet most changes happen as a result of wider influences. Some examples are getting married and adapting to someone else's patterns, travelling abroad and encountering another culture's cuisine, becoming more affluent and able to afford a wider range of foods. Often it is other people who make the difference.

If you are taking part in a Carbon Conversations group your facilitator may suggest creating a food time line. It's good to do this in a group and discuss the outcome with others but you can also do this by yourself. Draw a line horizontally across a large sheet of paper. At the start of the line (left) write your date of birth and at the end (right) write the current year. On the line mark all the points at which your diet changed. You might highlight eating school dinners, going to a pub for the first time, leaving home, travelling abroad, starting a family and so on. Younger people may remember the first time they tasted new foods such as coffee or seafood. Older people may remember when foods such as muesli, avocado pears or pizza first became widely available in the UK. Then reflect on what made the changes stick. People? Pleasure? Health advice? Social trends? Availability? Changes in technology such as the advent of microwaves? Understanding other changes may help you see how to make the climate-friendly options, you'd like to adopt, stick.

Talk with family and friends

Other people are almost always involved in changes you want to make to your diet. If you don't include those you care about or live with in your plans you will almost certainly come unstuck.

Talk to them. Explain your concerns. Ask if they share them. Negotiate. Involve them. Be prepared to compromise. Expect to experiment. Ask for support. You will find suggestions on how to raise tricky issues in Chapter Six.

Take it slowly and plan

Don't rush into anything. Decide on some steps that would lower the impact of your diet and then for each one ask yourself questions like these:

Who else will be affected if I make this change? How will they feel? What do I need to discuss with them? For example, if you would like to cook a vegetarian meal once a week, how will the rest of your family feel?

What will make this change easy and what will make it difficult? With the example of the vegetarian meal you might need to think about the practicalities of where you will shop, what recipe you will use, and how long the new dish will take to cook. It may help to order a supermarket delivery rather than struggle to find unfamiliar items, explore a vegetable box scheme or look up recipes online.

How can I make this plan realistic? Think about the obstacles and how you will overcome them. Decide how you will cope with setbacks. For example if you decide to stop drinking bottled water the day will come when you find yourself stranded without your reusable bottle and need to buy yourself a drink. How will you make sure you don't punish yourself for this? How will you ensure that you don't use an incident like this as an excuse to give up?

When am I going to do this? Is this a change you'll carry out every day or once a week? Can you pick the least stressful time to start it? Give yourself a realistic time-scale.

You can also use the technique of Force Field Analysis which we described in the last chapter to explore whether a particular change is likely to work for you.

Keep a sense of proportion

Acknowledge that you have mixed feelings about food. It's quite normal to feel bad about the origins of many food items but love preparing them, adore their taste and enjoy introducing others to their delights. Acknowledge the conflict. Talk about the fact that you sometimes feel guilty or sad about your impact. Remember that you are not single-handedly responsible for the global food system. You are not its creator and not its biggest player. Choose the part you play in it. Minimise the damage your lifestyle causes. Lend your voice to the campaigns that might change it. And then get on with enjoying everything that a good meal with family and friends can offer.

What about at work?

Workplaces can influence the way their employees eat through:

- the times allowed for breaks;
- the provision (or lack) of fridges and microwaves for workers' use;
- the provision of canteens and subsidised meals;
- the type of food on offer in canteens and at catered events.

Some workplaces also provide large numbers of meals to the public as part of their core business, (for example the health service, schools and the hospitality and catering sectors). These employers have the opportunity to take decisions that affect the carbon footprint of the meals provided as well as influencing the eating habits of the public. As an employee you may feel that you have little power but it is worth thinking about what happens in your workplace and what effect you could have.

The food you eat at work

Lunch breaks are often short. Fewer companies run their own canteens than in the past and where they do, catering is often provided by an outside contractor.[39] Some provide little in the way of kitchen facilities or rest rooms for their employees. The temptation to grab an unhealthy and unsustainable snack can be high. As one Carbon Conversations participant put it:

"The carbon footprint of what I'm eating at work is the last thing on my mind. I'm usually tired, stressed and thinking about the next meeting. The food is just fuel to see me through the working day."

Improving the sustainability of the food people eat at work can also mean addressing their wider needs for proper breaks and good facilities.

If your company does have a staff canteen it's worth finding out how it is run. If the catering is done in-house, the catering manager may be willing to explore more sustainable options. If it is provided by an outside contractor, it is worth asking about the nature of the contract, when it is due for renewal and whether it contains any sustainability clauses. The guide *Getting Started: the Really Simply Guide to Buying More Sustainable Food*[40] is full of good suggestions for organisations and their catering departments. It also has good advice on who to talk to and what questions to ask.

If people in your company make their own lunch arrangements, try thinking about the culture that has grown up around this. Are people encouraged to take proper breaks? Is there adequate provision of a kitchen and staff room? Do people socialise or share food at lunch time or are they hunkered down at their desks with a sandwich while they check their Facebook page? Try talking with colleagues about how you could make lunch breaks healthier and more sociable. An informal lunch club where people bring in their own home-made lunches and eat them together in the staff room is also a cheerful social setting where people can share approaches to food, recipe tips and preferences – helping them to feel competent and part of a community. If there is inadequate provision of facilities or if people are struggling to take breaks they are entitled to, you may be able to get help from your Trade Union, if you are a member.

The food your company supplies

Large organisations can have a powerful influence on the public's eating habits. A huge number of meals are eaten in hospitals, schools and universities as well as in staff canteens, restaurants and cafes. If the food in these places is healthy and sustainable then these types of food become the norm. If people like what is provided there, they may try to replicate it at home. Some public

> ❝ We have had some events where we put food on, but because we pay an outside company to manage the project, that outside company tends to organise the food, so I haven't really had much control over that. And it's not been my task, so I haven't thought about challenging what kind of food we have: maybe I should.
>
> Julie Pickard

sector organisations are making big efforts to provide more sustainable food and you will find good examples in both the health service and in education. For example, by sourcing local, fresh and organic food the Royal Cornwall Hospital Trust has cut carbon emissions from road transport by two thirds and it now spends over 80% of its food budget with local companies, with over 40% of that going directly on Cornish produce.[41] Nottingham Trent University has increased the vegetable content and reduced the meat content of many of its canteen dishes and with the money saved has been able to source more ingredients with a high environmental standard.[42]

If you work for a large public sector organisation, check out their policy on food procurement and see whether they are among the best or the worst performers. If your employer seeks staff feedback on the canteen or other catering provision, use this opportunity to suggest more sustainable food. Try talking to colleagues about your concerns and, if change is needed, find out who is responsible and whether it would be possible to approach them.

At the other end of the scale, many companies provide food for events they organise. If you are involved in organising a conference, or just in organising sandwiches for a team meeting, explore the sustainable choices that would be within your budget. You will find checklists to help you in Public Health England's guide *Healthier and More Sustainable Catering*.[43]

Rules of thumb

A sustainable diet is a healthy diet
Following a sustainable diet is also good for your health.

Go easy on meat, fish and dairy
Reduce the amount of meat, fish and dairy produce you eat. Substitute beans, pulses, nuts and seeds.

Fruit and veg are fantastic
Prioritise foods from the bottom two layers of the pyramid. Put vegetables, fruit and grains at the heart of your diet.

Avoid air freight: choose local and seasonal
Out of season, perishable fruit and vegetables clock up high emissions as they are usually flown in. Local, seasonal fruit and vegetables have the lowest emissions.

Favour fresh and unprocessed
Reduce the amount of processed foods in your diet, especially frozen foods and items with multiple ingredients.

Avoid waste
Only buy fresh foods you are sure you will use. Learn to use up leftovers. Reduce the amount of food you throw away.

❓ Frequently asked questions

If I was going to do just one thing to reduce my food footprint, what should it be?
Reduce the amount of meat and dairy produce in your diet.

Shouldn't I support 3rd World countries by buying their fruit and vegetables?
Third World economies do better when they export higher-value goods. For example, it is better to buy South African wine than South African grapes. The grapes only return 8500 Rand to the South African economy per tonne of CO_2 emitted in their transport. The wine returns 150,000 Rand per tonne of CO_2.[45] Very little of the price of fruit and vegetables grown in Third World countries reaches the people who work on the farms, unless they are part of a Fairtrade scheme. Growing for the global market has also proved damaging to many local economies in the Third World and in some cases has threatened water supplies.

Is it always better to buy food produced closer to home?
Almost always. The exceptions come with some out-of-season foods. During winter, the emissions from tomatoes grown outdoors in Spain and trucked to the UK will be lower than the emissions from tomatoes grown in Holland in heated greenhouses and trucked here. Similarly, if you want to eat out-of-season apples in July, the new crop imported from New Zealand by sea will have a slightly smaller footprint than British apples that have been kept in cold storage for 9 months.[46]

What if I have to drive to get to my local producers?
Car trips round the countryside in search of locally produced food are not a good idea. Per kilogram of food moved, the family car is the least efficient means of transport. Look for local produce that is delivered (like a vegetable box) or sold in places you can reach by walking or cycling.

How can you tell where something has come from?
Individual items like fruit and vegetables should be labelled with the country of origin. Meat labelling is confusing as some meats can be sold as British (or Scottish or Welsh) if the 'last substantial change' (such as curing pork into bacon) took place in that country. Items with multiple ingredients are even more confusing, but are likely to be made from ingredients sourced from around the world.[47]

Does organic food have a lower footprint?
Some research suggests that it does, mainly because it uses less nitrogen fertiliser. Other research suggests that it doesn't, mainly because it is less productive per hectare. Research (and debate!) on this issue continues.[48] If you are taking wider health, environmental and biodiversity issues into account organic small-scale production has advantages.

Do the vegetables I grow myself have a lower footprint than the ones in the shops?
Not necessarily. You can clock up a surprising footprint driving to an allotment or having manure delivered. Lack of experience can also mean crop failures that wouldn't happen to an experienced farmer. Despite this, growing your own vegetables is a wonderful experience that brings you closer to nature and makes you appreciate where your food really comes from. Do it if you enjoy it. Otherwise you can have the best of both worlds by signing up to a local, vegetable-box scheme or Community Supported Agriculture scheme which supports local growers.

Why is so much organic food imported?
While there has been a huge increase in demand for organic foods, the UK organic food industry is both small and small-scale. Supermarkets prefer to deal with large producers and the overseas ones tend to be cheaper. About 80% of organic food sold in the UK has been imported.

Local? Seasonal? Organic? Fairtrade? Which is the best?
Local is best in terms of the CO_2 in transport. Seasonal is best in terms of the CO_2 in storage. Organic may better in terms of the CO_2 in production. Knowing which is best for a particular product is difficult, so aim for food that is local, seasonal and if you wish – organic. For items that can't be grown in the UK, you can support Third World producers by choosing Fairtrade products where they are available.

Is it OK to drink bottled water?
The stuff that comes out of your taps is perfectly wholesome and, if you don't like the taste, you can filter it quite easily. Packaging and transporting water in bottles from one end of the country to another and across continents creates CO_2 for no real purpose. Bottled water in the UK mostly comes from Wales, France, Derbyshire and Scotland – though some comes from as far as Fiji.

Is it better to wash up by hand or with a dishwasher?
Don't wash up under a running tap – use a bowl. Whether a dishwasher or washing-up by hand uses less water depends on your washing-up style. Hand-washers use 10–50 litres depending on how they go about it. Dishwashers use 15–30 litres, depending on the model.[49]

If climate change brings food shortages, will GM crops help solve the problem?
Probably not. A 2008 UN report by the IASSTD (International Assessment of Knowledge, Science and Technology) representing the views of 400 scientists found little place for GM crops in solving world food problems.[50]

What about eating out?
Fast food restaurants are part of a highly mechanised industry and usually sell a lot of meat. The food is intensively grown, highly processed and has probably clocked up a lot of food miles. That's before you examine what is in it and who was exploited to bring it to you. Local, independent restaurants that are part of the local economy, offering a low-carbon menu and trying to source ingredients locally are something else entirely. Enjoy celebrating there![51]

Will reducing food waste help reduce our carbon emissions?
Globally, between 30 and 50% of all food produced never reaches a human stomach.[52] In 2012, 7 million tonnes of food was wasted in the UK. 4.2 million tonnes of this came from households, the rest from retailers, food manufactures, restaurants, commercial organisations, agriculture and horticulture. The average household throws out about 3 kg of useable food each week (160kg a year). It happens because people buy too much, fail to plan meals, don't store food properly and lack confidence in using up leftovers. On average each UK household could save 640 kg of CO_2e a year by avoiding unnecessary food waste.[53]

You say ships are a good method of transport for bringing us food but aren't they responsible for other pollution?
Yes. Some of the dirtiest oil is burnt by the shipping industry producing sulphur emissions which cause acid rain and upset the balance of many ecosystems. New EU and international limits have been set recently.[54]

Food sovereignty or food security – what's the difference?

Food security is defined by the World Health Organisation as a situation where "…all people at all times have access to sufficient, safe, nutritious food to maintain a healthy and active life."[55] The idea has become contentious as fears have grown that plans for food security are dominated by large corporations and their search for profits. For example the G8's 'New Alliance on Food Security and Nutrition'[56] has been widely condemned as a move that will lead to expropriation of land and the impoverishment of small farmers.

The movement for food sovereignty is an alliance of small producers, peasant farmers, local consumers and environmental organisations. Its best known representatives are La Via Campesina. Advocates of food sovereignty argue that the people who produce, distribute and consume food should be at the heart of decisions about the food system – not the big corporations. They emphasise the value of small producers, local knowledge, skill and control and the importance of working with nature.

More information

This section lists a small number of books and websites with good, accessible information that will help you fill in the background and follow up facts you are not clear on. You will find more detailed sources and a wider selection of reading in the Notes.

I'd like to know more about…

…campaigns

La Via Campesina, http://viacampesina.org, and the *International Planning Committee for Food Sovereignty*, http://www.foodsovereignty.org/, both campaign on food sovereignty.

WaterAid, http://www.wateraid.org/uk/, and *Action Water*, http://www.actionwater.org.uk/, are NGOs bringing safe water to the world's poorest people.

…community supported agriculture

You'll find details of a scheme near you on the *Soil Association* site, http://bit.ly/soilassoc-support.

…cooking with vegetables

VegBox Recipes lists what is seasonal, what you're likely to find in your veg-box and how to cook it, http://bit.ly/vegbox-recipes.

…the food system

Eat your Heart Out: Why the Food Business is Bad for the Planet and Your Health, Felicity Lawrence, Penguin 2008, is an easy read and a good account of what lies behind our cheap food system.

…food waste

Love Food, Hate Waste has great recipes and advice on how to buy the right amount, use up leftovers and store food safely, http://www.lovefoodhatewaste.com/.

… healthy, sustainable eating

People, Plate and Planet, Laura Blake, Centre for Alternative Technology, 2014, describes a number of dietary options that will make a difference, http://bit.ly/blake-2014.

Laura's Larder will calculate the emissions from your daily diet, http://bit.ly/lauralarder.

What is a Good Sustainable Diet? Tara Garnett, FCRN, 2014, has a good discussion of factors to consider in moving the global food system towards sustainable diets, http://bit.ly/Garnett-2014.

The organisation *Eating Better* helps individuals move towards eating less meat and more food that's better for us and the planet, http://www.eating-better.org/.

…local food

Making Local Food Work has resources and news on local food networks, http://bit.ly/makinglocalfood.

…organic food

The *Soil Association* promotes sustainable, organic farming and champions human health, http://www.soilassociation.org.

…reducing my water use

Read *Water: Use Less – Save More*, Jon Clift, & Amanda Cuthbert, Green Books, 2006.

…seasonal food

Eat the Seasons will tell you what's in season when in the UK and provide you with weekly updates, http://eattheseasons.co.uk.

…sustainable farming

The Food Ethics Council is a charity aiming to create a food system that is fair and healthy for people and the environment, http://www.foodethicscouncil.org.

Sustain is a charity that promotes "food and agriculture policies and practices that enhance the health and welfare of people and animals, improve the working and living environment, promote equity and enrich society and culture." http://www.sustainweb.org.

…virtual water

Read *Virtual Water: Tackling the Threat to Our Planet's Most Precious Resource*, Tony Allan, I.B. Tauris, 2011.

…what's happening in Scotland?

Community Food and Health (Scotland) promotes a healthy diet to Scottish communities with resources, publications and projects, http://www.communityfoodandhealth.org.uk.

Greener Scotland is a one stop shop for advice on greener and healthier eating, http://bit.ly/greenerscot-eating.

CHAPTER 5

Consumption and waste

"Man transforms raw materials into commodities and commodities into garbage."
Herman Daly, Steady State Economics

A junkyard worker sorts e-waste in Nanyang, China

Spending money 'spends' CO_2 as well. The average UK citizen is responsible for about 3.5 tonnes of CO_2 through their purchases of household goods, home improvements, clothes, entertainment and other services. In this chapter we look at some big questions:

- Can we reduce our CO_2 emissions without reducing our current levels of consumption?
- Can the ecosystems we depend on survive in an expanding economy?
- Does continued economic growth create the kind of society we want?

We also look at some personal and practical questions:

- How are our status and our sense of identity linked to the purchases we make?
- How can we tell how much CO_2 our purchases are responsible for?
- How do we feel if we try to reduce our impact, and buy less?

carbonconversations.org

What's the problem with stuff?

There is carbon embodied in everything you buy, from the shoes on your feet to a holiday trip. Somewhere, energy has been used – in extracting raw materials, turning them into goods, transporting these goods and selling them. Your house, your car, your clothes and your computer have all taken energy to make. Even services, like household insurance, a ticket to a football match and internet use have a carbon cost. The insurance company has offices to run. The football club has a stadium to maintain and its team may fly all over the world. The internet requires a vast array of servers to store its data. All of these use energy. At every step, CO_2 is emitted.

When you throw something away, more greenhouse gases are emitted. First there are the energy costs of removing waste, whether it's a skip full of builder's rubble, a black bag or a box of recycling. Then come the energy costs of recycling or burying rubbish in landfill. Finally, the stuff that is left to rot slowly emits methane, one of the most powerful greenhouse gases.

In general, the more you spend and the more you throw away, the more greenhouse gases you are responsible for. As we'll discuss in more detail, some purchases are more carbon-intensive than others. But, in general, consumption equals CO_2.

Rich countries, like the UK, consume a lot – far more than in previous generations, and far more than poorer countries. Within the UK, wealthy people consume much more than poorer people. Our high level of consumption is made possible by:

- cheap energy from fossil fuels – coal, oil and gas – that produce CO_2;
- free use of the natural world's resources – water, air, forests, the land, the sea and all their biosystems – sometimes called 'Global Commons' because their benefits can't easily be divided up between individuals or nations;[1]
- cheap labour from people in less-developed nations;
- continued economic growth; as production expands the price of goods falls, making them available to more people.

The problem is:

- our use of these 'Global Commons' and the damage done to them isn't reflected in the price we pay for goods;
- the economic system assumes that nature is endlessly able to support whatever is done to it.

> *Economic growth is not the only important thing, but happiness and health too. People in China realise we have a lot to do!*
> **Chinese students**

> *Our relatives in Bangladesh are already suffering the consequences of climate change – mass flooding and cyclones. These people are not to blame for the problem. Most of them are rural people who depend on agriculture to earn a living.*
> **Sarah Ravenscroft**

In reality, we are dependent on the natural world to support us and our economies. History is littered with stories of civilisations that have collapsed through ignoring this basic truth. We should not imagine we are exempt.

Environment and economics

A country's prosperity is often judged by the figures for its Gross Domestic Product (GDP) – the cost of producing everything in the economy during one year. Economists see growth in GDP as positive – a sign that the country is getting wealthier and that its citizens are enjoying a better standard of living.

Others argue that GDP is a poor measure of a country's wellbeing and ecological health. Some are concerned that continued economic growth may be unsustainable.[2]

Beached boats in the Aral Sea which shrank by 90% in 50 years, due to intensive cotton production

- Economic activity depletes and damages natural resources (air and water quality, forests, seas and ecosystems) without accounting for this damage in its costings. No price is paid.
- GDP says nothing about whether the growth brings positive benefits (better housing for example) or is simply clearing up after negative events. For example, the costs of dealing with flood damage and road accidents are included in GDP and are seen as contributing to economic growth. Similarly, GDP can't tell you whether activity is happening in industries that solve environmental problems or in industries that create them.
- GDP doesn't tell you whether everyone is benefiting from growth or just a few. In many countries, increased GDP has left many people in poverty as the benefits are not equally shared.
- Economic growth doesn't necessarily bring a better quality of life. Congestion, pollution and degradation of ecosystems all accompany growth beyond a certain point.
- Advocates of unlimited economic growth ignore the finite limits of the earth. If everyone in the world lived like we do in the UK, we would need three planet's worth of natural resources.[3]

Recent turmoil

In 2008 the world economic system fell into turmoil. The banking crisis made it clear that our prosperity is fragile. Questions began to be asked. The Queen challenged a group of economists, asking: "Why did nobody notice?" while activists from the Occupy movement questioned whether capitalism itself was fit for purpose.[4] Fundamental questions began to be raised about the kind of society people want to live in. As the peak of the crisis passed, the discussion became more muted but the questions remain.

- Why should ordinary people pay for bankers' mistakes?
- Does the power of global corporations and the financial system threaten democracy?[5]
- Is it possible to reform the world economic system so that it delivers stability, prosperity – and a solution to climate change?

In the UK between 2010 and 2014 the coalition government's response to the crisis was to cut public spending as a way of reducing the budget deficit. Economic growth stalled before picking up slightly in 2013. The poorest people have borne the brunt in reduced services, job losses and a growth in part-time and poorly paid work. The gap between rich and poor has grown wider.[6] Environmental issues have slipped off the agenda.

This is the context in which we now look at our chances of bringing the economic system and our patterns of consumption into line with what we know about climate change.

Conventional economics

Conventional economists think that climate change can be solved by 'de-coupling' economic growth and our use of resources: greater efficiency, more renewables, cradle to cradle recycling and careful use mean that we can do more with less energy. In essence, the economy is 'de-carbonised'. Often creating the right kinds of markets, in particular a market for carbon, is seen as key. The Stern report,[7] produced for the UK government in 2006, took this approach. Similar arguments are presented on an international scale in the follow-up 2014 report *Better Growth, Better Climate*. Here, Stern and a team of fellow economists argue that continued economic growth is compatible with dealing with climate change. Much of what they propose is sensible and necessary, such as major investments in public transport and renewables, and a focus on the development of cities. The big question however is whether their proposals will deliver the scale of carbon reduction that is necessary. Unfortunately, the answer seems to be 'no'. Their ten-point plan is only designed to show actions that are compatible with maintaining economic growth. As they themselves admit, these "would not be sufficient to achieve the full range of emissions reductions likely to be needed by 2030 to prevent dangerous climate change."[8]

Stern's first report received widespread approval but it has not been implemented by the UK government. At the time of writing we do not know whether *Better Growth, Better Climate* will lead to practical action either.

The Green New Deal

One of the most interesting responses to the financial crisis came from the Green New Deal group who saw it as an opportunity to kick-start the process that Stern recommended. Their name echoes the US New Deal programme of the 1930s. This regulated the financial sector and used government investment for big infrastructure projects such as rural electrification and school building. This created employment, provided the country with essential services and drew the US out of recession.

In a similar fashion the Green New Deal's economists propose:

- financial controls on the banks, tackling tax evasion, and offering encouragement to big investors such as pension funds to invest in sustainable projects;
- £50 billion investment per year to transform the UK's ageing infrastructure and create jobs – developing a renewable energy supply, transforming the transport system, making all existing buildings energy efficient and building new energy-efficient homes.

The authors argue that this programme could provide decent, well-paid jobs across the country for 1.5 million people, restore growth, be financially neutral and provide much needed stability.[9]

Challenges to growth

Not all economists accept that growth can continue however. Herman Daly, once an economist at the World Bank, was one of the first to argue that it can't, in his 1977 book *Steady-State Economics*.[10] He argued for a steady-state economy – one that doesn't keep growing, is stable in size and stable in its throughput of resources. Crucially it has room for both nature and human well-being. Daly and his colleagues suggest that a steady-state economy would be governed by four principles.

1. Maintain the health of ecosystems and the life support services they provide.
2. Extract renewable resources (like fish and timber) at a rate no faster than they can be regenerated.
3. Consume non-renewable resources (like fossil fuels and minerals) at a rate no faster than they can be replaced by the discovery of renewable substitutes.
4. Deposit wastes in the environment at a rate no faster than they can be safely assimilated.

More recently the well-respected economist Tim Jackson has revived interest in these ideas. As we saw in our discussions of rebound in Chapter One, energy efficiency doesn't deliver all the benefits hoped for. In *Prosperity Without Growth*, Jackson explains that it just isn't possible to decouple growth and the impact of our resource use enough. As incomes increase and the population grows, carbon emissions continue to rise, albeit more slowly. We certainly need energy efficiency. We certainly need investment in renewables. But we also need to leave most of the reserves of fossil fuels in the ground and run the world economy without continuous growth. We need to learn to live comfortably whilst consuming less.

Most people associate a shrinking economy with instability and poverty. This is the usual experience during a serious recession. Unemployment rises, inequality increases, essential services disappear and people suffer. Gradually attention is beginning to focus on how to shrink the economy without causing these problems. The work of Tim Jackson and fellow economist Peter Victor has been at the forefront of this[11] and you will find a local, practical version in the ideas of the group Steady State Manchester.[12] Not surprisingly, there are many opposing voices. Most business leaders find it impossible to imagine a world without economic growth. You can make up your own mind by reading some of the articles and books listed in More Information.

Looking at the future

It's clear that if we are to reduce carbon emissions, some reduction in the level of consumption in developed countries will have to be made. It's also clear that we could still lead comfortable lives.

- Some items would become more expensive, as environmental costs are factored into their price.

> *I am very lucky to have a 'green-collar' job already, helping manage a number of important sites for the Wildlife Trust. In the future, there should be great 'green-collar' opportunities in the production of renewable energy, energy conservation and sustainable building.*
>
> Iain Webb

- Our levels of consumption would fall but quality might increase: goods would have to last longer and be repairable. We would buy fewer items less frequently, so overall costs would not necessarily rise.
- We might have less 'stuff' but more leisure time.
- 'Green-collar' jobs would be created in new industries like renewable energy.
- More goods would need to be produced locally, boosting local economies.
- Once basic needs were met, economies would need to concentrate on activities that were sustainable and not resource or carbon-intensive.
- Inequality would need to be addressed, so that resources were fairly shared.

Reducing consumption in a growth economy is not easy. It's hard to participate fully in modern society if you don't buy the objects and services offered. People's sense of themselves – their identity – is also tied up with their purchases. There is constant pressure to consume. Advertising cleverly implies that you will be happier if you buy, and be left behind if you don't.

Why do we buy?

Most people try to make wise purchases but many say that they buy things which they later feel they don't really need or which don't bring them much satisfaction. Some people use shopping as a social outing. Others say they feel compelled to buy in order to remain involved in ordinary life. Meanwhile, research suggests that our high levels of consumption don't make us happy. Our reasons for spending money are complex.

Meeting basic needs

We live in a society where many of our basic needs – for food, clothing, shelter and safety – are met in ways that carry a high carbon price.

Need is the obvious reason for any purchase, but it can be deceptive. Once basic needs for food, shelter and clothing are satisfied, more complex social needs are constructed. A child 'needs' a pair of designer trainers, not because he would otherwise go barefoot to school but because his life will be miserable if he doesn't fit in. A commuter 'needs' a car, not because it's the best way to get to work but because the bus service is unreliable. My computer 'needs' to be upgraded, not because it is worn out but because new software is not compatible.

Similarly **our need to be safe** has been transformed. Earlier generations feared industrial accidents, poverty and illness. They expected the welfare state to provide a safety net in times of need. Today our fears are more diffuse. Some people fear the random attacks of terrorism or muggings. Nuclear accidents, climate change or fracking feature on some people's lists. For others it's the

> ❝ I love clothes. I have a cupboard full but I do wear them. Clothes let you say who you are. You can wear different clothes and be a different person. Buying nice things is part of having self-respect and taking pleasure in life. But I never throw anything away. I alter my clothes or turn the material into something else. I run clothes swaps and I encourage other people to alter garments that don't fit or turn them into something else useful.
>
> **Mary Evans Young**

unpredictable nature of modern employment and the loss of reliable jobs. Still others are made anxious by nanotechnology or genetic modification. The sense of being at the mercy of global events can lead people to try to buy safety. Owning a bigger car with more safety features, a house in a quiet neighbourhood or lots of life insurance might all fit into this category. Sociologist Ulrich Beck refers to this pressure on people to find individual solutions to unmanageable global risks as 'tragic individualisation'.[13] It's not surprising that many of us are caught up in it.

Our feelings of **love and care** lie behind many purchases. There is nothing wrong in wanting the best for your family or in expressing love through providing as well as you can. The difficulty is that many of the obvious ways of fulfilling these basic human impulses are also high-carbon: lavish presents, overseas holidays, the biggest house we can afford. Our desires feel like they are our own but society forms the ways we express them. Finding low-carbon ways to express our deepest feelings is an important task.

Identity, social acceptance and status

Everyone wants to **belong**. In previous generations you might have been defined by the job you did, the church or faith group you were born into, the area of town you lived in or your parents' class and job. In modern society the items we buy help define the groups we belong to. We signal membership of a particular subset by our style of clothes and accessories, the music we listen to and our choice of phone, car and activities. Not having things, or not being able to share activities with friends and colleagues can be a source of misery. Children often use clothes and toys to identify their group. For some people, having the right phone (or computer, or car) is key to taking part in conversations about upgrades or engine efficiencies. Many people would rather fall into debt than admit that they can't afford something that many of their friends own or do. Sometimes the social pressure or the desire for approval is obvious. You might buy a new suit to impress a job interviewer. More often the pressure is more subtle.

Self-esteem and self-image are often in play. Purchases can make people feel good about themselves, however temporary the feeling turns out to be. Having the right clothes, phone, car or postal address helps people feel they will be acceptable to others. Think about how you feel if you find yourself dressed wrongly for an occasion. If you're a strong character you may shrug it off, but many people will feel a deep sense of shame.

The phrase 'retail therapy' suggests that shopping has also become a common solution to **coping with bad feelings**. People shop in the hope of feeling better – usually in the hope of feeling less depressed. The lift is always temporary, sometimes lasting no longer than the trip home. It quickly becomes clear that the new T-shirt or CD is not the gateway to a happier life.

Material possessions often mark our **status** as well. They show where we stand in society. More, bigger, faster or newer usually means better, more successful, more popular or more admired. Not having material possessions is usually seen as a mark of poverty or failure. Nobody likes to appear poor or unsuccessful and it can be hard to find a way of resisting this pressure. People who have few possessions frequently aspire to have more. Parents often work hard to provide

> ❝ When I reflected on the things I need to buy I realised that a lot of the so-called needs are really a marketing strategy developed by companies to make us buy more. I can manage with little and purchase good quality things that last longer.
> **Euri Vidal**

carbonconversations.org

their children with a better life than the one they knew. The idea that we might need to make do with fewer consumer items and spend more of our income on cleaning up the mess of the world, is tough on people who started out with very little.

Fulfilment

In modern society, most new or exciting experiences – whether it is white water rafting, an unusual food or a surprising gadget – come with a price ticket. Novelty is a huge attraction. So is the possibility of enrichment through travel, sport, books, music or art. Many people will tell you that their best memories are often of people rather than the expensive meal, hotel or sporting fixture, but money has often been spent somewhere in the process. No-one would want our lives to be robbed of new and fulfilling experiences but finding low-carbon ways of achieving this is essential.

Bargains, lemons and illusions

It can be hard to tell a bargain from a lemon or from an illusion. Marketers are skilled at playing on our desires to be smart shoppers, on our gullibility and on our dreams. They know how to make us believe that our lives will be improved by buying their products. They subtly tell us we'll be happier, sexier and more successful if we have their particular brand. Bargains often persuade us through the door. The promise of massive reductions, two for the price of one or second one half-price – persuade us to buy things we don't really want or need. You will be a strong person if you are never seduced by an advertiser's pitch.[14]

Meanwhile, modern goods are often designed for a short life or are difficult to repair. Many shopping trips are caused by the irritating discovery that some previous bargain no longer works.

Affluence and good lives

Most of us have met an irritating person over forty who tells the tale of how they were happiest as a child playing with a cardboard box or messing about in the woods. "We didn't have much but we were happy," goes the refrain. I'm old enough to have said this myself but also to remember my parents (born c1920) and my grandparents (born c1890) saying the same thing. Clearly people have lived good lives in all kinds of different circumstances.

If you talk to people who have lived in less affluent times or who grew up in less affluent countries it becomes clear that the relationship between material goods and a good life is complex.

> **❝** Consumerism is an uphill struggle for a parent. Everything from desires for mobile phones to junk food is qualified with "But (insert name of other child) has an iPhone 6" etc. It's not their fault. I watch my daughter's face as she leafs through science and wildlife magazines - her eyes are drawn to the advertisements and her powers of critical thinking aren't developed enough. You can't shield them from advertising, and I wouldn't want to shield her from her peers - the last thing I want is for her to grow up in a 'home school' bubble! All you can do is try and develop their powers of critical thinking. We try and turn it into a game, "Spot the lie in the advert, or what are they NOT telling you...
>
> **Tanya Hawkes**

Across the generations, what seems to matter most to people are the following:

- a basic level of security about housing, health and money;
- good, satisfying relationships with family and friends;
- a sense of meaning in life (which might come from work, family, community involvement, politics or religious faith).

Once people have emerged from deep poverty, the pleasures of material goods seem to lie less in the satisfactions that the objects themselves bring, and more in their social meaning. We use material objects to show membership of a social group, confirm identity or demonstrate success. As an item fades from fashion it is quickly discarded because it no longer ensures that place. People often compare themselves with those who have more rather than with those who have less. Many see themselves as 'middling' or poor when in fact their household income is well above average. The median household income in 2011-2012 was £23,200 after tax and benefits.[15] This means that half of UK households lived on an income less than this.

Looking back several generations it is clear that we could be happy with much less but that we would need to be part of social groups who were also happy with less. We would need to find ways of feeling respected, valued and included that were not so dependent on material objects. You may remember the graph in Chapter One which showed how quality of life peaked in the 1970s, declining from then on, despite increasing material prosperity.

Some people find it easier than others to stand out against the dominant social trends. What about you?

The positive side of stuff

It's important not to treat all material objects as bad. It doesn't help to despise them. There are many positive aspects to the objects we surround ourselves with.

Making objects our own

We are not passive consumers of the objects we buy. We use them purposefully and not always in ways that the manufacturers and designers intended. We play with them, encounter the world through them and solve problems with them. To a child a plastic beaker may be a cup, a hat, a weapon or an object of affection. Teenagers who face exams bring with them a range of lucky mascots from their old teddy bears to their new mobile phone. One person twines cheap plastic flowers into her bicycle basket for decoration. Another uses an abandoned car to house her goats. A third uses nail polish to mark his child's belongings for school.

> **❝** *I love wearing my son Tom's cast-off clothes because they remind me of him, now that he's left home; and I like the way in which the thoughtful presents we bought him, or just the functional clothing we gave him when he needed it as a child, can be recycled. It's him recognising, as an adult, that they can not only fulfil a different practical need but also an emotional one as he chooses to re-present them to me, knowing what they will mean to me.*
>
> Jem Whitely

carbonconversations.org

Creativity

Almost all the objects we use have been designed with creativity and ingenuity. Many have changed the way we live. Some are marvels of human inventiveness. Objects also tell a bigger story – the story of our history, culture and human creativity. Former Director of the British Museum, Neil McGregor, created a popular radio series called *The History of the World in a Hundred Objects*[16] in which he did precisely that. He used a chopping tool to describe humankind's entry onto the world stage, while a Victorian tea set became the starting point for talking about the British Empire. What would you use to tell the stories of our own times? The bike or the car? The typewriter or the photocopier? The washing machine or the nylon shirt? The television or the mobile phone?

Personal stories

Each item also tells a personal story, embodies a relationship, creates a sense of who you are and who you have been. Throughout life, we continue to play with our objects, invest them with meaning and mourn their ends. An older person, moving into residential care, will agonise over

❝ The internet is really valuable to me. I'm not referring to social networking sites, but to the ease of communication with close friends and family when they are abroad for long periods of time through programs such as Skype.

Hannah Baker

❝ My sewing machine with a walking foot has kept me sane for 20 years by letting me create wonderful things in leather and fix my canvas tent. It has travelled with me wherever I have been and I cannot image life without it.

Frances Platt

❝ Sitting in my grandmother's chair brings back fond memories of playing in her house and my deep connection to her.

Pam Candea

140 carbonconversations.org

the objects they are able to take with them and what must be left behind. Sometimes the most mundane objects become invested with meaning: "I felt so sad when we got rid of our old car," a woman told me. "It's a lump of useless metal and plastic. But we'd given it a name, used it and abused it, cared for and hated it over ten years. I felt 'she' was part of the family."

In Carbon Conversations groups we ask people to describe purchases they feel pleased with and purchases they regret. Sometimes people bring pictures of their favourite belongings and sometimes the object itself. What are your cherished objects?

Tracking down the CO_2

Since there is CO_2 embodied in everything you buy, the big questions are:

- How much CO_2 is in each item?
- Are some purchases worse than others?

It's certainly true that some products and activities – an hour's jet-skiing for example – are very CO_2-intensive. Others, like paying someone to baby-sit, are CO_2-light. Getting exact figures for any item is difficult. Research is being done but there are no easy answers at present. The only thing you can be sure of is that when you spend money you 'spend' CO_2 as well. In general:

- the more you spend the bigger your footprint;
- the higher your income, the bigger your footprint – people who earn more usually spend more as well.

Only by reducing what you spend can you be sure of reducing your CO_2 'spend' as well. We suggest three different ways of looking at the problem.

Look at income

Research suggests that there is a strong correlation between income and carbon emissions.[17] As household income rises, so do the carbon emissions of that household. The number of people in the household also has an effect. In larger households some purchases (for example washing machines, cars, household goods) are shared, but others (such as clothes, toiletries, phones, entertainment) are duplicated several times. Larger households have higher consumption emissions than small ones.

The table below takes account of these factors and shows the average carbon emissions due to consumption for a number of household incomes after tax. If you want an idea of your individual consumption footprint, look for your household income in column one (add together the incomes

Household income and individual CO_2 emissions in tonnes[18]

Household income after tax		Number of people in house				
		1	2	3	4	5
low	below £12,000	2.6	2.2	2.0	1.7	1.5
below average	£12,000 – £17,000	3.5	3.0	2.6	2.3	2.0
average	£17,000 – £23,000	4.2	3.7	3.2	2.8	2.4
above average	£23,000 – £33,000	5.2	4.5	3.9	3.4	3.0
high	£33,000 – £48,000	6.3	5.4	4.7	4.1	3.6
very high	above £48,000	9.3	8.0	6.9	6.0	5.2

of every earner after tax). Then, find the column with the number of people over the age of three in your household. Each person in your household will be responsible for the emissions listed in that column against that household income. For example, one person in a one-person household with an income after tax of £20,000 will be responsible for 4.2 tonnes of emissions, through their purchases. Each person in a three-person household with a joint income after tax of £20,000 will be responsible for 3.2 tonnes of emissions each, or 9.6 tonnes for the household.

This is still a fairly crude measure. It assumes that everything you buy has an average carbon intensity, and that you are responsible for the CO_2 emitted by money you have saved as well as money you have spent. It doesn't take account of whether money is spent on carbon-intensive or carbon-light products. Nor does it give credit for spending money on energy-saving measures, or for investing in renewables schemes or environmental funds.

If you have an above-average income it is important not to feel ashamed of the CO_2 emissions associated with it. They are to be expected. What a higher income gives you however is choice.

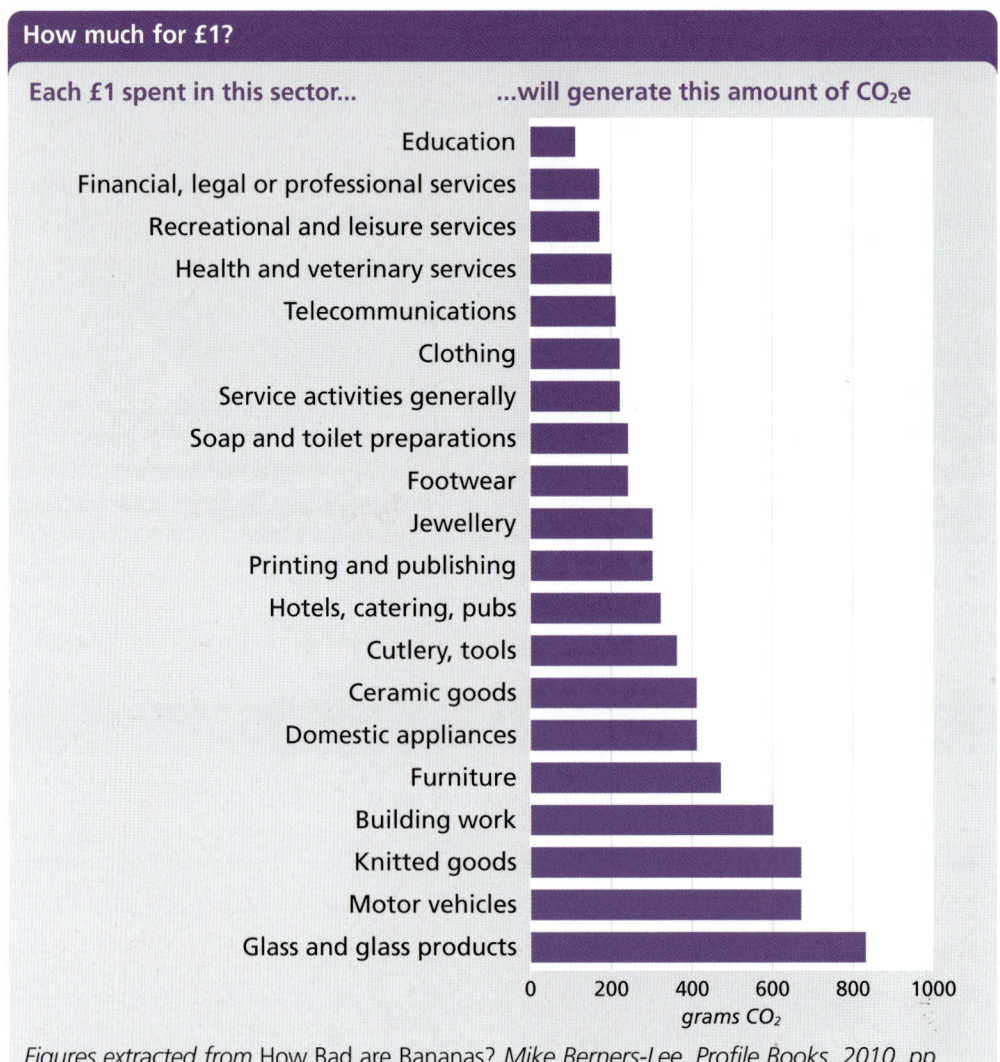

How much for £1?

Each £1 spent in this sector... ...will generate this amount of CO_2e

Sector	grams CO_2 (approx.)
Education	~75
Financial, legal or professional services	~150
Recreational and leisure services	~175
Health and veterinary services	~200
Telecommunications	~200
Clothing	~210
Service activities generally	~220
Soap and toilet preparations	~230
Footwear	~240
Jewellery	~290
Printing and publishing	~300
Hotels, catering, pubs	~325
Cutlery, tools	~375
Ceramic goods	~420
Domestic appliances	~425
Furniture	~475
Building work	~600
Knitted goods	~680
Motor vehicles	~690
Glass and glass products	~830

Figures extracted from *How Bad are Bananas? Mike Berners-Lee, Profile Books, 2010, pp 200-203,* updated using Office for National Statistics data.[19]

These choices may not be easy – you may find yourself going against the norms of the social group you belong to – but there are choices nonetheless.

Look at spending

In reality, some industry sectors are more carbon-intensive than others, so it matters where you spend your money. The table opposite gives some examples.

Look at each product

Calculating emissions for every product is a difficult task. There are two ways of doing this. In the first (usually called the bottom-up approach) each product has to be tracked across its lifecycle from:

- 'plough to plate', in the case of food;
- 'cradle to grave', for products that go to landfill;
- 'cradle to cradle', for items that are recycled.

The British Standard PAS 2050 provides certification for individual products.[20] You may see some of these labels on products in the shops, for example Walker's crisps at 75g, Boots Botanic Shampoo at 161g and a one litre passion fruit and mango smoothie at 750g CO_2.

The alternative is to take what is called a top-down approach, starting from the whole economy, looking at the carbon emissions of the relevant industry sectors and by some magical maths arriving at a good estimate for individual products. This is the approach taken by Mike Berners-Lee in his book *How Bad are Bananas?* The table overleaf lists the footprints of some common purchases.

The wider impact

CO_2 is not the only issue with many of the goods we buy however. In Chapter One we talked briefly about Johan Rockstrom's idea of the nine planetary boundaries. Mining for minerals and precious metals, and disposing of plastics and other waste has had devastating effects on biodiversity in some parts of the planet.

Many of our goods are made with 'conflict resources' – raw materials sourced from countries where their extraction is tied up with corruption, armed conflict, human rights abuses and complete disregard for the environment.[21] The electronics industry is a particular concern. Gold, tin, tantalum and tungsten from the Eastern Congo are used in our mobile phones and in many other consumer electronics.

Many of our goods are also made in countries with low standards of worker protection and where child labour is

T-shirt – 650 g CO_2

Car – 6 tonnes CO_2

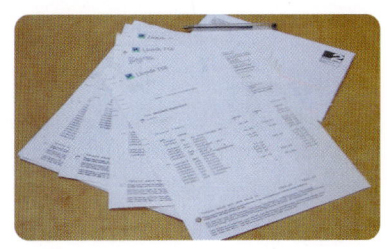

Bank account – 200 g CO_2 per year

Enough bricks for a 4 m x 2.5 m wall – 1.25 tonnes CO_2

carbonconversations.org

The carbon footprints of some common goods and services

	Kilograms CO_2
Clothing and household goods	
A year's worth of clothing	225
A year's supply of toilet roll	75
A new carpet 4m x 4m	76-290
A £500 gold necklace	200-400
A £100,000 mortgage at 5%	800
A new small Citroen car	6000
A new Landrover Discovery	35,000
Entertainment	
A paperback book	1
A bunch of 10 red roses, flown from Kenya	3.5
A bunch of 10 red roses, from a heated greenhouse in Holland	21
A trip to the swimming pool	13.5
A night in a hotel	25-60
A year's worth of newspapers	142-270
A new television	220
Communications and IT	
A year's worth of mobile phone use @ 2 mins a day	47
A year's worth of mobile phone use @ 1 hr a day	1250
A year's worth of emails	135
A year's worth of letters (assumes 5 letters a day and 2 catalogues – junk mail for example – a week)	480
A single web-search from an efficient laptop	0.0007
A single web-search from an inefficient desktop	0.0045
A new simple laptop	200
A new IMac	720
Having the builders in	
A new house	80,000
A £20,000 kitchen refit	10,000
2 kw array of photovoltaic panels	3,500

Information derived from How Bad are Bananas? Mike Berners-Lee, Profile Books, 2010

used. Somewhere, someone's health and well-being is likely to have suffered in bringing us the luxury goods we now treat as everyday items.

There are a number of good campaigns working to stop the use of conflict minerals and improve the conditions of workers in overseas factories. You can support these by joining the campaigns, writing to manufacturers and donating money but also through your choice of products and your careful use of the world's precious resources.

Children working in a wolframite (tungsten ore) mine in the Congo

What can you do?

It's important to remember that all the products and services you buy have a carbon impact. It will help to spend your surplus income in the lower-carbon sectors of the economy, but if you really want to reduce your carbon footprint you may also need to reduce your overall consumption and live on less. It is people with above average incomes who face the difficult choices. People on low incomes make less impact.

High and low-carbon items

High-carbon items use a lot of fossil fuels to make, and include cars, building work, machinery and many household goods. Examples of carbon-heavy purchases would be:

- new carpets or a kitchen refit;
- a meaty meal in a restaurant that is refitted each year;
- flying lessons.

Items likely to be low-carbon are: second-hand goods; labour-intensive services; and labour-intensive products. Carbon-light consumption might include:

- antiques, collectables and new works of art;
- baby-sitting, massage or gardening services;
- hand-crafted furniture or hand-made clothes.

> ❝ My footprint was really low but a new relationship with someone whose income and lifestyle are very different from mine has brought with it challenges for us both. Since we moved in together my footprint has increased by 50%. On the other hand my partner's footprint has reduced significantly so there is actually a net gain, but it's made me think again about what people with higher incomes should do. My solution is to 'tithe' myself on my income, investing 10% of it in renewables, wind-farms and forestry projects. This simulates the kind of taxation we might see in a post-carbon society.
>
> Peter Harper

carbonconversations.org

A few, beautiful, long-lasting, hand-made garments will be responsible for less CO_2 than a cupboard full of throwaway, poorly-made items from a sweatshop. You will sometimes find that there are high-carbon and low-carbon routes to the same goal. If you want to get fit, a jog in the park uses less carbon than a trip to the gym. If you want to socialise with friends, a home-cooked meal will have a lower impact than a trip to a restaurant. Buying second-hand and getting things repaired are also good routes to a lower-impact life. It is also important to think about the wider impact of what you buy. Try asking yourself:

- How was the natural world valued as this product was made?
- How long will it last?
- What will I do with it when I no longer want it?
- Who benefited from its production?
- Who suffered or was exploited?
- Is there a lower-carbon option?

Rebound

If you save money, be careful what you do with it. Buying second-hand clothes is not much help if you then blow the money saved on a flight abroad. Any money saved needs to be spent in a lower-carbon sector of the economy. Consider options like:

- energy-saving measures in your home;
- working less (negotiate a 4-day week, or drop a shift)[22];
- investment in an ethical fund or a renewables project;
- donations to an environmental charity.

Beyond personal action

There are many ways of acting collectively to reduce the impact of our consumption. You might like to give time to one of the many organisations working to change the global picture. There are organisations focused on the working conditions in overseas factories that supply us. There are organisations working to stop the use of conflict minerals. You could support an organisation persuading your pension fund to divest from fossil fuel companies, an organisation providing micro-finance to people in third world economies so they can start their own businesses, or an organisation persuading multinationals to pay a fair share of tax. The choice is yours. There are details of some of these organisations in More Information.

> We're social creatures and we like to talk about our possessions. We like to admire each other's stuff – an interesting picture, a piece of music, a new jumper. If you can't share in these conversations you're isolated and excluded. I grew up in a home where what was valued was the pleasure stuff could bring rather than its cost or its newness. When I first realized the effect of income on emissions the thing which really helped was being part of a social group who shared that understanding. Without that it would have been hard.
>
> Alex Randall

Enjoy yourself

You sometimes meet people who have become obsessed with the impact of their purchases. The ingenuity of the products available and the creativity that went into their design is lost on them. Consumed by guilt, they forbid themselves the pleasure of objects and are angry at anyone who dares to enjoy shopping. Make sure this doesn't happen to you. Enjoy the purchases you do make.

Practical steps

The table below gives star ratings for a number of actions you could take. As before, the greater the number of stars, the greater the impact the action is likely to have. What might you do?

Practical steps		I'm already doing this	I would consider this	This would be really hard
Shop for items that will last	*	☐	☐	☐
Buy goods made from recycled materials	*	☐	☐	☐
Avoid disposable items	*	☐	☐	☐
Use items until they are worn out	*	☐	☐	☐
Get items repaired or repair them yourself	*	☐	☐	☐
Recycle everything that can be recycled	**	☐	☐	☐
Spend more money on labour-intensive items and services and less on high-carbon goods	**	☐	☐	☐
Reduce total amount of waste by 50%	**	☐	☐	☐
Look for low-carbon entertainment - e.g. substitute time with friends or self-entertainment for energy-intensive trips and purchases	***	☐	☐	☐
Look for low-carbon sport/exercise - e.g. halve a three-times-a-week gym habit	***	☐	☐	☐
Donate £500 to charities alleviating the effects of climate change	***	☐	☐	☐
Spend £1,000 less a year	****	☐	☐	☐
Invest £2,500 in renewables	*****	☐	☐	☐
Work less, earn and spend less, enjoy more leisure time	*****	☐	☐	☐

Waste – what's the problem?

Where's the CO_2 in rubbish? It comes in two forms.

- Everything you throw out (packaging, uneaten food, unwanted items and shopping mistakes) has used energy in its creation. Somewhere along the line, CO_2 has been emitted.
- Getting rid of rubbish produces more CO_2 – when it is collected, and when it is dumped or recycled.

Getting rid of waste accounts for about 3% of your CO_2 emissions. Most people are familiar with the slogan 'Reduce, reuse, recycle'. EU directives and overflowing landfill sites have led governments to try to reduce the stream of rubbish people dump in their bins.

This approach doesn't deal with all the problems of waste and resources however. Most modern products are designed for a short life. Many are composite products that can't be recycled. Other materials can only be recycled a limited number of times because it is hard to separate them properly. For example the steel from cars is melted down with other car parts, including copper, paint and plastic coatings. This lowers the quality

The UK is running out of places to bury its rubbish

of the recycled steel so that it cannot be used to make a new car. Although the original product is saved from landfill, the recycled one often ends up there. Many products contain toxins that continue to cause damage whatever is done with them. A modern television for example contains 4,360 different chemicals, some of which are toxic.[23] Others could be reused if the TV was designed with that in mind. The 'reduce, reuse, recycle' approach is useful but it is working at the wrong end of the problem.

The circular economy

An alternative approach is to think of waste as a resource and develop the idea of a circular economy.[24] Conventional economies are linear. Raw materials are taken from the environment, used and then thrown away. A circular economy takes its inspiration from living systems. Waste is designed out. Technical 'nutrients' flow just like biological ones do. There's a constant cycle of renewal.

In a circular economy, products would be designed so that each element could be extracted and reused. Instead of thinking of products as objects that come to an end of their useful life we

> *I went on Haj in 2006. This is an annual event when 4 million people converge in one place, it really makes waste visible. Sometimes you couldn't see the pavement for the polystyrene and plastic just lying there. It made me realize we need bigger solutions.*
>
> ## Ammar Waqar

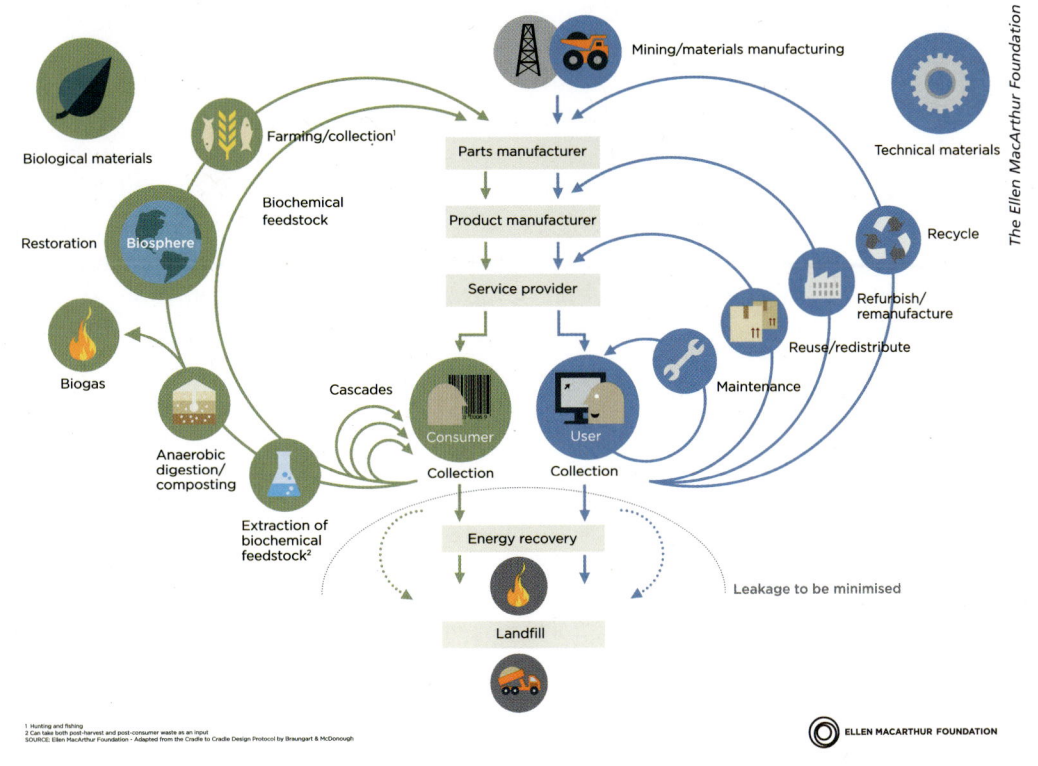

The circular economy – an industrial system that is restorative by design

would think of them as providing services which people want to enjoy. When the materials had finished providing one service they would be disassembled and used to provide another.

A circular economy would:

- design out waste;
- think in terms of systems and services rather than individual products;
- eliminate the use of toxic chemicals;
- emphasise resilience and effectiveness rather than efficiency;
- shift towards the use of renewable energy.

This is a challenging view for industry but it has been embraced by a number of big companies who see it as the future.

The circular economy tackles the problems of waste and resources but it doesn't tackle the bigger economic problems. Critics worry because:

- it assumes that the world economy can continue to grow;

> **❝** *I could not bear the thought of sending around 4,000 nappies per child to landfill. There is a massive choice of brands and types of reusable nappy and loads of information online. We've used them since bringing the baby home and for us it's just part of our routine.*
>
> **Charlotte Scott**

carbonconversations.org

- a move towards substituting technical nutrients with biological nutrients will put additional stress on ecosystems;
- endless recycling isn't possible because materials degrade over time;
- it assumes that all industry's energy needs can be met by renewables, even if economic growth continues;
- it doesn't take account of the energy which products use in their life time.

The idea of the circular economy can be seductive. It might encourage us to think that we can still have everything we want, if only industry would sort it out. Although the circular economy is a great idea we still have to be careful with what we have and make do with less.

Our feelings about waste

How do you feel about objects that come to the end of their useful life? Are you sad to let them go? Pleased you can buy something new? Worried about what to do with them? People's feelings about waste are complex and tangled up with emotions that most people rarely speak about and which are often unconscious.

The love of the old and the lure of the new

Our feelings about acquiring new objects and getting rid of old ones take us surprisingly close to feelings about mortality. We talk about them in terms of life and death. Products have a lifecycle. An old car is deemed dead. As Michael Braungart says in his book Cradle to Cradle "In Western society, people have graves, and so do products."[25]

Some people find it hard to throw anything away. As new items are purchased, they fill the loft, the garage and the garden shed with old ones that might come in useful one day. Throwing stuff out can feel like getting rid of an old friend or a part of ourselves. We may be:

- protecting ourselves against an accusation of being wasteful;
- driven by a fear of shortages that comes from an earlier period of poverty;
- protecting ourselves against the fear of death.

To place something in the ground or send it to landfill can remind us of our own mortality. We too will come to an end and need to be recycled. If we have been attached to an object, placing it in the bin can feel like the death of a part of ourselves.

The other side of the coin is our love of the new. The virgin product speaks of our vitality, our power and our control. It's the old, discarded object that is done for, not us. We can endlessly renew ourselves through our purchases.

The clean and the dirty

Our feelings about waste have a lot to do with how we have learned to think about what is clean and what is dirty. Anthropologist Mary Douglas argued that this is one of the fundamental distinctions that cultures make and we learn to make it in early childhood.[26] Is this object clean and good? Or is it dirty and dangerous?

Waste in our culture, as in many cultures, is seen as dirty and dangerous. It has to be dealt with through prescribed rituals, in specialised ways, according to learned rules. Reflect on the way you feel about something before and after it has been designated waste. The newly sliced piece of bread on your plate is designated clean. 10 minutes later the unwanted portion of it is designated dirty. There is no material change in the bread. It is no more damaged or unhygienic. It has simply been reclassified. The same might be said for an empty tin of beans or a discarded jumper. Once something is designated as waste, it seems to change its characteristics. It feels unattractive, shameful and dirty, and must be dealt with in the proper way.

Most people fear getting it wrong with regard to waste of any kind, whether it is faeces or any other kind of rubbish. The possibility of shame and humiliation are never far away. One consequence of this is that situations where it isn't clear which category something belongs in can be a source of anxiety. If you're no longer sure whether something is waste or not – what should you do?

The introduction of domestic waste recycling produced just such an anxiety. The rules were changed and people were asked to adjust their understanding of what was clean, what was dirty, what was pure, what was dangerous. The complaints that people made were often that they didn't know what went where, that the rules were incomprehensible, inconsistent or kept changing, or that recycling itself was dangerous. People were being asked to move from a simple classification – everything that is waste goes in the black bin – to a complex one where some waste was valuable and some waste was not, and where different rules applied to each different type.

Problems were compounded when those who administered recycling schemes placed themselves in the position of punitive enforcers, for example, refusing to take waste that was not in the right place (beside the bin and not in it or classified in the wrong way), leaving a humiliating mess outside the owner's front door.

Recycling rules

Persuading the public to recycle produced anxiety but gradually people became comfortable with the new arrangements. Demolishing the category of waste and thinking instead of resources and nutrients is another step change but it might help us see our relationship to the natural world in a different light. We might feel more respect for the eco-systems that provide us with what we need and be less likely to imagine ourselves as gods.

Practicalities

As a consumer, it is useful to remember the 'four Rs' – reduce, repair, reuse, recycle. Concentrate on the first three. If you can reduce, repair and reuse there won't be so much need for recycling.

Reduce

Try to stop the amount of stuff that comes into your house.

- Think before you buy – do you really need it or will you be getting rid of it in a few months time?
- Go for good-quality items that will last.
- Avoid disposable items (whether they are nappies, razors, paper hankies, or cameras).
- Choose items with less packaging and remember to take your own carrier bags when you shop.
- Refill and buy in bulk if you can.
- Stop some of the junk mail, with the help of the Mail Preference Service and Royal Mail (see More Information).

Repair

You can repair a surprising number of everyday items yourself. The London-based charity *Restart* offers tutorials and online guidance on how to repair electronics. The US-based online community *Ifixit* is creating a database of repair manuals for common household items that are found in the UK as well as the US. If you're not into DIY, seek out your local repair people, use them and tell your friends about them. See More Information for details about *Restart* and *Ifixit*.

Reuse

Try to extend the life of your stuff.

- Buy second-hand, where appropriate.
- Use your local *Freecycle* scheme to advertise anything you want to give away or to find free stuff you need (See More Information) and donate unwanted, usable items to charity shops
- Borrow or hire items that you need rarely.
- 'Upcycle' old items by using them to create something new. For example you could rework a dress from a charity shop rather than making a garment from new cloth. You will find inspiration on the upcycling sites listed in More Information.

Recycle

Local councils vary in what they recycle. The best ones now collect garden waste, food rubbish, cardboard, newspaper, glass, cans, tetrapaks (juice and milk cartons), some plastics and clothes and shoes. Some local councils also have collection points, usually at supermarkets or community centres.

It's important to follow recycling rules exactly. Waste is separated at the depot but the machines can't distinguish between a clean and a dirty bottle or spot when a piece of polystyrene packaging has got mixed up with the plastic bottles. One wrong plastic bottle in the mix can lead to the whole batch not working. Dirty tins and bottles or greasy food-stained paper will lower the quality of the recycled material and may lead to it being rejected by quality control.

All local councils have Household Waste Recycling Centres (often known locally as the dump or the tip) where you can take scrap metal, fluorescent tubes, white goods, electrical goods, mobile phones, printer cartridges, batteries, hard-core, soil, timber, textiles, shoes and furniture. They will also dispose safely of paint, engine oil and garden chemicals.

The WEEE (Waste Electrical and Electronic Equipment) regulations make producers of these goods responsible for their recycling or disposal at the end of their life. The retailer who is selling you a new item may collect it for you. Otherwise, contact your local council for guidance.

Getting stuck

Emotionally, it is probably harder to save carbon from this part of your footprint than from any other. It is the area which produces the biggest challenges to people's sense of what makes a good life and the area which most often makes people feel frustrated, angry or helpless.

Aspiration and social contracts

People born in the second half of the twentieth century were born into a set of interlocking assumptions: life will get better, opportunities will increase, each generation will be better off than the last, aspiration is good.

You can think of these assumptions as one part of a social contract between individuals and society. Work hard, pay a fair share of tax, be a responsible citizen and you can expect to be better off than your parents, with a decent job, a comfortable home, a high standard of living and a share of luxury goods.

- The rushed, stressful culture of many modern workplaces leads to last-minute decision making and little time to research sustainable options.

But there are opportunities too. Increasingly, organisations are taking on the challenge of sustainable procurement. Research suggests that five things are crucial.[27]

- support at senior level;
- a coherent, corporate approach;
- a positive approach to change;
- time, resources, knowledge and capacity;
- clear cost benefits.

Government departments and agencies have to comply with the Government Buying Standards.[28] These set sustainability standards for purchases in a wide range of products including furniture, construction materials, ICT, electrical goods and food. They also provide specifications for contracts. Support to both public and private sector organisations is provided by WRAP[29] who offer training and advice. Big organisations often have sustainable purchasing champions, whose job is to encourage low-carbon spending and train other staff in what this means.

Can you find out what your employer's policy is on sustainable procurement? Can you look at how sustainable your own department or work area is? As an individual, trying to cut down on unnecessary purchases, buy sustainably or increase recycling can be a way to exercise your creativity at work and feel more powerful.

Rules of thumb

A high income usually equals high emissions
Try to spend in the low-carbon sectors of the economy

Beware of rebound
Be careful what you do with any money you save

Try to live on less
Think about what really makes you happy

Think before you buy
Shop for items with a long and flexible life

Remember your 'R's
Reduce, Repair, Reuse, Recycle

> *I needed a model house to take to public events and fairs so my son made us a flat-packed dolls' house. I was quite proud of that resource. It's kept in a sack-bag that used to contain vegetables. We could have bought a packaged dolls' house with lots of plastic furniture and dolls but it would not have been quite what we wanted and it would probably have been sourced from China. Instead we have something that looks sustainable even down to the packaging.*
>
> Julie Pickard

carbonconversations.org

Frequently asked questions

My mortgage eats all my money – is that carbon free?

The price of a house is made up of its construction costs and the profit made by previous owners who are rewarded by the high value of land and the lack of supply in the market. Your mortgage payments cover both the price of the house and the bank's costs and profit. The construction industry is one of the high-carbon industries so a new house or a house that has had a lot of renovation work is responsible for a lot of CO_2.

If building work involves that much CO_2 doesn't that make eco-renovation a bad idea? Shouldn't I spend my money in a lower-emitting sector of the economy?

Like any building work, eco-renovation is responsible for emitting a lot of CO_2, but with eco-renovation carbon will be saved in the long-term as the building's energy demand is reduced. Doing this work sooner rather than later is important as it speeds up the date at which carbon begins to be saved. Some building methods and materials have less embodied carbon than others. Timber-framed houses, lime mortar and organic insulating materials are all winners.

My aromatherapist holidays in Thailand. Does that make it a high carbon industry?

The aromatherapy is still low-carbon! What people do with the money they earn counts as their carbon footprint, not yours.

What about my savings? When I lend money surely it's busy producing CO_2?

Again, it's a question of whose footprint it is. The goods that companies make, using your savings, will be bought by others and will count towards their footprints. When you cash in your savings or spend the interest, whatever you buy counts towards your footprint.

My savings are in ethical investments so that's OK isn't it?

It's worth thinking about where your money is invested and supporting low-carbon options if you can. Ethical investment funds are concerned with a range of issues so you need to check which ones your fund emphasises. The Dutch bank Triodos does not invest in oil/energy exploration or extraction. The Ecology Building Society only puts its money into low-carbon developments. Look out for Community Renewable projects (usually wind farms) that you can invest in.

Should we be worried about the impact of IT?

The data centres that store the information we access online all run on electricity. When you plug in your laptop and connect to the internet, you're not just using electricity at home, you're also using electricity across the world. The infrastructure supporting the internet and telecommunications accounts for less than 1% of global emissions and some companies are taking steps to move data centres to cooler locations (where they require less cooling) and to move towards using renewable electricity.[32] These infrastructure emissions make up a small part of the average UK citizen's consumption footprint. Nonetheless, try to keep a check on your use.

Doesn't our recycling just end up in China?

No. Most of our paper, cardboard, steel and glass are recycled in the UK. Cartons (the kind that hold juice) go to Sweden. A lot of plastic recycling is shipped to China because China is a major manufacturer of plastic items. It goes as a backload on the boats that bring the goods we import.[33]

What happens to electronic waste?
European regulations mean that old electrical goods must be collected and disposed of safely but we repeatedly hear that e-waste is being exported (often illegally) to countries with lax regulation.[34] It is important to recycle electronic waste. The materials used in it are valuable and can be reused, but many of them are toxic. They should not be left to leach into the environment and the waste needs to be handled in safe conditions in order to protect workers' health.

Doesn't it cost more to recycle things than to make new ones?
No. Recycling saves energy and water, reduces pollution and saves on raw materials.

I enjoy my job but it earns me a lot of money. What should I do?
A generous amount of high-quality, local, energy-efficient goods and services are yours for the asking! Think about creating an energy-efficient home, buying wonderful art and employing people on fair terms to help you with jobs you don't want to do yourself. Next, invest in ethical, low-carbon funds and pensions. If you run your own business, make sure it is a leader in low-carbon activity. Finally, give generously to environmental and development charities that help countries suffering from the effects of climate change.

I'm on a low income and can't afford high-quality green services and products. What should I do?
People earning under £15,000 usually have low carbon footprints so you shouldn't worry. Concentrate on reusing and repairing, sharing with others and buying good quality goods when you can. You can also campaign, lobby industry groups and write to your MP, demanding more sustainable products at fair prices.

If everyone stops buying stuff won't the economy go into recession?
The economy as a whole needs to change direction and provide the goods and services that a low-carbon society needs. Our actions are a small part of showing what we want and living according to our principles.

Isn't the real problem population growth?
No. Globally, the rate of population growth is slowing as better education and a raised standard of living lead to people having fewer children. World population is predicted to stabilise at around 9 billion. The problem is the resources used by each person. If that can be reduced, population itself is not the issue. See More Information for details of statistician Hans Rosling's engaging explanations of this.

Are there any examples of sustainable development we can look at now?
Some people argue that isolated rural areas like Ladakh in India, which have changed little in centuries and have a careful and respectful relationship to the local ecology, provide a model. Others point to cities that are moving in the right direction, arguing that purely rural solutions will not solve the problems of huge urban areas. For urban solutions check out Malmö and Hammarbysjöstad in Sweden. For rural solutions explore the Ecovillage Movement – see More Information.

More information

This section lists a small number of books and websites with good, accessible information that will help you fill in the background and follow up facts you are not clear on. You will find more detailed sources and a wider selection of reading in the Notes.

I'd like to know more about...

...campaigning

Labour Behind the Label supports garment workers' efforts worldwide to improve their working conditions, http://www.labourbehindthelabel.org/.

Global Witness campaigns against resource-related conflict and corruption and associated environmental and human rights abuses, http://www.globalwitness.org/, while the *World Development Movement*, http://www.wdm.org.uk, campaigns against the root causes of poverty and inequality and has a particular interest in climate change.

On the money front, the *Jubilee Debt Campaign*, http://jubileedebt.org.uk/, is a global movement demanding freedom from the slavery of unjust debts and a new financial system that puts people first, while the *Tax Justice Network*, http://www.taxjustice.net/, campaigns on the harmful impacts of tax evasion, tax avoidance, tax competition and tax havens.

...economics

Economics: the User's Guide, Ha-Joon Chang, Penguin, 2014, is a clear, amusing introduction to the subject.

Green Economics: an Introduction to Theory, Policy and Practice, Molly Scott Cato, Routledge, 2009, will introduce you to the ecological perspective.

Prosperity without Growth: Economics for A Finite Planet, Tim Jackson, Earthscan, 2009, makes the arguments about the problems of growth.

...ethical and sustainable consumption

Confessions of an Eco-Sinner: Travels to Find Where My Stuff Comes From, Fred Pearce, Eden Project Books, 2008, is a gripping story about the supply chains of household goods and the people who make them.

Growth Fetish, Clive Hamilton, Pluto Press, 2004, is a lucid account of the connections between growth, environmental damage and human happiness.

Ethical Consumer, www.ethicalconsumer.org, evaluates products and companies on a range of ethical criteria.

...how to stop junk mail

The *Mailing Preference Service*, www.mpsonline.org.uk, will stop junk mail that is addressed to you. To stop unaddressed advertising that is delivered by Royal Mail, write to Royal Mail Door-to-Door deliveries. Royal Mail, First Floor, Kingsmead House, Oxpens Road, Oxford, OX1 1RX.

...population

Look at Hans Rosling's documentary *Don't Panic*, http://bit.ly/Rosling-panic, or his Ted talk *The Best Stats You've Ever Seen*, http://bit.ly/TED-Roslingstats.

...recycling and waste prevention

Reduce, Reuse, Recycle: an Easy Household Guide, Nicky Scott, Green Books, 2007, is a short, sweet A-Z guide.

Recycle Now, www.recyclenow.com, has guidance by region and local authority.

Wastewatch, www.wastewatch.org.uk, has guidance and an online sustainable lifestyles community.

...repairing and upcycling

Restart, http://therestartproject.org and *Ifixit*, http://www.ifixit.com, have workshops, tutorials and online manuals about how to repair electronics and other everyday items.

Upcycle That, http://www.upcyclethat.com/, will help you find creative uses for old objects.

...sharing, swapping and reusing

Bookmooch, www.bookmooch.co.uk and *Read It, Swap It*, http://www.readitswapit.co.uk, let you swap books.

Ecomodo, http://www.ecomodo.com/ and *Streetbank*, http://bit.ly/Streetbank-share, will help you share skills and borrow items from your neighbours.

Freecycle, www.freecycle.org and *Freegle*, www.ilovefreegle.org, help you give away unwanted possessions and find goods you need for free.

LETS (Local Exchange and Trading Schemes), www.letslinkuk.net and *Time Banks*, www.timebanking.org, help people swap their skills without money changing hands.

...visions of the future

Malmö, http://bit.ly/Malmo-sustain and Hammarby Sjöstad, http://www.hammarbysjostad.se, are interesting examples of sustainable urban design in Sweden.

The *Eco-Village Network UK*, www.evnuk.org.uk, promotes rural, low-impact communities. Findhorn, www.findhorn.org, is a well-known example.

Zerocarbonbritain: Rethinking the Future, Centre for Alternative Technology, CAT Publications, 2013 supplies the technical vision.

...what's happening in Scotland

Changeworks, www.changeworks.org.uk, runs waste prevention schemes in Scotland and their site has good information for individuals, businesses and community projects.

Greener Scotland, www.greenerscotland.org, has information and advice on waste reduction in Scotland.

CHAPTER 6

Talking with friends, family and colleagues

Climate change isn't always a welcome topic amongst friends

When I was a young woman I was told that there were certain subjects I shouldn't discuss in polite company. Sex, death, politics, religion and money were top of my aunt's list. Today we might add climate change to the list of taboo dinner-party topics. All too often its mention leads to embarrassed silence or angry debate.

What is more distressing is when people close to you – your friends and family – are also unhappy to talk about the subject. Although many say that family and friends are their strongest source of support in facing climate change, it is also common to find that the subject leads to friction. In this chapter we discuss the need for support from those close to you and suggest some strategies for coping with difficult conversations.

carbonconversations.org

The nature of the problem

Most people are concerned about climate change. A 2013 study of UK attitudes found that just under three-quarters of the British public accept that the world's climate is changing. Nearly two-thirds said that they were concerned about it.[1] These attitudes do not always translate into action however. Another study by the RSA[2] found a similar number of people expressing concern but asked some deeper questions about what this meant to them. This report concluded that most of those who said they were concerned were better described as 'unmoved'. They rarely spoke about climate change to anyone else and if they did the conversations were short, mostly less than ten minutes. These people accept that climate change is real but they do not match this with much sense of connection to the issue. The feelings, the sense of urgency or the actions that you might expect are missing.

As we discussed in Chapter One, these responses are familiar to therapists working with people who are faced with distressing knowledge. People don't usually deny the facts of a painful situation. Instead, they protect themselves by denying the meaning, the importance or the permanence of those facts. Therapists refer to this form of denial as disavowal.[3] We acknowledge the facts as true but behave as though they are not. You can probably think of examples from your own life. A young person faced with yet another job rejection will tell you that it doesn't matter or that she doesn't care. A woman faced with evidence of her husband's affair convinces herself that she must be mistaken. Someone faced with spiralling debts may retreat to dreams of winning the lottery or simply carry on as if nothing has happened, failing to tell their family the bad news.

Disavowal creates splits in the mind that allow us to carry on as usual. We can both know and not know something at the same time. Fact is split off from feeling. Our actions are split off from their significance. We don't actively deny the truth. We simply park it in a separate box in the mind and behave as if it doesn't matter. This is what allows a conversation to slip seamlessly from wondering if recent floods are connected to climate change to chat about cheap flights and holidays. If someone challenges us, re-making the connection and reminding us of the painful reality, we are likely to react angrily. Our defences are both necessary and convenient – necessary in that they stop us from being overwhelmed and convenient in that they allow us to avoid facing difficult truths. You may be familiar with some of the following responses.

- It's not my responsibility, it's up to government/industry/China/the US.
- I don't see what I can do about it.
- I don't think it's that pressing.
- I can't make a difference – the plane will go anyway, whether I'm on it or not.
- I won't be here, so I'm not bothered.
- There'll be time to sort this out once we've dealt with the economy.
- Don't point the finger at me – I care – I just don't choose to show it by growing a beard and wearing sandals.

> *While our travel choices were once a common topic of conversation among my friends and family, my choice to remove flying from my life has been met with little interest, if not active avoidance of discussion surrounding the reasons for which I made this choice.*
>
> **Catherine Cherry**

There is of course some truth in some of these statements. Bigger systems influence everything from how we travel to work to how we raise our children. On our own, we are just a small part of the picture. There are plenty of big players who are also responsible. There are other pressing political problems and many ways of approaching this one.

The question we address in this chapter is how to hold conversations that will help people become engaged, rather than stay in an unmoved state. A lot of advice in this field focuses on how to persuade the general public to take small steps that might help or to become politically engaged. We draw on some of this work in this chapter but our focus is different. We are not talking about campaigning or about promoting behaviour change but about conversations with the people we meet day to day – our families, friends and colleagues. Here, it's relationships and feelings that matter, and small moments as well as big ones. How can we:

- Hold a conversation about climate change that doesn't end in upset or embarrassment?
- Help others feel that the subject is important to them and that they can do something about it?
- Manage conflicts about the subject with people we love and like?
- Cope with our own feelings when the topic comes up?

This chapter suggests some strategies that may help.

How it feels in practice

About one in seven people are both concerned about climate change and actively engaged in doing something about it.[4] If you're reading this book you are probably one of them.

If you have become more active and talkative about climate change you have probably noticed shifts in your relationships with other people. It's usually the negative changes that stay in people's minds. For example:

- people are awkward or embarrassed if I raise the subject;
- people avoid me;
- people see me as smug;
- people see me as a puritan, trying to impose my views on them;
- people like to wind me up about it;
- I've stopped talking about it to friends and family;
- I've withdrawn from some social groups because of it.

There are a number of issues in play here.

The information trap

Many of us imagine that information is the answer. We see our task as 'to get the message across' or 'raise awareness'. We hope that telling others the facts that have shocked us will be enough to change their minds. We can hardly wait to spill them out. "Did you know…?/The fact is…/Research says…" Unfortunately facts on their own don't change minds. If they did, the world would be a very different place. Most people are very good at:

> ❝ Like a lot of people I'm aware of the resource issues and poor working conditions that lie behind a lot of the goods and services we take for granted but I'd rather not think about them. It's really difficult if you do – it opens up the issue of should I even buy this at all?
> **Ammar Waqar**

- screening out information they think doesn't apply to them;
- splitting off information that makes them feel uncomfortable;
- splitting off information that challenges their sense of identity and expectations of life;
- listening with 'confirmation bias' – making the facts they do hear, fit the world view they already hold.[5]

Facts only make sense when we are ready to hear them. We need to be in an open, receptive frame of mind, free of distractions and other worries. If you want someone to listen to you talking about climate change you need to create a situation where they can be receptive to challenging news.

This is not what most people want to hear when they have the urgency of climate change pounding in their own heart. Once you have acknowledged the reality of climate change yourself it is hard not to feel strongly about the silence of others. You feel desperate to convince them. Their lack of action can seem inexplicable. They can seem complacent and irresponsible. A woman described walking through the shopping centre in a daze, staring at other people, wondering how they could still pick items off the shelves. A man described how he devoured every scrap of information he could lay his hands on and then manically regurgitated it to anyone who would – or wouldn't –listen.[6] Our sense of urgency, our despair and our underlying anxiety can overwhelm others and make us poor communicators. Like the Ancient Mariner in Coleridge's poem we pour out an endless stream of facts to anyone who we can stop.

Anxiety leads to poor communication

In these states of mind we appear to be focused on the subject but we are actually focused on ourselves and our own distress. Sometimes we are trying to get rid of that distress. Sometimes we are looking for someone to be angry with. Sometimes we are pleading for someone else to take responsibility. What we communicate is the need for someone to deal with our feelings and so people respond accordingly. Sometimes they try to reassure us, telling us it can't be as bad as we imagine. Sometimes they retaliate. Sometimes they try to comfort us with stories of how government will deal with it. If we then react with frustration, the conversation is likely to break down.

If you recognise yourself in this description, the first step is to find another way to deal with your own distress. You need to talk through your own feelings about the issue before you try to convince, help or educate anyone else.

Projection and scapegoating

It would be a mistake to think that the problem lies simply with our own feelings however. Once you have declared your interest in climate change you can easily become a scapegoat for others.

> *There were lots of things that I knew in the back of my mind, as if I knew and didn't know at the same time. I feel so much internal conflict between wanting to have a low-impact lifestyle and wanting to live comfortably and 'normally'. It helped to discuss these things without being made to feel guilty for the things you just can't do anything about, and I realised that with each small decision you can build up to a large overall impact.*
>
> Rebecca Miller

This is the process that therapists call projection, where people attribute their own feelings to someone else.

If someone does feel anxious about climate change they may see the cause of their anxiety in you, rather than in the situation. "Don't wind me up," "Stop going on about it" or "Let's talk about something nicer" are common responses. If someone feels ashamed of their own inaction they may project their self-critical conscience into you. If they see you as a nagging parent who is trying to tell everyone else what to do they can feel absolved from responsibility. They no longer have to experience the nagging inner voice and they can blame you for getting on their back. One friend begins every conversation about holidays with the phrase, "I know you'll disapprove but…" By making me responsible for her own disapproval she takes her flights with a clear conscience.

Achieving the right state of mind

It's easy to forget the times when communication has gone well. They seem less remarkable than the times which end in hurt or embarrassment. You can learn a lot from reflecting on them. You will probably find that:

- you were calm;
- you weren't desperate about the outcome;
- you were feeling confident and positive about yourself;
- you were interested in the other person;
- you connected to the other person's feelings and experience;
- you listened more than you spoke.

These are all aspects of creating what we call a 'safe space' for conversation. This is much easier to do if you are feeling good yourself. If you start out anxious, upset, angry, judgemental or defensive the conversation is unlikely to go well. If any of these negative feelings are dominant for you, find support for yourself before trying to engage with others.

Creating the safe space

A 'safe space' is one in which people feel safe to share experiences, express feelings and explore ideas. It is a milieu where people can expect to be listened to without being judged. It has an atmosphere where people feel that others will try to understand their point of view and that they can dare to take risks, experiment and try out new ideas. This might mean admitting to weakness, being able to laugh at yourself or agreeing to try something new. The 'safe space' isn't cosy or self-congratulatory. It can be challenging but it does have kindness and empathy at its heart.

> ❝ Once I'd realized the seriousness of climate change I was gripped by a terrible urgency that I've since seen in others. I'd launch in with my fears for the future, my bitterness about governments and corporations and my demands that people should start doing something, right now this minute. My index finger was wagging and I could see people moving away. Gradually I realized that this approach engendered fear and denial in others. People switched off. I realized I needed to provide the time and space for people to come to their own conclusions.
>
> Pam Candea

We try to create this kind of space in the Carbon Conversations groups that this book was created for. If you can create it in your interactions with others you may find your conversations about climate change go better.

Existing relationships

When you are talking with family, friends or colleagues, existing relationships always come into play. With family and friends we assume that there is a basic level of trust that will see us through and can be surprised to discover that it doesn't always do so. The people we are closest to are often the people we also argue with the most. When someone knows you well, they also know how to wind you up or hurt you. Like any other contentious subject, climate change can be pulled into the dynamics of a marital dispute or sibling rivalry. It can provide fodder for the politics of housework or the workplace.

Traditional gender roles provide a common trap. If the woman of the house feels responsible for reminding everyone else of their domestic duties (tidy your room/wash up/put your clothes in the laundry) then the small actions that help to reduce a family footprint (turn off the lights/close the fridge door/take a short shower) can get pulled into this dynamic. She feels additionally burdened. Others feel absolved of responsibility and see her as a nag. The mirror image of this is the man who takes responsibility for anything seen as practical or technical. If Dad reads the meters, puts up the draught stripping and drools over the photovoltaic catalogues, then carbon reduction can be seen as just another of his hobbies.

In most families there are other dynamics too, some crude, some subtle. My brothers love to wind me up and climate change provides the perfect topic. In another family the teenage children felt that their parents' refusal to provide them with endless fashion items and electronic gadgets was further evidence of their parents' meanness. In a third family, a father saw his son's refusal to fly overseas for a family gathering as an act of deliberate disrespect.

Close friends can be a great source of support but amongst groups there are often powerful norms about the way to behave. Norms such as flying overseas for a hen weekend, buying a new outfit every weekend or upgrading your car every three years are hard to challenge. Groups like conformity and if you stand out you may find yourself under pressure. Banter, mockery and gossip are some of the common ways in which groups put pressure on their members to conform.

At work there are often strong cultural norms about the kind of chat that takes place in coffee breaks or in after-work socialising. It's common to enquire about holidays, home improvements or recent outings. These conversations tend to follow predictable patterns. You're expected to be enthusiastic about exotic holiday destinations or a new conservatory, and commiserate about

> ❝ I went to a talk that Mark Lynas did in Wolvercote, and he had slides about how the village would look if we didn't do something. I was quite shocked. My first reaction was to count ahead twenty, thirty years, and think, 'Oh well, I probably won't be here then,' but my second reaction was to think, 'Actually my child and grand-children will be here.' It makes me sad to think that the world will be a very different place for them.
>
> Judith Secker

bad weather, missed flights and substandard builders. Announcing that you're not flying anywhere this year, that your building work is an eco-upgrade or that you've given up eating meat disrupts the predictable flow of chat. Awkwardness descends. In formal work relationships, power and responsibility play a big part. As with anything else she does, a respected manager will be able to bring her team with her on climate change. If there is already friction, her climate change initiative is likely to be treated in the same way as anything else she tries. There may be grumbling, a half-hearted response or subtle sabotage.

In all these relationships we are sometimes naive in the way we introduce climate change. We expect support and are surprised to discover that another aspect of the relationship has come into play. The power balance between friends, the history of domestic arguments or the resentment of junior colleagues can take us by surprise. We expect agreement and are surprised to discover friction. Recognising that a conversation goes on at more than one level can help.

Levels in a conversation

Most conversations take place at several levels. We often focus on the content, such as planning a holiday, arranging a meeting or talking about climate change. This is the surface level and what goes on underneath can be just as important. You can think of a conversation as having four levels: the content, the mood or emotions felt by the people involved, the agenda each person has and their perceptions of each other.

Content is the subject matter – what's on the news, how's the family, what is it urgent to do this week?

Mood and emotion refer to how people feel. A conversation can have a dominant mood, for example, light-hearted, serious, depressed, awkward or excitable, which may change during the course of the conversation. Each person will also have their particular feelings. For example, one person might feel comfortable, excited and curious. The other person might feel the same way but they could equally well feel edgy, anxious, suspicious or cross.

The agenda refers to what people hope to get out of the conversation. Most people are hoping to get something out of a conversation, if only to pass the time of day or show that they feel well-disposed towards another person. These agendas are often covert or semi-conscious and can shift during the course of a conversation. For example you might be trying to persuade the other person, prove them wrong, show superiority or flirt. Sometimes your agenda will coincide with someone else's. Sometimes your agendas will clash. The other person may be happy to

> ❝ If you understand the seriousness of climate change, there's no way that you can frame the issue positively. This makes it hard to raise directly with people who haven't begun to think about it - you can frighten people, put them off completely or end up dumping on them. My approach is to come at it sideways, with a related issue that also matters to them but which is more straightforwardly soluble. I point out how so many issues are related and move from there to climate change. I talk about collective solutions and the importance of working together to change our society for the better.
>
> Rich Hawkins

share your agenda but they might be trying to change the subject, persuade you of an opposite point of view or end the conversation.

Perception refers to how we see others. We often start with unfounded assumptions about others. We perceive them in particular ways, which can have little to do with how they feel about themselves, or with what they are saying to us. For example you might see someone as overbearing or timid, as behaving like a parent or like a child. In turn, they might be seeing you as a role model and wanting your approval, or seeing you as an inferior and someone to be pushed around. Even with people we know well, we can slot them into our existing expectations: Dad's a joker, Tom's lazy, Saffron's an airhead.

Some examples

Here are three examples, one from a domestic situation and two which are climate change related.

> A woman says to her husband: "Have you thought about supper?" The content is a factual question. Her mood is edgy and irritable though she's attempting to conceal this because she doesn't want a row. Her perception is that her partner is lazy and thoughtless because it's already 7.30 and he's checking his email again. Her agenda is to get him to make supper. He replies: "Not really", which is factual and true (the content). His mood is irritable in return because he feels wrong-footed. His perception of his wife is a parental one – mother telling him off. His agenda is not to lose face.

> A group of flatmates have agreed to turn lights off when they leave the room but Jack comes into the empty kitchen to find every light blazing. He goes into the living room to speak to the others and says "Hey, guys, I thought we agreed we'd turn lights off when we're not using them?" The content is the agreement about lights, but Jack's mood is hurt and his tone is reproachful, his perception of his friends is that they don't care and his agenda is to shame them into action. Dan replies "Cool it mate, a few minutes won't hurt." Dan's mood is resistant and irritable, his perception of Jack is that he's behaving like a little dictator and Dan's agenda is to show that he can't be pushed around.

> In a workplace chat over coffee Denzil has connected recent floods with climate change. Karen challenges him: "Do you really think it's worth doing anything?" The content is a factual question but Karen's mood is hurried, critical and impatient, her perception is that Denzil is a misguided do-gooder and her agenda is to reinforce her belief that there's nothing more she should do about the problem.

> ❝ Over a leisurely lunch the conversation moved from one couple's trip to S. Africa to another's excitement about their forthcoming river cruise. They shared delight at places visited, wildlife seen and wonderful experiences. I felt unable to join in and in the end couldn't wait for them to leave. I felt distanced from them and silenced by feeling that it would be rude to challenge guests. Increasingly I try to take the initiative. I say in a very matter of fact tone that I don't want to fly anymore and then share my plans. People seem to just hear that as information, although I often hear an expression of curiosity in their 'Oh' response.
>
> **Jane Orton**

In all these examples you can see that focusing on the content will get you deeper into trouble. A battle is likely to ensue, feelings will get hurt, each person will retire wounded with their original position entrenched. Reflect back on some of your own climate-change conversations and see if you can identify what was happening at each of the four levels.

Content
- What was the other person talking about?
- What were you talking about?
- Were you talking about the same thing?

Mood/emotion
- Were your feelings and those of the other person similar or different?
- Did your feelings change as the conversation went on?
- Did the mood of the conversation shift as it went on?

Agenda
- What were you trying to do?
- What was the other person trying to do?
- Were your agendas compatible?
- Did they shift during the conversation?

Perception
- How did you perceive the other person?
- What did you imagine they were thinking of you?
- How did the other person perceive you?
- What did they imagine you were thinking of them?
- Did anyone's perceptions change during the course of the conversation?

You may have remembered a conversation that went better than those in our examples but many people recall conversations that came unstuck in similar ways. How can you get past this? Start by focusing on the emotion and mood of the conversation.

Achieving empathy

Empathy means:

- imagining what it is like to be someone else;
- listening, accepting and respecting their point of view;
- showing warmth and understanding;
- avoiding blame, criticism and judgment.

> **❝** My family are supportive but they have their blind spots. In one chat with my dad he was enthusiastically telling me how he was refusing plastic bags in the shops but it then transpired that he'd just come back from a weekend trip to Las Vegas. Other things I've been able to influence them on - they're growing their own veg and getting solar panels. I feel it would be healthier to raise issues and talk them through but I'm afraid of undermining my relationship with them so some no-go areas remain.
>
> Rich Hawkins

The paradox of empathy is that the more people feel understood and respected, the more open they are to reflecting for themselves and the more likely they are to shift their opinion or alter their behaviour. Identifying someone else's mood is the first step towards empathy. Try observing the shifting moods in some of the conversations you take part in. You may be surprised at how rapidly they can change. What seems to make someone open up or close down? How do different people show enthusiasm or irritation? How do they show approval or disapproval? Sometimes it is worth checking out and giving time for the other person to respond. Try asking: "You seem irritated – is that right?" or "I get the sense that you're feeling quite put upon by this."

You may be surprised at how this can open up the conversation, as in this example between a manager and a member of her team:

Manager: "Have you made any progress with the travel-to-work survey?"

Team member: "It's on my list."

Manager: "You seem irritated by my raising this again…"

Team member: "No, no, not at all…"

Manager: "I wouldn't be surprised if you were irritated. It's difficult being asked to add something else to your job role."

Team member: "Well, I am a bit pissed off I suppose. I just get flack from the rest of the team."

The manager could have closed this conversation down by responding to the irritation with a demand of her own such as "I want your report on my desk by Friday'". By taking a more empathic route, she opens up the possibility of solving the problem. Here's an example between two friends. Kate has always taken the lead in the friendship.

Kate: "I think you feel I'm always banging on about this."

Ruby: "Well it does seem like every time I suggest we do something fun together you come up with a reason for why it's going to wreck the planet."

Kate: "Sounds like you feel I'm a bit of a kill-joy."

Ruby: "Yeah – it depresses me. I feel I can never do anything right. It's as if all my enthusiasm for life is being trampled on."

In this example, Kate manages not to retaliate. By identifying with Ruby's annoyance, she allows Ruby to express what she feels. This creates space for more understanding between the two of

> ❝ I remember when a client's sustainability team were trying to improve recycling rates, they decided to remove the waste bins under everyone's desks. This would probably have been a good idea - having no bins means people have to think about what to do with their waste paper, and they're more likely to recycle it - except that they forgot to tell everyone it was happening. So there was a dirty protest. For at least a week after the bins disappeared, the sustainability manager came into work in the morning to find her desk littered with items that would previously have gone into the bins. It was a good lesson in the value of talking.
>
> **Anne Augustine**

them. Empathic conversations usually check what the other person is feeling by reflecting back the mood or feeling you are picking up from them. They also use more open questions than closed ones. Closed questions invite yes/no answers. Open questions invite the other person to carry on talking and express what they feel or think. Try questions like:

- It sounds like you feel…
- Are you feeling that…?
- What do you think about…?
- How does that make you feel?
- What happened next?
- How did that work out?

If you can stop trying to convince someone else and instead become interested in what they feel and think you are likely to have better conversations.

Appreciating the real dilemmas
Another important aspect of empathy is appreciating the real dilemmas that people face. With regard to climate change you have encountered many of these in the previous chapters of this book and will have struggled with them yourself. For example:

- the dilemmas of being part of an international family;
- the feeling that you are being asked to curtail your aspirations;
- the conflict between doing what feels best for your family and what feels right for our collective future;
- the sense of unfairness – that those who cause the most emissions are not doing much to check them;
- the shock of realising that a high income makes you a high emitter;
- the traps created by the way society is organised, such as the systems of transport, settlement, provision of goods and services, which lock us into high emissions.

Each of these dilemmas plays out differently in people's lives. Sometimes they create genuine and painful obstacles. Sometimes people reach for them as reasons to do nothing. Again, if you explore these issues through open questions, paying close attention to the feelings they bring up, you are likely to have a more fruitful conversation. At certain points you will almost certainly find that you are hitting ambivalence and resistance – your own as well as that of other people.

Ambivalence and resistance

Don't be surprised when you encounter ambivalence. Faced with the need for major social and personal change, most people have mixed feelings. People simultaneously want to know and don't want to know about the impact their lives have on our climate. One day they feel inspired to change, the next they long to stay the same. One moment they feel it's a really important issue, the next that they don't really care. You've probably noticed this ambivalence in yourself. One day you're really keen. The next it all feels too much. You find yourself involved in "Yes, but…" conversations, sometimes with someone who is trying to help you but just as often with yourself.

"I could take the bus but…"
"I agree it's important but…"
"I'd like to do more but…"

You become a master at showing just why any suggestion is impractical, dangerous, irrelevant or just plain unhelpful. Often, you feel someone else's resistance before it is put into words. They fidget, their glance travels away, they move uncomfortably in their chair. They nod, as if they're agreeing with you, but actually they're collecting their thoughts in order to block what you are saying. William Miller and Stephen Rollnick suggest that the most important thing in these situations is to 'roll with the resistance'.[7] The metaphor comes from judo where instead of hitting back you use the other person's momentum to your advantage. Conversations about climate change shouldn't be battles but resistance *is* a signal to respond differently. Don't argue. Don't retaliate. Don't oppose the resistance directly. Instead, try to approach from a different angle. Ask more questions. Suggest another perspective but don't impose it. Acknowledge that we all have mixed feelings. Elicit what the other person feels. See them as a resource in finding a solution.

Imagine that in a conversation about public transport, someone says to you: "I'd like to use the bus but it takes so long and the times are so inconvenient". Listed below are seven possible responses you could make. The first three are likely to lead to an entrenched argument or an awkward silence. The last four 'roll with the resistance'.

1. If you look through these timetables you'll see that they've really improved lately.
2. I get the bus most days and I've found it works out really well for me.
3. I think we have to put our own convenience to one side when we're thinking about climate change.
4. It sounds like you don't really like the idea of buses.
5. It sounds like you've had bad experiences trying to use buses in the past.
6. What would your dream public transport system be like?
7. Time is such a pressure isn't it? Maybe that's the first thing to think about, rather than the nitty-gritty of bus timetables.

In the heat of the moment it can be hard to follow good advice, but if you practise listening for the resistance you will quickly find that your tactics in conversation change. There are some common forms in which resistance to acting on climate change is expressed. You may recognise some of these in yourself as well as in others. For each one we've suggested some moves that could 'roll with the resistance'.

"I'd love to but…"

There is a common longing to be an exception. We all hope that others will take the brunt of change and that we can be excused. Academics feel that their work is so important they must be allowed to fly. Country dwellers argue that their off-road vehicle is a necessity. Parents justify their long commute with the need to live near a good school. Young people feel they have as much right to explore the world as previous generations. Older people claim a right to some rewards after a lifetime of hard work. Other phrases of this kind you will hear are "I just don't have the time…", "I don't think I'm extravagant…" "I make up for it by…" Try asking:

> ❝ I came to the travel meeting feeling 'this is a waste of time'. I'd thought I was mostly pretty good when it came to having a low-impact lifestyle but when I looked at my travel footprint it dwarfed everything else because of the flights home to see family. I felt stuck between a rock and a hard place. I'd have written the whole thing off if I hadn't had an outlet to talk about it. That's what Carbon Conversations offers. It allows things to be complicated and allows your life to be real, without judgment.
>
> Rebecca Miller

- How would society need to change for you to be able to change?
- Is there anything you could do that would contribute to that change in society?
- How would you feel if that change had taken place?

If you're lucky the conversation may move into a discussion of what people are afraid they will lose if they take climate change seriously. It may help to talk about your own desire to be an exception or your own ambivalence. It may also help to focus on the losses people fear. Once loss is spoken about it often seems less significant. Try statements and questions like:

- It sounds like you've got really mixed feelings about the actions we all might need to take.
- I found the idea that I might have to give stuff up really difficult at first. It was only when I realised that I was also gaining something that I stopped feeling resentful.
- In my daydreams everyone else has to do stuff and I'm allowed to carry on regardless. It's been tough acknowledging that my reasons for thinking I'm an exception don't really stack up.

"It's all so complicated…"

Some people use their confusion as a reason for retreat. Sometimes their focus is on small technical distinctions. They fret over dilemmas such as whether it is better to buy hothouse flowers grown in the UK or air-freighted ones from Kenya and whether washing up by hand is better than using the dishwasher. (The truth about the flowers is that both options are unsustainable and the truth about the washing up is that both options can be carried out with very little hot water.) The questions do need a proper answer but you may find that your helpful information is met with disinterest or a change of subject. Focusing on small issues like these can be a way of diverting yourself from the big ones and convincing yourself that it is all too complicated to tackle.

Similarly, conversations that appear to be about technical disputes can have more to do with feelings of despair or irritation. It's easier to feel exasperated that the experts can't make up their minds than to feel angry about the scale of the changes that are asked of you. Remarks that begin…

- "I read in the paper…"
- "My builder says…"
- "Someone told me…'"

…often relate back to an urban myth such as the idea that wind turbines are hopelessly inefficient or that it uses less energy to leave the heating on all day than to turn it off. Technical conversations can also be about hopeful but unrealistic solutions which will avoid some of the pain or difficulty of major changes. These are often referred to as greenwash. The claims made for insulating wallpaper or the idea that biofuels can supply our energy needs are good examples.

Your approach here needs to be two-fold. You need to use your intuition to feel what might lie behind the question and your knowledge to reply to its technical aspect. Don't answer the technical side on the basis of your gut feeling! And don't respond to a feeling with a technical lecture! On the feeling side, try interventions like:

> ❝ We need to fix the big picture but we need to look at the small things too. Just because we can't do everything doesn't mean that we shouldn't do what we can. It doesn't help to get into an 'all or nothing' frame of mind. If you do, you end up doing nothing!
>
> **Claire Melling**

carbonconversations.org

- It sounds like you could just give up in despair.
- Some of the technical detail is tough, isn't it?
- I can understand why you're irritated/confused/annoyed.
- It would be great if there were some magic answers, wouldn't it?

On the technical side, recognise your own limitations, be supportive of people's curiosity and encourage their questioning. If you genuinely have the technical answer at your fingertips it can help to offer it with confidence if this is really what is being sought. If you are not a technical expert, ask the person for the sources of their information. This often makes it clear that there is no real foundation for the 'facts' being offered or casts doubt on them. If there is a trail leading back to a source, follow it up. Look out for vested interests and question unlikely new technologies that are going to save the world.

"I'm too small to make a difference"

Variants of this are, "It's not my responsibility", "It's probably too late" and "I've got other things to worry about". These statements often signal a retreat into hopelessness. People find climate change overwhelming and can't see the point in doing anything. It can help to reflect back to someone that they may be feeling hopeless or powerless. It can also help to ask questions that put them back in touch with their deeper motivations for acting. Try reflecting back the feelings that might be behind the statement, for example:

- It sounds like you're feeling rather hopeless/powerless/overwhelmed/insignificant.
- It sounds like you feel that nobody takes account of you.
- It sounds like you long for someone else to clear up this mess.

Asking questions that connect someone to their own strengths can also help, for example: "What has given you strength in the past?" or "What usually makes you stick at difficult tasks?"

'It's all right for you…'

Variants of this are, '"You want everyone to be like you…" and "You've been conned, now you're trying to convince everyone else…" The dominant emotion is resentment. The person is probably feeling hedged in or pushed around. They project onto you that you have life easy, that you're a bit of a dictator or that you're stupid. This makes it much easier to disagree with you. It's tempting to retaliate with stories of your struggles, a denial that you've ever tried to influence anyone or a vivid account of the catastrophes that climate change will bring. Take a deep breath and try to stay calm. Sometimes it can help to reflect back the feeling. Try:

- It sounds like you're feeling hedged in/pushed around/exasperated with the subject.
- Do you resent all this talk about climate change?

This may open up a discussion of the person's feelings that is fruitful but sometimes this kind of projection is the signal to back off and close the conversation for the time being. Try something like:

- I think I've really annoyed you. I'm sorry.
- Let's leave this for now and go for lunch.

Sometimes this is enough to let the person reassess their view of you. You may get an apology in return or at least the possibility of returning to the subject another time.

Promoting self-efficacy

If you want someone to join you in making changes or to make changes on their own account, you have to believe in them. They need your respect. You have to support their sense of self-efficacy. Think about times when you have tried to make changes or tackled a difficult project yourself. How did you overcome self-doubt? How did you deal with setbacks? How did you stay hopeful? It was probably easier when you had someone backing you. Realistic encouragement matters. It will help if you can:

- believe in other people's willingness to act;
- nurture people's potential;
- credit people with what they achieve;
- praise what is done well.

Climate change can be a difficult topic in this respect. Our own disappointment at political failures or at the complacency of the majority can lead us to denigrate the first 'baby steps' that other people take. Look at the difference between three possible responses in a tea-break conversation at work. Maria says: "I'm concerned about climate change too – I always do the recycling properly." Which of Tod's replies is most likely to encourage Maria to do something more?

1. "Well that's not exactly going to save the planet, is it?"
2. "That's a great first step – what else are you planning on?"
3. "That's good – how did you get the family on board?"

In the first response, Tod speaks from his irritation at Maria's complacent belief that doing her recycling is enough. In the second, he praises her but immediately makes it clear that he thinks what she's done is inadequate. In the third, he praises her and asks her to tell him more, an approach that is likely to open up the conversation, put her in touch with her abilities to organise her family and give him some clues about what else he could suggest to her.

Supporting other people in this way comes from a state of mind that is not always easy to achieve. It's dependent on a degree of hope and faith in other people's good will and on being able to keep your own anxiety and anger in check. Don't be surprised if you don't always manage this. Do think about the circumstances that make it easier to achieve. Choosing when and where you talk about climate change can help.

Pick your time and place

Climate change and carbon reduction often come up at times and in places that make the conversation hard. People often report feeling that they are on the back foot as the norms of the conversation restrict what it is acceptable to say. Socially, many issues are framed in ways that assume that climate change has no connection to them. For example, it's common to see tax as a burden rather than as a necessary policy to help deal with climate change. Similarly, driving a car is assumed to be a right rather than an environmental problem. Look at the examples below. The dominant assumption or framing is in brackets at the end of each one.

1. The meeting room was hot and my boss told me to open the windows; I didn't feel I could scrabble around looking for the heating controls. (The most important thing is to get on with the meeting.)
2. Everyone else in the pub was happy that green taxes are being removed from fuel bills. I wanted to disagree but I knew I was on a hiding to nothing. (Tax is a burden, you're a mug if you want to pay it.)
3. My dad announced over Christmas dinner that he was inviting (and paying for) the whole family to join him in Goa to celebrate his sixtieth. (The most important thing is family: you're disloyal and ungrateful if you don't come.)
4. My friend asked me to sign a petition against congestion charging. (Driving a car wherever you want to is a right, tax is a burden.)

5. My cousins showed me the bargain clothes they'd bought from a discount shop and expected me to congratulate them on their smart shopping. (Price is the most important aspect of any purchase.)

In situations like these you need to decide if this is a moment to stay quiet, assert yourself mildly or assert yourself strongly. Asserting yourself can be hard as you're driving against the flow of the conversation. If you think back to the levels of a conversation that we talked about earlier, you need to pay attention to both the agenda and the perceptions of the people taking part. Is your agenda of talking about climate change compatible with other people's agendas of (say) running an efficient meeting or getting uproariously drunk? If you assert your agenda, how will you be perceived? Will you be seen as a welcome messenger, as the meeting's time waster or the party's killjoy? Strategy matters. Are you likely to get a good outcome by raising the subject? If not, you may do better to stay quiet for the time being.

Often you will do better if you can pick your own time and place for a conversation. Frame what you want to say positively, in a way that you think will appeal to the other person. Think about:

- Who do you want to talk to – everyone in the family/work-team/group of friends, or just one or two people?
- What kind of outcome are you looking for? Do you want your viewpoint acknowledged? For the other person to show interest? Or are you looking for a promise of change on their part? Weigh up what is realistic.
- When is likely to be a good time? Avoid rushed situations when people are tired or distracted. Try to make it a pleasant occasion. Make sure you listen.

In the first example above, the person did as her boss instructed. She didn't want to run the risk of annoying him or shaming him in a tense meeting. Later, she contacted the Facilities Manager to find out where the heating controls were and then had a quiet word with her boss about how to turn the heating down if the situation recurred. In the last example, the person admired the clothes her cousins had bought but then, in a lull in the conversation, explained how she had been thinking recently about the impact of the clothes she herself bought and had decided to change her shopping habits. One cousin shrugged and said "Whatever…" but the other one was more interested and they managed a short conversation about it.

In both these examples the person managed to take control of the agenda of the conversation and manage the perceptions the other person was likely to have of them. Keep your expectations realistic as well. Most people hate to lose face and prefer to make up their own minds. They may not shift their position through one conversation but if you have listened as well as spoken, treated them with empathy and respect and supported them in their good intentions, you will probably have made a difference.

Your own needs

People vary in how much they like to talk about issues that are troubling them. We all have our own ways of dealing with upset and anxiety. These often have their roots in childhood. Were you a child who actively sought comfort from others? Or one who retreated to their room and cried alone? Do you come from the tradition of the stiff upper lip? Or did your family prefer to talk through difficulties? Do you like to get on and solve a problem by yourself or are you someone who can't get started till you're sure of the support of others?

Climate change produces strong feelings. You may be anxious about what the future holds for you or your children. You may be ashamed of living in a culture that pays so little attention to such an important issue. You may feel guilty about everyday actions that you haven't managed to change. You may be angry at politicians for their inaction. You may despair of humanity ever getting its act together. The process of trying to live a low-carbon life produces another set of strong feelings. People often feel grief, anger, frustration and sadness as they struggle to make changes that are difficult for them. Some people are eager to talk about these feelings and feel better for doing so but we don't all seek support in the same way. Which of these examples is most like you?

Emma comes from a family where talking was the norm. She finds it easy to share her feelings with her partner Jenny. When they meet up in the evening they tend to ask how the other's day has gone and it feels quite natural if climate change comes into the conversation, along with their feelings about it.

John is a rather bluff, practical man who looks for his wife Carol's support in the form of praise for his achievements and quiet agreement when he's in a mood of anger or despair. He needs her to admire his draught-stripping and be pleased at the change that the solar panels have brought. If he rails: "Bloody Lawson" when the climate change denier comes on the TV, this is not an invitation to a political discussion but a request for agreement. "Bloody Lawson indeed" is enough for him to feel acknowledged. Carol is not a great talker either. She gains comfort from her connectedness to the natural world and finds that spending time quietly in her garden is the best form of support she knows. She has one friend who she turns to if something is really troubling her but she finds it difficult to express herself in words and is anxious about wasting someone else's time.

Matt's political activity is his main forum for discussing climate change. The conversations tend to be about campaigning and strategy and ignore people's reasons for being part of the group. He has introduced the idea of spending a short part of each meeting checking in on how people are feeling about the issues they are facing. This has increased the group's willingness to offer more personal support to each other.

Dan's religious beliefs are the touchstone for what he does in all aspects of life. Connecting climate change to his other spiritual and ethical concerns grounds him. His main source of support is regular discussions with other church members.

The need for hope

The question of hope often comes up amongst people who are deeply involved in climate change. How can we keep hope alive? How can we protect ourselves from despair? Hope needs to be realistic. False optimism helps no-one. During the struggle against fascism in 1920s Italy, the Italian socialist Antonio Gramsci coined the famous phrase 'Pessimism of the intellect, opti-

> ❝ I am frightened about the future and what it holds for my son. I keep myself from thinking about it too much because it can send me into despair. I'm also careful about talking about my despair to others because I'm afraid of bringing them down and that they might get stuck in their own dark place. I know I can get out of mine. I keep hope alive by being active, increasing the circle of people who understand. Who knows? One day I may talk to someone who has the power and influence to make a big change.
>
> Pam Candea

mism of the will'[8] which appeared on the masthead of his newspaper, *L'Ordine Nuovo*. He meant that one should always look at the difficult truth, refuse illusion and yet still find the determination to fight for what one believes to be right and just. Contemporary activist Shaun Chamberlin coined the phrase 'dark optimism' for the way he feels, describing it as:

> "…a way of seeing life which is not afraid of seeking the truth – even when that truth is unpalatable or feels overwhelming. By exploring the unknown we can see it for what it is, rather than what we might fear it to be. Where there is darkness present we face it with an indomitable belief in the potential of humankind."[9]

Buddhist writers Joanna Macy and Chris Johnstone titled their book *Active Hope*,[10] expressing their view that hope is a practice or an act of doing rather than a belief or a state of mind. However you think of it, it is important to find some way of acknowledging the real difficulties we face and keeping realistic hope alive. These are some of the things people have told us about how they manage this:

- "I accept that this isn't something to think about all the time, I allow myself to compartmentalise it, put it somewhere manageable."
- "Spending time in nature helps me. It gives me a quite different perspective."
- "I surround myself with people who feel the same way as I do, so I have a sense of companionship and solidarity."
- "Seeing the creativity that goes into low-carbon technologies cheers and encourages me."
- "Humour helps – being able to laugh, not necessarily about climate change but about anything."
- "I treasure all the ordinary things of life, like a meal with friends, a family birthday or a sunny day."

Managing despair

Sometimes talking seems to bring you down. Sometimes you find yourself blaming good friends or winding up your family in the ways that only close relatives can. Sometimes you catch yourself in a punitive mood. You stamp on someone's naïve optimism. You're grudging about the good work someone has done. You demand the impossible from the people you love. Feelings of despair and impotence often lie behind such experiences. They can also indicate burn-out or at any rate the need for a break from campaigning and organising. It's essential to keep a sense of proportion. In a world where many do little and the few do a lot, it is easy to feel the weight of the future bearing heavily on you.

Try not to punish yourself or others. Look for the real sources of pleasure in life. This might be time spent with family, time spent outdoors or time spent on an old hobby or much loved pursuit. Remember that one reason for acting on climate change is to preserve what matters in life to you. If you are able to balance your commitment with a life that is fruitful in other ways you will not only have a better time yourself but be a better role model for others.

> **"** Perhaps the most important thing is to get people out of their comfort zone, tell them about carbon emissions, help them reflect on their own impact, and then encourage them not to focus on the grass they are stepping on, but on the forest they can make grow.
> **Euri Vidal**

Sources of support

Think about how you find support and whom you usually turn to. Think about whether your concerns about climate change can be shared as openly as you wish with the people you usually share your problems with. If no-one ever listens to you, appreciates you or gives you support in your attempts to live appropriately with climate change you will find life difficult. If support doesn't exist amongst your immediate circle, then start looking more widely. Think of joining a group who are actively working on some aspect of climate change. Try attending meetings or lectures on the subject. Look for online discussion groups. There's someone out there who will appreciate your support and can offer the same to you!

Lessons from cognitive approaches

So far we have concentrated on the emotional experience of talking about climate change and the way it affects our relationships with people we care about or work with. A lot of research has been done on the more cognitive and behavioural aspects of people's responses to climate change. These approaches concentrate on people's ideas, attitudes and behaviour, rather than on their emotions, relationships and social connections. Most of this work is aimed at understanding how big communication campaigns should approach the issue, but you may find some of it useful at the smaller scale of family, friends and colleagues as well. Which appeals make people sit up and think? What approaches make them change their behaviour? Does the language we use make a difference? Should we appeal to people's self-interest or to their deeper values? Do different sections of the population respond in different ways? You will find pointers to some of this work in the More Information section but here we summarise the conclusions we have drawn from our readings of it.

Information is not enough
As we mentioned earlier, people screen out information they think doesn't apply to them. Don't lecture people or thrust leaflets in their hands. Try to create a setting where people can be interested and are willing to listen. Beware also of the paradox where some people confuse having accepted a fact as true with doing something about it. It is easy to feel that if you are concerned about something you have also done something.[11]

People make snap judgments
Most people try to fit new facts to their existing views rather than altering their views because of new information. We use rules of thumb and gut feelings to help us make up our minds. This means that it will help to think about how the facts of climate change fit with someone's existing attitudes. If you're talking to a business audience you are more likely to get a hearing if you dress in a way that accords with their expectations of a serious speaker and present your arguments in frameworks they are used to. The same goes for any other audience too. Craft your presentation so that it appeals to the particular people you are talking to.[12]

Trusted messengers
'Trusted messengers' are more likely to get a hearing. People are more likely to listen to people who are already trusted leaders in their communities. Trade unionists are more likely to pay attention to a trade union leader, church members to their priest, university students to a fellow student and so on.[13]

Adapt to your audience
Tailoring what you say to your audience helps. Not everyone responds to the same type of message. Speaking the language of your audience and framing what you say in terms that interest them will help. There are a lot of different ways of dividing up the population from theories that focus on class or cultural identity to approaches such as social marketing, that work out how to sell carbon reduction to different audience segments.[14]

Climate change feels distant
It's easy for climate change to feel distant and unconnected to ordinary life. Most people's time horizons don't extend much beyond the next few years and they find it hard to be concerned about events that may be 30 years in the future. It can be just as hard to feel concerned for long about people you will never meet in places you have never seen.[15] Try to make connections to people's actual experiences. Gardeners and outdoor types may be aware of weather patterns changing. People with relatives overseas may know a lot about droughts, floods and storms in other countries. Parents may be thoughtful about their children's future.

The value-action gap
There are always gaps between people's values and their actions or between their attitudes and their behaviour.[16] We are all creatures of conflict and our best intentions often come to naught in the face of our own desires and social systems that make it hard for individuals to change on their own. You'll do yourself no favours by gleefully pointing out someone else's inconsistencies. Try to explore the conflicts people experience. Open up a conversation about the difficulties.

Money-saving appeals are counter-productive
Money-saving appeals and appeals to self-interest don't work in the long-term. You may get some short-term gains by telling people that carbon reduction saves money. The trouble is that many of the actions people need to take will cost money or demand a serious change in their lifestyle. If people are encouraged to act solely from self-interest, many people will not consider the deeper changes that are needed.[17]

Values matter
Strengthening people's intrinsic values such as their concern for others and for 'bigger than self' issues, their care for nature and their desires for fairness will help create the climate for social action and political change that is needed.[18]

Small steps don't automatically lead to big ones
People hope that there is a virtuous escalator that will carry you from small steps to big ones. There isn't.[19] If all you ask of someone is a small step they will often do as requested but feel virtuous and stop right there. You need to frame the small step as the first on a big journey.

Framing matters
Frames are unconscious structures in our minds – bundles of words, thoughts and feelings – that shape how we see the world. The way an issue is framed will dictate how we see it. If climate change is framed as an environmental issue it will be seen as a minority concern. If wind turbines can be framed as eyesores the public will easily reject them. If action on climate change is seen as 'helping the environment' it will be seen as optional. Changing the way an issue is framed can be difficult but it is worth thinking carefully about how language can make you fall into unexpected traps.[20]

Frightening people doesn't help
Stories of disaster make people shut down. Although their interest is raised in the short term, so is their anxiety and they quickly put their defences back in place. Sometimes the response to fear is to ignore the subject altogether but fear can also lead people to pursue illusory solutions.[21]

Speaking personally helps
The story of your journey may inspire others. Understanding your motivation may help others share your concerns. Speaking from the heart is more appealing than a list of numbers or a screen full of graphs.[22]

Use stories
Stories, practical examples and a positive message all help.[23] People like to be entertained. We learn through stories and examples as much as through facts and figures. Stories make the dry facts personal and help people identify with an issue. A story doesn't have to be long – some of the best stories are over in a couple of sentences. Practical examples can inspire, make the issue concrete and graspable, and help people see that there is something positive that they can do. Although your overall message may be serious, people also need to feel a sense of realistic hope.

Rules of thumb

Listen
Empathise, accept, offer support, don't judge.

Speak from the heart
Express what you feel, notice your own responses, reflect.

Understand ambivalence
Accept that we all have mixed feelings and struggle with our inner conflicts.

Roll with the resistance
Focus on feelings and find a new angle if you hit a brick wall.

Don't expect instant change
Work through the complex feelings so that change becomes permanent.

Nourish your creativity
Take care of yourself and seek support.

Frequently asked questions

Other people aren't empathic towards me, why should I empathise with them?

It's tough if others are always cold or critical. It's possible that they are being defensive. They may be protecting themselves from feeling exposed. They may be scapegoating you. Recognise the resistance and back off for a time. Remember that you don't have to like everyone and that not everyone will deserve your best empathic response!

When I try to understand other people's points of view, they assume I'm agreeing with them. Surely we need to argue our case?

There's a difference between being a doormat, having a pointless, angry argument and enjoying an assertive exchange of views. Sometimes when people are struggling to avoid an unpleasant row they back down and end up feeling like the doormat. There will be times when you want to make it clear that although you've been interested to hear what someone else thinks, you wish to disagree. Before reaching that point it can be helpful to explore with the other person why they think what they do, what has influenced them and how they have arrived at their point of view.

Surely people need to know that we're facing catastrophe?

It's true that there are many worrying and depressing aspects of the future we face. However a morbid fascination with disaster doesn't help if you are trying to get persuade others. Sometimes people are attracted to ideas of catastrophe because they are frightened themselves: passing that fear onto others is a way of trying to deal with the fear. Sometimes people are so angry at what is happening to the world that catastrophe feels like a just punishment: frightening others with the possibility of disaster becomes a form of revenge. Ask yourself why you are attracted to the idea of disaster. Research tells us that these stories don't lead to engagement and that there are better ways of trying to involve people.[24]

Information changed my mind. Why do you say it doesn't change other people's?

All of us forget the times when information passed us by or we dismissed it as irrelevant. We don't remember the occasions when we got up to make the tea when climate change came on the news or picked up a leaflet and put it straight in the bin. The information only made sense to you at a point when you were ready to absorb it. Think about what created that moment for you. Information is important only when people are ready for it.

Most of my difficult conversations just arrive. I feel I don't have much control over them. What do you suggest?

Try to balance these occasions with ones that you create yourself. If you'd like to talk to someone about climate change, think about making the time and space to do so on your own terms. Decide what would be a realistic outcome for you. Prepare what you want to say. Think what you would like to hear about from the other person. Listen well. Keep the first conversation short unless they clearly want to continue. Meanwhile, have some prepared responses for those difficult times when you've been ambushed. Some people find they can use humour to deflect the conversation. Some turn attention to the tactics of the other person, for example, "You love to wind me up, don't you?" This sometimes has the effect of disarming the other person and allowing a change of subject. Some people risk a direct challenge such as, "I think you're using this to get at me about other things you're cross about." Work out how to withdraw from conversations that don't seem to be going anywhere.

Don't we just need to get on with things instead of talking all the time?

We need to do both. Not enough people – only 14.5% – are 'getting on with things'.[25] Most are avoiding any real engagement. You may be surprised to find how many people share your concerns but feel too powerless, hopeless or disillusioned to do anything. Talking with them about how they feel is often the first step towards action.

Don't we need more good news stories?

We need to distinguish between realistic, inspiring examples and illusory, utopian daydreams. We certainly need the former and we hope we've put plenty of examples in the stories throughout this book. Think critically about the value of the good news stories and projects you hear about. Are they genuinely good examples or greenwash? Real solutions or daydreams? Widely applicable or minority pursuits? Grab the former and talk about them wherever you can.

People ignore me to my face, then three months later I find them lecturing me on the urgency of climate change or the benefits of home insulation. What's going on?

Most people don't change overnight. You have probably been part of a gradual process in which your friends shifted their attitudes. Many people find it humiliating to admit that someone else helped to change their mind. Most people like to think that they have arrived at their point of view independently. Be flattered. Treat their change of view with good nature and humour.

I volunteered to be Green Champion in my workplace but people either ignore me or delight in winding me up. What can I do?

This tends to happen when there is not proper support for the Green Champion scheme. Sometimes it has been introduced as a piece of greenwash. Sometimes there have been good intentions but not enough thought given to what is involved. Are you given enough time for these responsibilities? Is there sufficient support from senior management? Has a budget been allocated for the changes that are needed? If your answer to these questions is 'no', think about who you can talk to about changes to the scheme that might be needed.

Shouldn't we be teaching children? It's their future and they're the ones who will have to make the big changes.

Each generation seems to hope that the next one will solve the problems they have failed to address. It's easy to get primary school kids to identify with endangered species and help with the recycling but this rarely lasts into their teenage years. It's also very easy to make children feel anxious about an issue like climate change. Children have very little power or control. They can't dictate where they go on holiday, what they eat, how their homes are heated or what fashions will make them feel acceptable to their friends. Even more than adults, children need to feel safe if you are addressing a difficult subject like climate change. Most talks given to schools take little account of this and children can end up feeling alarmed and fearful. A more positive approach is to develop children's interest in the natural world and offer them plenty of enjoyable experiences that can act as an antidote to our high consumption culture and give them the skills to deal with an uncertain future. Research suggests that people who spent time playing freely outdoors as children tend to have a deeper sense of connection to the natural world and more pro-environmental attitudes.[26]

Don't we need a spiritual re-engagement with the natural world?

Some writers on eco-psychology emphasise the idea of spiritual re-engagement with nature.[27] Spiritual connections are important for some people but not for everyone. The major faiths all have views on the relationship of people to the natural world and people with religious faith frequently find support through their religious practices. For other people spirituality and religion are turn-offs. Do what feels right for you but don't try to impose your spiritual or religious beliefs on others – it's unlikely to help.

Climate change spells d-i-v-o-r-c-e in my household. How do I stay true to my values and save my marriage too?

It sounds like you are struggling with a number of difficult conversations. This may not be the best time to add climate change to the list of flashpoints. Look at how to improve communication with your partner in general – much of the advice we give earlier in this chapter can apply to other conversations as well. If things are looking really bad, try making an appointment with Relate, the family counselling charity. Come back to climate change issues once you are both feeling better about the relationship.

I've persuaded people that this is a serious issue but I don't have the technical expertise to tell them what to do next. What do you suggest?

If you haven't taken part in a Carbon Conversations group, try to organise one by looking on the Carbon Conversations website or contacting The Surefoot Effect who run the programme. If you have taken part in a Carbon Conversations group, think about training as a facilitator and helping to run a group. This will give you the confidence you lack. You will be paired with someone who can support you with complementary skills.

More information

This section lists a small number of books and websites with good, accessible information that will help you fill in the background and follow up facts you are not clear on. You will find more detailed sources and a wider selection of reading in the Notes.

I'd like to know more about…

…climate change and psychology

The *Climate Psychology Alliance*, http://www.climatepsychologyalliance.org/, and *Psychology for a Safe Climate*, http://psychologyforasafeclimate.org/, carry a good selection of articles and resources on a variety of psychological approaches to climate change.

Rosemary Randall's blog, http://rorandall.org/, carries regular short pieces with a psychosocial approach to climate change.

…cognitive and behavioural approaches

Don't Even Think About It: Why Our Brains are Wired to Ignore Climate Change, George Marshall, Bloomsbury, 2014, is a lively, enjoyable, informative read which knits together many diverse approaches.

Talking Climate carries regular updates about research on communication, behaviour change and social psychology, http://talkingclimate.org/.

Creating a Climate for Change: Communicating Climate Change and Facilitating Social Change, Susanne C. Moser and Lisa Dilling, Cambridge University Press, 2007, is a good, academic introduction.

…communication and listening skills

Listening to the Other: a New Approach to Listening Skills, Caroline Brazier, O Books, 2009 is a good introduction.

Online, try *Active Listening*, Kathryn Roberston, 2005, http://bit.ly/Robertson-2005.

…denial and disavowal

Living in Denial: Climate Change, Emotions and Everyday Life, Kari Norgaard, MIT Press, Cambridge MA, 2011, describes how denial operates in a community through shared assumptions and conventions.

Engaging with Climate Change: Psychoanalytic and Interdisciplinary Perspectives, edited Sally Weintrobe, Routledge, London, 2013 contains a number of articles discussing these concepts.

States of Denial: Knowing about Atrocities and Suffering, Stanley Cohen, Polity Press, 2011, is the classic sociological text on the subject.

…ecopsychology

Vital Signs: Psychological Responses to Ecological Crisis, edited Mary-Jayne Rust and Nick Totton, Karnac, 2012, is a collection of essays mainly from an ecopsychological viewpoint.

Ecopsychology UK brings people together around this approach, http://www.ecopsychology.org.uk/.

...family relationships
The New Peoplemaking, Virginia Satir, Science and Behaviour Books, Palo Alto, 1989.

Families and How to Survive Them, John Cleese and Robin Skynner, Cedar Books, London, 1993.

*They F*** you up: How to Survive Family Life*, Oliver James, Bloomsbury Books, 2006.

...loss and grief
'Loss and Climate Change: the Cost of Parallel Narratives', Rosemary Randall, *Ecopsychology*, September 2009, 1(3): 118-129, http://rorandall.org/publications/.

Grief Counselling and Grief Therapy, J. William Worden, Routledge, (2nd edition) 1991.

...psychosocial approaches
Psychosocial Contributions to Climate Sciences Communications Research and Practice, Renee Lertzman, 2014, http://bit.ly/Lertzman-2014, is a good introduction.

A New Climate for Psychotherapy, Rosemary Randall, *Psychotherapy and Politics International* 3 (3): 165-179, http://rorandall.org/publications/, takes this approach.

Politics, Identity and Emotion, Paul Hogget, Paradigm Publishers, 2009, is a wide-ranging example of this approach.

...what happens at work
Understanding Organisations, Charles Handy, Penguin, London, 1993 (4th edition) is a good introduction to the dynamics of the workplace.

NCVO's guides on working with people will improve your skills, http://bit.ly/NCVO-guide.

...values based approaches
Common Cause, http://valuesandframes.org/, is the gateway to organisations working from a values and frames perspective, and to the research that backs up this approach.

CHAPTER 7

Moving on

"What helped me act on climate change? Realising I wasn't alone, seeing I didn't have to do it all at once, planning to act with friends."

Some people will have read this book as part of a Carbon Conversations group. Others will have read it alone. In either case you may be wondering what to do next. Is reading a book or taking part in a group the end of the story? We hope that you will feel inspired to continue exploring carbon reduction in your own way, but overleaf we suggest some possible routes to follow.

Personal plans

At the start of this book we were clear that individuals cannot solve the problems of climate change on their own. Governments need to make international agreements, put the right policies in place and regulate for change. Industry needs to deliver new technologies and systems. Nonetheless there is much that individuals can do. We think that most people with an average or above average carbon footprint can halve it without much difficulty. People whose footprint is already below average should be able to bring theirs down to about half the national average. These are challenging targets but we have found that people who take part in Carbon Conversations groups make reductions of about three tonnes almost immediately.[1] Here are some factors that may help you pursue the goal of halving your footprint.

Think long-term

Think about where you would like to be in five or ten years' time. How might you get there? How does carbon reduction fit with other long-term goals? Look for opportunities (such as a new job or a house move) that will offer you the chance to make big reductions in your CO_2 emissions. A written plan will help you make steady reductions year by year. If you start with an average 15 tonne footprint and reduce your emissions by 1.5 tonnes per year, you will reach the target in five years' time.

Monitor your footprint

Signing up to the *Carbon Account* or *iMeasure* websites[2] will help you keep track of your home energy and travel emissions. Taking part in a Carbon Conversations group will give you tools and activities for measuring your food and consumption footprints. It's only when you monitor your emissions that you can really see the difference you are making.

Keep climate change front of mind

Think of climate change and carbon reduction whenever you have a decision to take – large or small. Whether you're buying a bunch of flowers, choosing a restaurant, or taking decisions about work or holidays, try to work out the carbon implications. If there's a choice, go for the low-carbon option.

Remember relationships

Be realistic about your relationships with others. Be aware that your interest in carbon reduction can easily be pulled into other conflicts in your relationships, whether these are with friends, family or colleagues. Try to work with other people. Think about how to bring them with you but don't feel responsible for their decisions.

Be savvy about systems

It's easy to do things the conventional way: jump in the car, buy a new outfit, grab a ready-meal. Modern clothes are designed for warm houses and frequent washing. Transport systems are

> ❝ I started facilitating Carbon Conversations because I wanted to meet other people who had the same concerns and I strongly believe that knowledge sharing is more effective in small discussion groups. Not only do we learn from each other but it creates a strong support system for facing the difficulties.
>
> **Gomathy Sethuraman**

designed around the car. Work demands long hours that offer little time to cook or relax. We are all involved in complex systems that have high carbon impacts but which make life work smoothly, as long as we play the game. As you try to reduce your carbon footprint you will need to find other ways of working with these bigger systems. Sometimes this will be straightforward, but at other times you will come up against obstacles that you can't shift. Don't take this as a signal to give up. There may be more options than you are aware of. Talking and working with others may help you find them. It is also useful to think about the policy and technology changes that would make a low-carbon lifestyle the easy option. Can you add your voice to demands for change?

Face the feelings

Be aware that climate change is a complex issue emotionally. It is easy to feel discouraged, particularly when government and industry seem to be paralysed, inactive or obstructive. It is also challenging to make some of the personal changes needed. Some of the choices may feel painful or unfair. However positive you mean to be, it is common to have days when you:

- block out the existence of climate change;
- long for someone else to take responsibility;
- deny (in words or behaviour) that you can do anything;
- feel like partying towards oblivion.

It can help to:

- acknowledge that there are losses as well as gains in low-carbon living, and mourn the experiences you are saying goodbye to;
- treat yourself well – a low-carbon life shouldn't be about guilt and deprivation but about smarter choices and new pleasures;
- reach out for support and comfort from others who are on the same journey;
- celebrate the changes you have achieved.

Stay connected

It is hard to stay engaged with climate change on your own, particularly if colleagues, family or friends are dismissive, uninterested or even hostile. Seek out others who feel the same way as you, and support each other.

Stay creative

Remember that everyone's solutions will be different. Checklists and advice can only take you so far. Your best plans will be integrated with your values and personal to you. Be creative and share your good ideas with others.

Communicate

See yourself as someone who can help others change. Talk to family, friends and colleagues. You are more likely to encourage and inspire others (and less likely to find yourself labelled as a nag or a misery) if you:

> *Having taken part in a Carbon Conversations group, I could see how powerful the process was and I wanted to learn how to harness that power myself. As a facilitator I've loved seeing how the people in groups gain strength from talking about their feelings.*
> **Rebecca Nestor**

- listen to people's dilemmas;
- empathise with their difficulties;
- speak personally and from the heart;
- appreciate each person's unique experiences and contributions;
- encourage, affirm and support others.

Be a role model

Demonstrate your beliefs through your actions. Make them look normal, enjoyable and easy. Arrive by bus, talk enthusiastically about your low-carbon holidays, serve a delicious seasonal meal, show off your newly acquired draught-stripping skills. Think about where you can show leadership on climate change and where you can find allies. You might be a leader in your team at work, in a faith or community group, a sports club or youth group, or just among friends or family. Everyone can be a leader somewhere. Allies are just as important. Spot the people who might support you: talk with them and work together.

Collective plans

Think about everything you can do with others.

Join or facilitate a Carbon Conversations group

If you haven't taken part in a Carbon Conversations group, think about joining one. If you have already taken part, think about becoming a facilitator. Carbon Conversations groups work on a cascade system. Once you have taken part, a short training course enables you to facilitate a group for others. You may have friends you would like to draw in. You might be able to start a group at work, or in a community or faith group to which you belong. Facilitators work in pairs and receive regular support during the first groups they run – ask your group facilitators for details or contact Surefoot for details, info@surefoot-effect.com.

Groups, communities and networks

Many Carbon Conversations groups are run by community groups who offer other activities such as home energy surveys, Open Eco House days, shared car schemes or local food initiatives that will help you reduce your footprint. You'll find groups with names like Aberdeen Forward, Low-Carbon Oxford North and Steady State Manchester, as well as numerous groups like Transition Cardiff and Transition Stirling who operate under the Transition Towns banner.[3] If you would like to work with others, check if there is a group of people somewhere near you who are already doing something of interest. If there isn't, your Carbon Conversations group might be the start of one. Many other organisations have responded to the climate crisis by setting up a specialist

> ❝ At the heart of my work for the Labour Party is the same belief in justice and fairness which informs my work on climate change. I want to work politically on climate change with a party that can actually do something. I'm very proud of the 2008 Climate Change Act. I am disappointed by the national party's ambivalence on fracking, but my local party are actively campaigning against it. These are the compromises of working with the political mainstream.
>
> **Tony Wragg**

group or network for their members. For example, the union UNISON has a *Green UNISON network*, the *Islamic Foundation for Ecology and Environmental Science (IFEES)* connects Muslims concerned about climate change, and there are a number of Christian networks.[4]

Political action

Political action could mean supporting online campaigns, writing to your MP, joining a campaign group, taking part in direct action, or simply being careful how you vote.

The *They Work for You* website[5] will put you in touch with your MP and help you find your way around the parliamentary system. At national and local elections check out the party policy and the personal views of candidates about climate change and inequality. Let them know that these are major factors in how you vote. You may have a difficult choice, but by this stage in our book that shouldn't surprise you. You may have to decide whether or not to vote on principle for someone who stands little or no chance of election. You may have to draw a balance between climate change and equality on the one hand, and other values you hold strongly on the other. If you are already politically committed, you might want to lobby your own party about its climate change and equality policies. If you rarely, or never, voted in the past perhaps it's time to stand up and be counted? If you feel the parties are all the same, perhaps it is time to help them be different?

You can explore online action through the websites of *Avaaz*, *38 Degrees*, *Change* and *350.org*.[6] *Avaaz* and *350* are international groups. *Avaaz* deals with a range of political issues, including climate change. *350* combines grass-roots organising with online petitions and mass public actions aimed at reducing world emissions to 350 ppm CO_2 in the atmosphere. *38 Degrees* is a UK organisation, running a variety of online campaigns, including climate-related ones. *Change* is an international organisation but it encourages people to start their own petitions about local issues. All these sites have tips on letter writing and will help you craft an effective email.

The *Climate Coalition* is a national coalition of non-governmental organisations (NGOs) who are concerned and active in work on climate change.[7] It works with sister organisations *Stop Climate Chaos Scotland* and *Stop Climate Chaos Cymru*. Member organisations range from the *Royal Society for the Protection of Birds* to *Greenpeace*. Many of its national groups, such as *Friends of the Earth*, *Greenpeace* and the *World Development Movement*, have local branches you can get involved with.[8] *Friends of the Earth* and *Greenpeace* work on environmental issues. The *World Development Movement* campaigns against the root causes of poverty and inequality, including climate change. The *Campaign against Climate Change*[9] has a network of local groups and a number of national campaigns. Their current focus is on the creation of a million climate jobs.

> **❝** When I was first involved in climate change my focus was on the importance of personal carbon reduction. Climate Camp politicised it for me. I went on a political journey of realising that this problem can't be solved by only acting within the normal political process. That led me towards direct action, mainly against open cast coal mining. It feels to me that there is no other option, though it can be scary. You need good training and support to chain yourself to bulldozers and deal with the police.
>
> Alex Randall

Direct action groups make a political point by disrupting the work of the big climate polluters. Check out *Plane Stupid*, *Greenpeace*, *Climate Rush*, the *Climate Justice Collective*, *Coal Action*, *Coal Action Scotland* or *Frack-Off*, if you are interested in this.[10]

Action at work

Many people have the potential to influence others at work. You may be a business owner, be responsible for setting policy, be a trade union member or be able to volunteer as your department's Energy Champion. Help for business is available through the *Carbon Trust*.[11] Some trade unions have environmental networks (notably, *Green UNISON*).

A specially adapted version of Carbon Conversations can also be run for workplaces, and has proved extremely effective in both public and private sector settings. It can be used with staff at different levels to promote engagement with an organisation's existing environmental policies, develop confidence and understanding amongst staff who are new to environmental responsibilities, and help companies meet Corporate Social Responsibility goals. Contact Surefoot (the Community Interest Company that manages Carbon Conversations) if you are interested in this.

Conclusion

Whatever route you take in dealing with climate change we hope this book has helped you feel confident that your voice and your contribution matter, individually, collectively and politically. Psychologically, we all need to find the place that Al Gore once described as lying 'between denial and despair'.[12] We need to cope with the human tendency to split off, repress and ignore painful realities. We also need to avoid the black pit of despair that can come from facing the truth, but which leads to apathy, cynicism and defeat. This is not always easy, but we hope this book has encouraged you to think that it is possible and given you some tools for the task.

> ❝ I'm one of the environmental champions at work. I think it's really important to raise the conversation about climate change and sustainability. Doing this makes you feel less alone and less overwhelmed. Once you start talking, you find that people who you wouldn't have expected to be sympathetic are interested. You find that there are real opportunities to do things that make a difference. You build up support and start to change the culture.
>
> Katherine Simpson

Notes

A full bibliography can be found on the Carbon Conversations website.

Notes to Introduction

1. When this individualism took root is a matter of debate. Most recently, many people connect it to globalisation and the economic and political changes initiated by Margaret Thatcher in the 1980s which swept away the post-war consensus about collective provision and the positive role of the state. Sociologists like Zygmunt Bauman in his book *Liquid Modernity* (Polity Press 2000) or Anthony Giddens in *Modernity and Self-Identity* (Polity Press 1991) relate it to broad trends in the post-war world which removed old certainties about the relationship between individuals and society. Others, for example eco-feminists like Carolyn Merchant in *Earthcare: Women and the Environment* (Routledge, 1996), go back further and relate it to what they see as the hubris of the scientific revolution, which underpinned industrialisation, and saw the earth as a resource to be exploited for human gain.
2. There are elements of experiential learning, deliberative dialogue, therapeutic group work and psycho-education in the thinking behind Carbon Conversations groups. For more information, see the *Facilitator's Guide to Running Carbon Conversations Groups*, Rosemary Randall, Surefoot, 2015.

Notes to Chapter One

1. Margaret Thatcher put climate change on the UK agenda with a speech to the Royal Society in 1988. 21 years later the 2009 COP talks at Copenhagen, which many had hoped would finalise an international agreement, ended in disarray. See the Margaret Thatcher Foundation's website for her speech, http://bit.ly/Thatcher-1988.
2. A YouGov poll in 2013 found that 39% of the UK population thought that the world is becoming warmer as a result of human activity, http://bit.ly/YouGovCC-2013. A DECC Tracker survey the same year found that 66% of people were concerned about climate change, *Public Attitudes Tracker – Wave 5 Summary of Key Findings*, DECC 2013, http://bit.ly/DECC-2013.
3. The facts about climate change in this section are taken from the IPCC's 5th Assessment reports, *Climate Change 2013: the Physical Science Basis: Summary for Policy Makers*, http://bit.ly/IPCC-2013, and from *Real Climate*, http://www.realclimate.org/. A good introduction to the science can be found in *The No-Nonsense Guide to Climate Change*, Danny Chivers, New Internationalist Publications, 2011. *Weather Reports from the Future*, a series of short videos from the World Meteorological Organisation gives a graphic picture of what the weather may be like in 2050, http://bit.ly/wmo-2014.
4. In general in this book we refer to CO_2 but use CO_2e when other greenhouse gases are also involved.
5. Temperature data: HADCRUTv3, http://bit.ly/hadcrut3; 'Uncertainty Estimates in Regional and Global Observed Temperature Changes: a New Dataset from 1850.' P. Brohan et al, *Journal of Geophysical Research* 111, D12106, 2006. CO_2 data: Mauna Loa (1959-2009), http://bit.ly/maunaL; Law Dome Ice Core, http://bit.ly/icecore.
6. For details of an 8% target and how it could be achieved, see the *Radical Emissions Reduction Conference Abstracts*, Tyndall Centre for Climate Change Research, 2013, http://bit.ly/tyndallreduct.
7. 'Planetary Boundaries: Exploring the Safe Operating Space for Humanity,' J.W. Rockstrom et al, *Ecology and Society* 14(2): 32, 2009, http://bit.ly/Rockstrom-2009.
8. *A Safe and Just Space for Humanity: Can we Live within the Doughnut?* Kate Raworth, Oxfam, 2012, http://bit.ly/Raworth-2012, and Kate Raworth's website, www.kateraworth.com.
9. *Public Perceptions of Climate Change and Energy Futures in Britain*, Alexa Spence et al, Ipsos-Mori, 2010, http://bit.ly/spence-CC-2010, and *Public Perceptions of Climate Change in Wales*, S.B. Capstick et al, Climate Change Consortium of Wales, Cardiff, 2013, http://bit.ly/capstick-2013.

10. See *Energy Use in the New Millennium: Trends in IEA Countries*, International Energy Agency, 2007, http://bit.ly/iea-energyuse.
11. Information about conflict minerals: *Raise Hope for Congo*, http://bit.ly/congo-minerals. Information about the cotton industry and the drying of the Aral Sea: *Environmental Justice Foundation*, http://bit.ly/EJF-Cotton-Water. This article from the *Independent* provides a brief account of China's air pollution problems, http://bit.ly/Independent-China.
12. 'A New Climate for Psychotherapy', Rosemary Randall, *Psychotherapy and Politics International*, Issue 3:3, John Wiley 2005, http://bit.ly/randall-2005, and 'The Difficult Problem of Anxiety', Sally Weintrobe in *Engaging with Climate Change: Psychoanalytic and Interdisciplinary Perspectives*, edited by Sally Weintrobe, Routledge, 2013.
13. The differences depend on how you calculate imports and exports and whether land-use, deforestation and other greenhouse gases are included or not. There is a good discussion of the issues in *How Bad are Bananas? The Carbon Footprint of Everything*, Mike Berners-Lee, Profile books, 2010. Figures for individual countries are published by the US Energy Information Administration: http://bit.ly/eia-energystats, and you will find a brief, readable discussion of the issues about imports in *Carbon Emission Accounting – Balancing the Books for the UK*, UKERC Energy Insight Briefing Paper, 2012, http://bit.ly/ukerc-2012.
14. These issues are discussed in *Environment: Treading Lightly on the Earth*, a free module from the Open University, 2010, http://bit.ly/open-environment.
15. Figures derived from Peter Harper's work. Full details of his 'Carbon Fingerprint' approach can be found at http://peterharper.org.
16. *Techno-Fixes: a Critical Guide to Climate Change Technologies*, Corporate Watch, 2008, http://bit.ly/corporate-tech, remains a good introduction to the technologies and their political implications. *Earthmasters: the Dawn of the Age of Climate Engineering*, Clive Hamilton, Yale University Press, 2013, focuses specifically on the problems of geo-engineering. For a defence of the 'technology will save us' argument, see *The God Species: How the Planet can Survive the Age of Humans*, Mark Lynas, Fourth Esate, 2011.
17. See pp 157-9 in *Heat: How we can Stop the Planet Burning*, George Monbiot, Penguin Books, 2007 and *Fuelling Hunger*, a 2013 report from Action Aid, http://bit.ly/actionaid-hunger. The problems created by using biofuels in power stations are well explained in a Guardian article *The Campaign Against Drax Aims to Reveal the Perverse Effects of Biofuels*, Charles Eisenstein, The Guardian, April 2014, http://bit.ly/eisenstein-2014.
18. The various policy options are well described and discussed in *Kyoto 2: How to Manage the Global Greenhouse*, Oliver Tickell, Zed Books, 2008.
19. *A Green New Deal*, Andrew Simms et al, New Economics Foundation, 2008.
20. *Climate Change 2013 the Physical Science Basis: Summary for Policy Makers*, IPCC 2013, http://bit.ly/CC2013-summary.
21. Aubrey Meyer's idea of 'Contraction and Convergence' describes how countries could gradually arrive at a fair allocation of carbon emissions: *Contraction and Convergence: the Global Solution to Climate Change*, Aubrey Meyer, Green Books, 2001.
22. See the critical report from Sandbag who are supporters of carbon trading: *Drifting towards Disaster: the ETS Adrift in Europe's Climate Efforts*, Damien Morris, Sandbag 2013, http://bit.ly/sandbag-disaster.
23. *Energy and the Common Purpose: Descending the Energy Staircase with Tradable Energy Quotas*, David Fleming, The Lean Economy Connection, 2007, http://www.teqs.net/ and *A Persuasive Climate: Personal Trading and Changing Lifestyles*, Matt Prescott, RSA, 2008, http://bit.ly/prescott-2008.
24. This idea is promoted by schemes like TEEB (The Economics of Eco-systems and Biodiversity), http://www.teebweb.org/, and REDD (Reducing Emissions from Deforestation and forest Degradation), the UN's controversial scheme to reward forest owners in the Global South for not cutting their forests down. Closer to home there is a good discussion of the issues in *Placing a Monetary Value on Ecosystem Services*, Chartered Institution of Water and Environment Management, 2012, http://bit.ly/value-ecosystem.

25. *Mapping Rebound Effects from Sustainable Behaviours: Key Concepts and Literature Review*, Steve Sorrell, Sustainable Lifestyles Research Group Working Paper 01-10, 2012, and *The Burning Question*, Mike Berners-Lee and Duncan Clark, Profile Books, 2013.
26. The idea that economic growth could continue forever in a world of finite resources was challenged in *Steady State Economics* by Herman Daly, Earthscan, 1977, and has since been developed by many other people, including the New Economics Foundation whose website is a good source of information about the writers and thinkers in this field. http://www.neweconomics.org/our-work. See also Naomi Klein's book *This Changes Everything*, Allen Lane, 2014, which offers an impassioned and convincing argument for de-growth and major political change.
27. *A Safe and Just Space for Humanity: Can we Live within the Doughnut?* Kate Raworth, op cit.
28. *The Genuine Progress Indicator 2006: A Tool for Sustainable Development*, John Talberth et al, Redefining Progress, 2006, http://bit.ly/Talberth-2006, and 'Beyond GDP: Measuring and achieving global genuine progress', Ida Kubiszewski et al, *Ecological Economics* 93 57-68, 2013, http://bit.ly/Kubiszewski-2013.
29. *The Song of the Earth*, Jonathan Bate, Picador, 2000 for a discussion of our longing to live in harmony with nature, explored through poetry and literature.
30. Simple, user-friendly version of DECC's *2050 Pathways Project* calculator: http://my2050.decc.gov.uk/. Explanations and full version: http://bit.ly/2050-guide.
31. *Zero Carbon Britain: Rethinking the Future*, the Centre for Alternative Technology, 2014, http://www.zerocarbonbritain.com/.
32. *Climate Futures: Responses to Climate Change in 2030*, Forum for the Future, 2008, http://bit.ly/CC-Futures.
33. *The Radical Emission Reduction Conference Abstracts*, Tyndall Centre, 2013, http://bit.ly/tyndallreduct.
34. *Living in a Low-Carbon Society in 2050*, ed. Horace Herring, Palgrave Macmillan, 2012.
35. Although the Montreal Protocol successfully outlawed CFCs and restricted HCFCs and HFCs on the basis of their Ozone Depletion Potential these also have a Global Warming Potential and even the 2007 revision of the Montreal Convention is not stringent enough from a climate change perspective. *The Benefits of Basing Policies on the 20-year GWP of HFCs*, J. Maté et al Greenpeace International, 2011, http://bit.ly/Mate-2011.
36. If you love numbers and want to know how the footprints of individual items are calculated, see *How Bad are Bananas?* Mike Berners-Lee, op. cit. and *Time to Eat the Dog? The Real Guide to Sustainable Living*, Robert and Brenda Vale, Thames and Hudson, 2009.
37. *Climate Change 2013 the Physical Science Basis: Summary for Policy Makers*, IPCC 2013, http://bit.ly/CC2013-summary.
38. 'Tropical Cyclones and Climate Change', Thomas R. Knutson et al, *Nature Geoscience*, 3, 157-163, 2010, http://bit.ly/knutson_2010.
39. *Global Warming may have Fuelled Somali Drought*, Jason Straziuso, Phys.Org, 2010, http://bit.ly/Straziuso-2010.
40. 'Growth in emission transfers via international trade from 1990 to 2008', Glen Peters et al, Proceedings of the National Academy of Sciences of the USA, Vol. 108, No.21, 2011, http://bit.ly/peterstrade-2011. Summary of the paper: http://bit.ly/guardian-trade.
41. *US National Climate Assessment*, http://bit.ly/whitehouse-cc.
42. *Sharing Nature's Interest: Ecological Footprints as an Indicator of Sustainability*, Nicky Chambers et al, Earthscan, 2000.
43. *The Burning Question*, Mike Berners-Lee and Duncan Clark, Profile Books, 2013, p. 32.
44. *A Safe and Just Space for Humanity: Can We Live within the Doughnut?* op cit.
45. *Myth Buster*, the UK Climate Change and Migration Coalition, COIN 2013, http://bit.ly/COIN-2013.
46. United Nations Population Fund, http://bit.ly/1p8EVlA, or Hans Rosling's TED Talk, http://bit.ly/TED-Rosling.

47. *Web of Power: the UK Government and the Energy-Finance Complex Fuelling Climate Change*, World Development Movement, 2013; *Dealing in Doubt: The Climate Denial Machine vs Climate Science*, Greenpeace, 2013, http://bit.ly/Greenpeace-2013; *Merchants of Doubt*, Naomi Oreskes and Erik M. Conway, Bloomsbury, 2010.

Notes to Chapter Two

1. In *Energy Consumption in the UK 2013*, the Department of Energy and Climate Change attribute 29% of UK energy consumption to the domestic sector. In reality the percentage is probably slightly less as the DECC figures do not include outsourced carbon (the embodied energy in imports other than fuels) in their total, http://bit.ly/govuk-consumption.
2. Our figures for home energy consumption come from a number of sources, including the DECC report cited above, research by Peter Harper (peterharper.org) and the reports from the Environmental Change Institute cited below. The figure for an average house is sometimes given as 5 tonnes. Some of the lower-consuming houses that affect the average are actually in fuel poverty, so the average consumption per household would be greater if these households were able to heat their homes properly. There are also differing opinions on the carbon intensity of electricity. We prefer to be pessimistic and have taken the higher rather than the lower figures for the existing emissions of a typical UK house. In actuality of course, homes show a huge range of emissions depending on factors like size, occupancy, location and the weather that year.
3. *Home Truths: A Low-Carbon Strategy to Reduce UK Housing Emissions by 80% by 2050*, Brenda Boardman, Environmental Change Institute, 2007, http://bit.ly/Boardman-2007. *Achieving Zero: Delivering Future-Friendly Buildings*, Brenda Boardman, Environmental Change Institute, 2012, http://bit.ly/boardman-2012.
4. In 2008 the Government published the *Code for Sustainable Homes* which laid out the environmental standards new homes should be built to. In 2014, the coalition government reviewed and weakened these standards and postponed the introduction of zero-carbon houses. *Code for Sustainable Homes*: www.planningportal.gov.uk.
5. Energy Performance Certificates rate buildings from A to G for their energy efficiency. They have to be issued whenever a property changes hands. From 2018 it will be unlawful to rent a house with the worst ratings (F and G). Some university lettings schemes and local authorities already impose this standard. See the Government's *Aide-Memoire*, http://bit.ly/energy-2011.
6. *Comfort, Cleanliness and Convenience*, Elizabeth Shove, Berg, 2003.
7. *Families and Households 2012*, Office of National Statistics, 2013, http://bit.ly/national-stats.
8. EPC register, https://www.epcregister.com/. The adviser page allows you to enter your EPC number and get advice about suitable upgrades, and the FAQs deal with common questions.
9. *Understanding Home Owners' Renovation Decisions: Findings of the VERD project*, Charlie Wilson et al, UKERC, 2013, http://bit.ly/Wilson-2013.
10. *The Effectiveness of Feedback on Energy Consumption: a Review for DEFRA of the Literature on Metering, Billing and Direct Displays*, Sarah Darby, Environmental Change Institute, 2006, http://bit.ly/darby-2006.
11. Information about the Green Deal and ECO: *Energy Saving Trust*, http://bit.ly/est-grants. Information about the Scottish Green Homes Cashback scheme: *Scottish Energy Saving Trust*, http://bit.ly/est-cashback.
12. The AECB promotes sustainable construction, particularly for small builders and designers, and offers an online database of members and services. They also publish a set of standards for environmental construction (CarbonLite) and promote the Passivhaus standard, http://www.aecb.net/, and http://www.carbonlite.org.uk.
13. PassivHaus buildings provide high levels of comfort with very low energy use. There are different schemes for new-build and retrofitted buildings. The PassivHaus Trust provides training in its exacting standards, http://www.passivhaustrust.org.uk/.

14. See *Fuel Poverty*, Department for Energy and Climate Change, updated August 2013, http://bit.ly/govuk-fuelpoverty, and *The Scottish House Condition Survey*, Scottish Government, 2013, http://bit.ly/govscot-housesurvey. Figures for Wales: http://bit.ly/govwales-fuelpoverty. For discussion of the issues, *Fixing Fuel Poverty: Challenges and Solutions*, Brenda Boardman, Earthscan, 2010.
15. 'Turning Lights into Flights Estimating Direct and Indirect Rebound Effects for UK Households', Mona Chitnis et al, *Energy Policy 55 (2013) 234–250*.
16. *Low Carbon Behaviour Change*, p 6, Carbon Trust, 2013, http://bit.ly/behaviour-2013.
17. The Government's Carbon Reduction Commitment Energy Efficiency Scheme applies to many large organisations and means they are taking active steps to reduce energy use. Many large buildings (those with a floor area over 500 square metres) will already be monitoring their energy as they have to display an Energy Performance Certificate (commercial buildings) or a Display Energy Certificate (public buildings) which rates them from A (good energy efficiency) to G (poor energy efficiency).

Notes to Chapter Three

1. The information in this section is taken from: *Social Trends 40 – Transport*, Office for National Statistics, 2010, http://bit.ly/trends40; *Transport Statistics Great Britain 2012*, Department of Transport, 2012, http://bit.ly/govuk-transport; *The National Travel Survey 2012*, Department of Transport, 2012, http://bit.ly/govuk-travel; *2011 Census Analysis – Method of Travel to Work in England and Wales Report*, ONS, 2012, http://bit.ly/census-travel; *The Car Dependency Scorecard 2012*, Campaign for Better Transport, 2013, http://bit.ly/bettertransport-car.
2. 2011 UK census, http://bit.ly/censusuk-2011.
3. 5.5 million British people live permanently overseas and another 500,000 live overseas some of the time, mainly through second home ownership. *Brits Abroad: Mapping the Scale of British Emigration*, Dhananjayn Sriskandarajah, and Catherine Drew, London, IPPR, 2006, http://bit.ly/Drew-2006.
4. *Commuting and Personal Well-being 2014*, Office of National Statistics, 2014, http://bit.ly/commuting-stats.
5. Although the EU has guidelines on sustainability and the use of biofuels, many people think that these do not go far enough. *Broken Biofuel Policies Still Driving Rainforest Destruction*, Greenpeace, 2010, http://bit.ly/greenpeace_biofuel.
6. For more discussion of the pros and cons of electric vehicles, *Sustainability without the Hot Air*, David Mackay, UIT, 2009, http://www.withouthotair.com/; *Zero Carbon Britain: Rethinking the Future*, Centre for Alternative Technology, 2013.
7. *Car Dependency Scorecard 2011*, Campaign for Better Transport, http://bit.ly/bettertrans-2011, and *Car Dependency Scorecard 2012* Campaign for Better Transport, http://bit.ly/bettertrans-2012.
8. 49% of cars on motorways exceed the 70 mph speed limit and 14% exceed it by more than 10 mph. *Transport Statistics Great Britain 2011*, Department of Transport, 2012, http://bit.ly/govtransport-2011. See also *Getting the Genie Back in the Bottle: Limiting Speed to Reduce Carbon Emissions and Accelerate the Shift to Low Carbon Vehicles*, Jillian Anable et al, UKERC and the Slower Speeds Initiative, 2006, http://bit.ly/Anable-2006.
9. *Car Sick: Solutions for Our Car-Addicted Culture*, Lynn Sloman, Green Books, 2006.
10. For a discussion of aviation policy, see *Aviation and Climate Change Policy in the UK*, Peter Lockley, Airport Watch, 2011, http://bit.ly/Lockley-2011.
11. Most of the figures in this table are taken from DEFRA's *Greenhouse Gas Conversion Factor Repository*, http://bit.ly/DEFRA-GHG. The figures for flights include radiative forcing at 1.9 and we have averaged DEFRA's figures for domestic and European flights to give one figure for short-haul flights. It is hard to find good figures for ferries and cruise liners. There is not a lot of good research and there are huge differences between different boats. A high-speed catamaran across the Irish Sea has much higher emissions than a slow ferry across the Mersey for example. Our figure for foot passengers is DEFRA's and is calculated based on the additional weight of foot passengers on a RO-RO ferry. We have assumed a similar figure for the few passengers who travel on cargo boats. Our figure for car passen-

gers is based on an analysis of Irish Ferries which gives 1.13 kg per car-km and we have assumed average car occupancy of three people: *A Study of the Carbon Footprint of Car-Transport with Irish Ferries*, Carbon Tracking Ltd, 2008, http://bit.ly/carbontrack-ferries. Our figure for cruise liners is the average from a New Zealand study which found a range from 250g to 2200g per passenger km: 'Carbon Emissions from International Cruise Ship Passengers' travel to and from New Zealand', O.J.A. Howitt et al, *Energy Policy*, 2010, http://bit.ly/Howitt-2010. The high figure for car passengers accounts for the weight of the car. Remember that ferry trips tend to be short and cruises long, so a cruise will always clock up high carbon emissions. For comparison, George Marshall in *Carbon Detox*, Hachette, 2007, calculated 700g per passenger-km for the Queen Elizabeth II, and gives a figure of 500g per passenger-km for fast ferries and 100g per passenger-km for slow ones.

12. Our imaginary future owes a lot to the analysis in *Zero Carbon Britain: Rethinking the Future*, Centre for Alternative Technology, 2013. The ideas about coach travel are Alan Storkey's and can be found in his 2005 paper *A Motorway Based National Coach System*, www.alanstorkey.com, and are also described in *Heat: How We Can Stop the Planet Burning*, George Monbiot, Penguin, 2006.
13. *Glasgow's Strategic Plan for Cycling 2010-2020*, Glasgow City Council, 2010, http://bit.ly/glasgow-cycle.
14. *The National Travel Survey 2012*, op cit.
15. 6000 miles of railway line were closed in the 1960s. 24,000 miles were added to the road system between 1985 and 1995, http://bit.ly/roads-uk.
16. Force-field analysis was developed by social theorist Kurt Lewin and is described in *Field Theory in Social Science*, Kurt Lewin, Harper and Row, 1951. It is widely used in organisations trying to manage change.
17. *Busting the 21 Days Habit Formation Myth*, Ben D. Gardner, University College London, 2011, http://bit.ly/Gardner-2011.
18. *Climate Change and Sustainable Consumption: What Do the Public Think is Fair?* Tim Horton and Natan Doron, Joseph Rowntree Foundation, 2011, http://bit.ly/horton-2011.
19. 'Missing Carbon Reductions? Exploring Rebound and Backfire Effects in UK Households', Angela Druckman et al 2011, *Energy Policy* 39, 3572–3581. See also *The Burning Question*, Mike Berners-Lee and Duncan Clark, Duncan, Profile Books, 2013.
20. http://bit.ly/southampton-travel.
21. Details of the Oxford policies, http://bit.ly/oxford-policy.
22. For an amusing view of offsetting view the short film *Cheat Neutral*, http://www.cheatneutral.com/.
23. *Transport Statistics Great Britain 2012*, Department of Transport, 2012, http://bit.ly/govuk-transport.
24. The report *Why Airport Expansion is Bad for Regional Economies*, Friends of the Earth, 2005 used government figures to show that foreign visitors arriving by air spent nearly £11 billion in the UK in 2004 but UK residents flying out spent £26 billion abroad – a loss to the UK economy of £15 billion pounds, http://bit.ly/foe-tourism.
25. *The Final Call: Investigating Who Really Pays for Our Holidays*, Leo Hickman, Guardian Books, 2008 and *The No-Nonsense Guide to Tourism*, Pamela Nowick, New Internationalist Publications Ltd, 2007.
26. *Briefing Paper*, Aviation Environment Federation, 2011, http://bit.ly/aef-2011, quoting figures from the Civil Aviation Authority's Passenger Surveys, and *Heat*, George Monbiot, Penguin, 2007, p.177, quoting a MORI poll.
27. *Quick Hits: Limiting Speed*, UKERC, 2006, describes how speed reductions could save significant amounts of carbon emissions, http://bit.ly/quickhit-2006.
28. *Controlled Motorways*, The Highways Agency, http://bit.ly/gov-speed, and *Fox Traffic Simulation* http://bit.ly/traffic-sim.
29. *Energy Consumption in the UK*, DECC, 2012, op cit.
30. *Shopping Trip or Home Delivery: Which Has the Smaller Carbon Footprint?* Alan McKinnon and Julia Edwards, Green Logistics, 2009, http://bit.ly/McKinnon-2009.
31. *Reported Road Casualties in Great Britain: 2011*, Department of Transport Annual Report, 2012, http://bit.ly/govuk-road, and *Safety in Numbers*, Cyclists Touring Campaign, http://bit.ly/ctc-safey.

Notes to Chapter Four

1. *Crop Production in a Changing Climate*, UNEP, 2006, http://bit.ly/unep-2006.
2. The IPCC estimates climate change will reduce average crop yields by between zero and two per cent per decade for the rest of the century, at the same time as demand increases by about 14 per cent per decade. *Climate Change 2014: Impacts, Adaptation and Vulnerability. Part A Global and Sectoral Aspects, Contribution of Working Group II to the Fifth Assessment Report of the Intergovernmental Panel on Climate Change*, Field et al, Cambridge University Press, 2014, http://bit.ly/Field-2014.
3. 'Dietary Greenhouse Gas Emissions of Meat-Eaters, Fish-Eaters, Vegetarians and Vegans in the UK', Peter Scarborough et al, *Climatic Change*, 125:179–192, 2014, http://bit.ly/Scarborough-2014.
4. Product Carbon Footprint Summary, Tesco, 2012, http://bit.ly/tesco-carbonprint.
5. The UK is 9% self-sufficient in fruit and 62% self-sufficient in vegetables: *Fruit and Vegetables and UK Greenhouse Gas Emissions: Exploring the Relationship*, Tara Garnett, University of Surrey: Centre for Environmental Strategy, 2006. Only 8% of farms in England are mixed: DEFRA report *Agriculture in the UK 2010*. The change from mixed farming to monocultural farming is documented in *Farmageddon*, Paul Lymbery, Bloomsbury, 2013. For a discussion of meat production see Simon Fairlie *Meat: a Benign Extravagance*, Permanent Publications, 2010. Other information in this table is taken from Tara Garnett, *Cooking up a Storm: Food, Greenhouse Gas Emissions and Our Changing Climate*, University of Surrey, Food Climate Research Network, 2008.
6. The role of fast food is clearly explained in Eric Schlosser and Charles Wilson's *Chew on This: Everything You Don't Want to Know about Fast Food*, Puffin 2006. See *Shopped*, Joanna Blythman, Harper Perennial, 2007 and *Tescopoly: How One Shop Came Out on Top and Why it Matters*, Andrew Simms, Constable, 2007 for discussion of how the supermarkets control large parts of the food chain and the wider economy. For an analysis of the environmental burden of UK patterns of food consumption on other areas of the world see, *Environmental Impacts of the UK Food Economy with Particular Reference to WWF Priority Places and the North-East Atlantic*, World Wildlife Fund, 2008, Donal Murphy-Bokern.
7. The workings of the food system are well outlined in *Eat Your Heart Out: Why the Food Business is Bad for the Planet and Your Health*, Felicity Lawrence, Penguin 2008. For discussion of the global problems see *Stuffed and Starved: Markets, Power and the Hidden Battle for the Worlds' Food System*, Raj Patel, Portobello 2008 and the chapter on food in *The Poverty of Capitalism: Economic Meltdown and the Struggle for what Comes Next*, John Hilary, Pluto Press, 2013. For a succinct description of the overlapping issues in the UK see *Square Meal: Why We Need a New Recipe for the Future*, Food Research Collaboration, 2014, http://bit.ly/square-meal. For a discussion of food sovereignty see La Via Campesina, http://viacampesina.org, or *Food is Different: Why We Must Get the WTO Out of Agriculture*, Peter M Rosset, Zed Books, 2006. There are numerous books discussing a better way forward for UK farming. You'll find an eloquent call for a return to mixed farming in *The Carbon Fields: How Our Countryside Can Save Britain*, Graham Harvey, Grassroots, 2008. *Feeding People is Easy*, Colin Tudge, Pari Publishing is an easy read around the global issues. Equally compelling is *Farmageddon*, Paul Lymbery, op cit.
8. See http://cultivateoxford.org/, for more information
9. Tara Garnett, 2008, op cit.
10. *Livestock's Long Shadow: Environmental Issues and Options*, H. Steinfeld et al, FAO, 2006, http://bit.ly/Steinfield-2006.
11. 'Trends and seasonal cycles in the isotopic composition of nitrous oxide since 1940', S.Park et al, *Nature Geoscience* 5, (2012) 261–265, http://bit.ly/Park-2012.
12. Over a 100 year period one tonne of methane has the same effect as 25 tonnes of carbon dioxide. The Guardian's *Ultimate Climate Change FAQ* has a good explanation, http://bit.ly/guardian-cc.
13. Figures on relative proportions of greenhouse gases in agriculture, *Zero Carbon Britain: Rethinking the Future*, Paul Allen et al., CAT Publications, 2013, pp 84-85, quoting DECC figures.
14. *Shooting Fish*, Benjamin Wielgosz, Sustain, 2005, http://bit.ly/Wielgosz-2005, and Rupert Murray's film, End of the Line. http://endoftheline.com/.
15. *Tackling Climate Change Through Livestock – a Global Assessment of Emissions and Mitigation Opportunities*, P.J. Gerber et al, FAO, 2013, http://bit.ly/Gerber-2013.

16. Steinfeld et al op cit, p.45.
17. *Wise Moves: Exploring the Relationship between Food, Transport and CO₂*, Tara Garnett, Transport 2000 Trust, 2003, http://bit.ly/Garnett-2003.
18. Garnett, 2008, op cit p.38. Garnett also suggests that the UK cold chain is responsible for 15% of total food chain emissions but this includes home refrigeration which we include in our calculations for home energy.
19. This figure is arrived at by comparing Tesco's figure for the carbon emissions of their frozen peas (Tesco's *Product Carbon Footprint Summary*, op cit) with the standard emissions factor of 0.44 kg CO₂/kWh for electricity used by the UK government, http://bit.ly/carbonsmart.
20. *Recycling of Plastics*, Sue Jackson and T. Bertenyi, ImpEE Project, University of Cambridge, 2006, http://bit.ly/Jackson-2006 and *How Bad are Bananas*, Mike Berners-Lee, Profile, 2010, p. 180.
21. Courtauld Commitment on packaging, WRAP, http://bit.ly/wrap-packaging.
22. *Making the Most of Packaging: a Strategy for a Low-Carbon Economy*, DEFRA, 2009, http://bit.ly/DEFRA-packaging.
23. 51% of UK food (in net terms by value) is imported, Garnett 2008, op cit, p. 5, quoting DEFRA. The UK has been dependent on imported food since the industrial revolution but recently many people have become interested in whether the UK could become self-sufficient and what kind of diet this would involve. See 'Can Britain Feed Itself?' Simon Fairlie, *The Land* 4, Winter 2007-8, http://bit.ly/Fairlie-2007, and *Zero Carbon Britain* op cit.
24. Agricultural products, food, beverages and tobacco accounted for 26% of European road freight calculated by tonne-kilometre in 2010-2011. *Road Freight Transport Statistics*, European Commission, 2012, http://bit.ly/EU-freight. In the UK DEFRA's 2006 report *The Validity of Food Miles as an Indicator of Sustainable Development* attributes 25% of all UK freight to the food system, http://bit.ly/DEFRA-food.
25. Urban food kilometres increased by 27% between 1992 and 2002 due to an increase in shopping for food by car, DEFRA, 2006, op cit.
26. 1 – 2% of supermarket turnover comes from locally sourced food. *Good Neighbours: Community Impacts of Supermarkets*, Friends of the Earth, 2005, http://bit.ly/foe-neighbours. See also *Supermarket Local Sourcing Initiatives: Moving us Further Away from a Sustainable, Local Food Economy*, Corporate Watch, 2010, http://bit.ly/corporate-food.
27. 'Food swapping' figures: *The UK Interdependence Report*, Andrew Simms, New Economics Foundation, 2007, http://bit.ly/Simms-2007.
28. Women's Environmental Network, reported in the Guardian, http://bit.ly/guardian-network.
29. CarbonSmart, UK Conversion Factors, http://bit.ly/carbonsmart.
30. Pyramid based on *Double Pyramid 2012: Enabling Sustainable Food Choices*, The Barilla Centre for Food and Nutrition, 2012, http://bit.ly/Pyramid-2013. The 'Livewell Plate' provides similar advice, *Livewell: a Balance of Sustainable and Healthy Food Choices*, J. McDiarmid et al, World Wildlife Fund, 2011, http://bit.ly/livewell-2011.
31. *From Field to Fork: the Value of England's Local Food Webs*, CPRE, 2011, p. 2, http://bit.ly/Protection-2011.
32. Local Government Regulator reported in the Guardian February 26th 2011, *'Local' Food Labelling Misleads Consumers, Regulator Reveals*, http://bit.ly/guardian-labelling.
33. Information on fruit seasons: *Eat the Seasons*, http://eattheseasons.co.uk, and http://www.freshplaza.com/. See also *Seasonal Food*, Paul Waddington, Eden Project Books, 2009.
34. Figures from Berners-Lee, 2010 op cit, from *Lifecycle Carbon Emissions from Food Systems*, Miguel Brandao, University of Surrey, 2008, http://bit.ly/Brandao-2008, from *Environmental Impacts of Food Production and Consumption*, C. Foster et al, DEFRA, 2006 and from Tesco's *Product Carbon Footprint Summary*, op cit.
35. *Virtual Water: Tackling the Threat to our Planet's Most Precious Resource*, Tony Allan, I.B. Taurus, 2011.
36. 783 million people do not have access to clean water and almost 2.5 billion do not have access to adequate sanitation. United Nations International Year of Water Cooperation, http://bit.ly/UN-water.

37. The concept is Tony Allan's. See *Virtual Water* op cit and *The No-Nonsense Guide to Water*, Maggie Black, Verso 2004. Fred Pearce provides a readable romp through the problems in *When the Rivers Run Dry: What Happens When Our Water Runs Out?* Eden Project Books, 2006. Online see WaterFootprint, www.waterfootprint.org.
38. Figures variously from: *Virtual Water* (Allan op cit); *Global Food: Waste Not, Want Not*, Tim Fox, Institution of Mechanical Engineers, 2013, (food and petrol), http://bit.ly/global-foodreport; *Water: Use Less, Save More*, Jon Clift and Amanda Cuthbert, Green Books Guides, 2006, (bicycle); *Waterfootprint*, www.waterfootprint.org (biodiesel from soy); and 'Water footprint of European cars' M. Berger et al, *Environ. Sci. Technol.*, 2012, 46 (7), pp 4091–4099 (car), http://bit.ly/Berger-2012.
39. *Workplace Canteens: – a Survey of Union Reps*, Labour Research Department, 2010, http://bit.ly/Labour-2010.
40. *Getting Started: the Really Simple Guide to Buying More Sustainable Food for Caterers, Chefs and Food Buyers Working in the Public Sector*, South East Food Group Partnership and Sustain, http://bit.ly/sustainweb-guide.
41. See Royal Cornwall Hospitals Trust, http://bit.ly/nhs-sustain.
42. *Healthier and More Sustainable Catering: a Toolkit for Serving Food to Adults*. Public Health England, 2014, http://bit.ly/govuk-sustain.
43. Public Health England, 2014, op cit.
44. *Econometric Modelling and Household Food Waste*, Erik Brittton et al, WRAP, 2013, http://bit.ly/Brittton-2013.
45. *Bioregional Solutions for Living on One Planet*, Pooran Desai and Sue Riddlestone, Totnes: Green Books, 2002.
46. Tara Garnett, 2008, op cit.
47. *Consumer Guide to Country of Origin Information on Food Labels*, Food Standards Agency, Scotland, 2012, http://bit.ly/foodstandards-2012.
48. The evidence is reviewed in 'Does Organic Farming Reduce Environmental Impacts? A Meta-Analysis of European Research', Hannah Tuomisto et al, *Journal of Environmental Management* 112 (2012) 309-320.
49. Berners-Lee, 2010, op cit, quoting DEFRA's Market Transformation Project.
50. *Agriculture at a Crossroads: Synthesis Report*, GM IAASTD, 2008, http://bit.ly/IAASTD-2008. For discussion of the GM industry's response see *The IAASTD Report and Some of its Fallout – a Personal Note*, Dr. Angelika Hilbeck, ETH Zurich, http://bit.ly/ines-IAASTD.
51. Read this interview with Will Nicholson for a quick view of the sustainability of the restaurant sector, http://bit.ly/Nicholson-sustain.
52. Tim Fox, Institution of Mechanical Engineers, 2013, op cit, http://bit.ly/global-foodreport.
53. The CO_2 e associated with avoidable food waste was 17 million tonnes in 2012. There are 26.4 million households in the UK (Families and Households, 2013, Office of National Statistics) which gives the figure of 640 kg per household. *Household Food and Drink Waste in the United Kingdom 2012*, WRAP 2012, http://bit.ly/waste-2012. Food waste is discussed in more detail in *Waste: Uncovering the Global Food Scandal*, Tristram Stuart, Penguin 2009.
54. See the regulations at http://bit.ly/govuk-shipping.
55. WHO definition, http://bit.ly/WHO-food.
56. Description of the G8's New Alliance on Food Security and Nutrition, http://bit.ly/feedthefurture-security. For a critique, War on Want's report, http://bit.ly/waronwant-food.

Notes to Chapter Five

1. 'The Tragedy of the Commons', Garrett Hardin, *Science*, Vol. 162 no. 3859, pp. 1243-1248, 1968. 'Revisiting the Commons: Local Lessons, Global Challenges', Elinor Ostrom et al, *Science* Vol. 284, pp 278-28, 1999, http://bit.ly/ostrom-1999.
2. Some different critiques of economic growth can be found in *Steady-State Economics*, Herman E. Daly, Earthscan 1977, in *Growth isn't Possible*, Andrew Simms and Victoria Johnson, New Economics Foundation, 2010, http://bit.ly/simms-2010, in *Prosperity without Growth: Economics for a Finite Planet*, Tim Jackson, Routledge, 2011, and on the website of the Centre for the Advancement of a Steady State Economy, http://bit.ly/steady-state.
3. *One Planet Living*, http://www.oneplanetliving.net/ and *Sharing Nature's Interest: Ecological Footprints as an Indicator of Sustainability*, Nicky Chambers et al, Earthscan, 2000.
4. *Queen Asks Why No-one Saw the Credit Crunch Coming*, Daily Telegraph, 2008, http://bit.ly/Telegraph-royall. Occupy Movement, http://occupylondon.org.uk/, and http://www.occupyuk.info/.
5. *The Poverty of Capital*, John Hilary, Pluto Press, 2013.
6. *Living Standards, Poverty and Inequality in the UK: 2013*, Jonathan Cribb et al, Institute for Fiscal Studies, 2013, http://bit.ly/Cribb-2013.
7. *The Economics of Climate Change: the Stern Review*, Nicholas Stern, Cambridge University Press. For a broader discussion of this approach see *A New Blueprint for a Green Economy*, Edward B. Barbier and Anil Markandya, Earthscan, 2012.
8. *Better Growth, Better Climate: the New Climate Economy Report*, The Global Commission on Economy and Climate, 2014, p.24, http://bit.ly/nce-2014.
9. *A National Plan for the UK from Austerity to the Age of the Green New Deal*, Green New Deal Group, 2013, http://bit.ly/greennewdeal-2013.
10. *Steady State Economics* op cit.
11. For Peter Victor's ideas about how to make the transition to a no-growth economy, *Managing without Growth*, Peter Victor, Edward Elgar, 2008.
12. *In Place of Growth: Practical Steps to a Manchester Where People Thrive Without Harming the Planet*, Mark Burton et al, Steady State Manchester, 2012, http://bit.ly/Burton-2012.
13. 'Living in the World Risk Society', Ulrich Beck, *Economy and Society*, Volume 35 Number 3, 329-345, August 2006.
14. *Advertising Effect: How Do We Get the Balance of Advertising Right?* Zoe Gannon and Neal Lawson, Compass, 2010, discusses how advertising creates unsustainable 'wants', http://bit.ly/Gannon-2011.
15. *Middle Income Households 1977-2011-12*, Office of National Statistics, http://bit.ly/onsgov-middleincome.
16. *A History of the World in 100 Objects*, Neil MacGregor, 2011, http://bit.ly/MacGregor-2011.
17. 'The Impact of Social Factors and Consumer Behavior on Carbon Dioxide Emissions in the United Kingdom', Giovanni Baiocchi et al, *Journal of Industrial Ecology*, Vol. 14, Issue 1, pp 50-72, 2010 and 'Who emits most? Associations Between Socio-Economic factors and UK households' Home Energy, Transport, Indirect and Total CO_2 Emissions', Milena Buchs and Sylke V. Schnepf, *Ecological Economics*, 90, (2013), 114-123, http://bit.ly/Buchs-2013.
18. Figures in the table adapted from *Understanding Changes in CO_2 Emissions from Consumption 1992-2004: A Structural Decomposition Analysis*, J.C. Minx et al, Report to DEFRA, Stockholm Environment Institute, York University and University of Durham, 2009 and from *The Distribution of Total Greenhouse Gas Emissions by Households in the UK, and Some Implications for Social Policy*, Centre for the Analysis of Social Exclusion, Paper 152, I. Gough et al, 2012.
19. Corrections based on *ONS Table 9, CPI Detailed Indices Annual Average: 1999 to 2013*, http://bit.ly/ons-cpi.
20. Description of how bottom-up product analysis works, Carbon Trust, http://bit.ly/Carbontrust-bottomup. Details of PAS 2050, http://bit.ly/PAS-2050.
21. *Global Witness*, http://www.globalwitness.org. Enough Project, http://www.enoughproject.org/conflict-minerals.

22. *21 Hours: Why a Shorter Working Week Can Help Us All Flourish in the 21st Century*, New Economics Foundation, 2010 explains why this is a good idea, http://bit.ly/Neweconomics-2010.
23. *Cradle to Cradle*, Michael Braungart and William McDonogh, Vintage, 2008, p. 110.
24. *Towards the Circular Economy*, the Ellen MacArthur Foundation, 2012, http://bit.ly/MacArthur-2012.
25. *Cradle to Cradle*, op cit, p.102.
26. *Purity and Danger: an Analysis of the Concept of Pollution and Taboo*, Mary Douglas, 1966, Routledge edition 2002.
27. *Implementing Sustainable Procurement: Overcoming Common Barriers*, Environment Agency and WRAP, 2012, http://bit.ly/wrap-2014.
28. *Government Buying Standards*, http://bit.ly/defra-buying.
29. *WRAP – Sustainable Procurement*, http://bit.ly/sus-proc.
30. *Income Inequality: Trends and Measures*, The Equality Trust, 2013, http://bit.ly/equalitytrust-2013.
31. *Living Standards, Poverty and Inequality in the UK: 2013*, Jonathan Cribb et al, Institute of Fiscal Studies, 2013, http://bit.ly/Cribb-2013, and *The Spirit Level: Why More Equal Societies Almost Always Do Better*, Richard Wilkinson and Kate Pickett, Penguin, 2009.
32. Internet infrastructure responsible for 1.9% of global emissions: *Smarter 20:20 The Role of ICT in Driving a Sustainable Future*, Boston Consulting Group, 2012, http://bit.ly/boston-2012. 61% of this is accounted for by end-user devices whose emissions are normally counted as part of the household or workplace footprint. The other 39% comes from data centres and telecommunications networks, giving a figure of 0.74% of global emissions. Greenpeace report some improvement in internet companies' commitment to reducing their environmental impact: *Clicking Clean: How Companies are Creating the Green Internet*, Greenpeace, 2014, http://bit.ly/clicking-clean.
33. Envirosort, http://bit.ly/envirosort.
34. For example, *Ghana Accuses UK Recycling Firm Envirocom of Illegal Fridge Imports*, http://bit.ly/Guardian-imports.

Notes to Chapter Six

1. *Public Attitudes to Nuclear Power and Climate Change in Britain Two Years after the Fukushima Accident: Summary Findings of a Survey Conducted in March 2013*, Wouter Poortinga et al, UKERC Working paper: UKERC/WP/ES/2013/006 2013, http://bit.ly/Poortinga-2013. The authors found that 72% of the population agreed that climate change is real, while 60% were concerned about it. Worryingly the same study found an increase in the proportion of people doubting the reality of climate change, rising from 4% in 2005 to 19% in 2013. *Public Perceptions of Climate Change in Wales: Summary Findings of a Survey of the Welsh Public Conducted During November and December 2012*, S.B. Captsick et al, Climate Change Consortium of Wales, Cardiff, 2013, found that Welsh people were a little more certain of the reality with 88% agreeing that the climate is changing.
2. *A New Agenda for Climate Change: Facing up to Stealth Denial and Winding Down on Fossil Fuels*, Jonathan Rowson, London: RSA, 2013, http://bit.ly/Rowsoncc-2013.
3. Disavowal is discussed in relation to climate change in 'A New Climate for Psychotherapy?' Rosemary Randall, *Psychotherapy and Politics International* 3 (3): 165-179, 2005, http://bit.ly/Randall-2005, and in 'The Difficult Problem of Anxiety in Thinking about Climate Change' in *Engaging with Climate Change: Psychoanalytic and Interdisciplinary Perspectives*, ed. Sally Weintrobe, Routledge, 2013.
4. Rowson, 2013, op cit.
5. Confirmation bias in relation to climate change is explained clearly in *The Psychology of Climate Change Communication: A Guide for Scientists, Journalists, Educators, Political Aides, and the Interested Public*, New York: CRED, 2009, http://bit.ly/Cred-2009.
6. These processes are described in more detail in 'Great expectations: the psychodynamics of ecological debt', Rosemary Randall, in *Engaging with Climate Change: Psychoanalytic and Interdisciplinary Perspectives*, op cit.

7. *Motivational Interviewing: Preparing People for Change*, William R. Miller and Stephen Rollnick, Guildford Press, 2002.
8. *Selections from the Prison Notebooks of Antonio Gramsci*, edited and translated, Quintin Hoare and Geoffrey Nowell Smith, Lawrence and Wishart, 1971.
9. *Dark Optimism*, http://www.darkoptimism.org/about.html.
10. *Active Hope: How to Face the Mess We're in Without Going Crazy*, Joanna Macy and Chris Johnstone, New World Library, 2012.
11. The limitations of the information deficit model are discussed in *Creating a Climate for Change: Communicating Climate Change and Facilitating Social Change*, Susanne C. Moser and Lisa Dilling, Cambridge University Press, 2007.
12. The Cultural Cognition project discusses these issues well. See 'Fixing the communications failure' *Nature* 463, 296-297, Dan Kahan, 2010 and *The Tragedy of the Risk Perception Commons: Culture Conflict, Rationality Conflict, and Climate Change*, Dan Kahan et al, Cultural Cognition Project, Working Paper No. 89, 2011, http://www.culturalcognition.net/.
13. *Creating a Climate for Change*, op cit.
14. The guru of social marketing is Doug Mackenzie-Mohr. His classic book is *Fostering Sustainable Behavior: an Introduction to Community-Based Social Marketing*, D. McKenzie Mohr and W. Smith, New Society Publishers, 1999. A much-used UK example is Chris Rose and Pat Dade's *Values Modes*, http://www.cultdyn.co.uk/valuesmodes.html. Futerra's 2010 pamphlet *Sell the Sizzle*, http://bit.ly/futerra-2010, and DEFRA's 2008 report, *A Framework for Pro-Environmental Behaviours*, http://bit.ly/defrareport-2008, also give a clear idea of the approach.
15. 'American Risk Perceptions: Is Climate Change Dangerous?' *Risk Analysis*, 25 (6), 1433-1442, 2005, Anthony Leiserowitz, http://bit.ly/leiser-2005.
16. 'Mind the Gap: Why Do People act Environmentally and What Are the Barriers to Pro-Environmental Behavior?' A. Kollmus and J. Aygeman, *Environmental Education Research*, Vol. 8, No. 3, 2002. For a critique of the behavioural approach: 'Beyond the ABC: Climate Change Policy and Theories of Social Change', Elizabeth Shove, *Environment and Planning A* 42(6) 1273–1285, 2010, http://bit.ly/Shove-2010. For an explanation of the psychoanalytic view of the mind's conflicts in relation to climate change, *Engaging with Climate Change: Psychoanalytic and Interdisciplinary Perspectives*, ed. Sally Weintrobe, Routledge, 2013.
17. *Common Cause: the Case for Working with our Cultural Values*, Tom Crompton, WWF, 2010, http://bit.ly/Crompton-2010.
18. *Common Cause* op cit.
19. *Simple and Painless: the Limitations of Spillover in Environmental Campaigning*, Tom Crompton and John Thogerson, WWF, 2009, http://bit.ly/Thogerson-2009.
20. The guru of framing is George Lakoff. *Don't Think of an Elephant! Know Your Values and Frame the Debate*, Chelsea Green Publishing, 2004, is a short summary, *Moral Politics: How Liberals and Conservatives Think*, University of Chicago Press, 1996, 2nd edition 2002, gives the detailed arguments. For UK applications: *Finding Frames: New Ways to Engage the UK Public in Global Poverty*, Andrew Darnton and Martin Kirk, Bond, 2011, http://bit.ly/Darnton-2011, and *Common Cause* op cit.
21. 'Fear Won't Do It: Promoting Positive Engagement with Climate Change through Visual and Iconic Representations', Saffron O'Neill and Sophie Nicholson-Cole, *Science Communication*, March 2009, Vol. 30 no. 3 355-379, and 'More Bad News: the Risk of Neglecting Emotional Responses to Climate Change Information', Susanne Moser, in *Creating a Climate for Change*, op cit.
22. The workshops designed by Marshall Ganz will help you craft a public speech that is both inspiring and personal. *Story of Self*, Marshall Ganz, 2009, http://bit.ly/ganz-2009.
23. *Story of Self*, op cit.
24. *Creating a Climate for Change*, op cit.
25. *A New Agenda for Climate Change*, op cit.

26. 'Learning to Love the Natural World Enough to Protect it', Louise Chawla, *Barn* nr, 2 2006:57-78, ISSN 0800-1669. A summary of this paper and other relevant research: Centre for Confidence, http://bit.ly/Chawla-2006.
27. *Ecopsychology: Restoring the Earth, Healing the Mind*, ed. Theodore Roszak et al, Sierra Club Books, 1995.

Notes to Chapter Seven

1. Research by Southampton University found that participants in Carbon Conversation groups made a mean reduction of 3.72 tonnes across the sample. 'It Helped Me Sort of Face the End of the World: the Role of Emotions for Group-Based Third Sector Initiatives on Climate Change', Milena Büchs, Emma Hinton and Graham Smith, accepted for publication 2015 in *Environmental Values*.
2. *Carbon Account*, http://www.thecarbonaccount.com/, *iMeasure* http://www.imeasure.org.uk/.
3. *Aberdeen Forward*, http://www.aberdeenforward.org/; *Low Carbon Oxford North* http://www.lcon.org.uk/; *Steady State Manchester*, http://steadystatemanchester.net/; *Transition Stirling*, http://www.transitionstirling.org.uk/; Transition Cardiff, http://cardifftransition.com; *Transition Network*, http://www.transitionnetwork.org/.
4. *Green Unison*, www.unison.org.uk/green/; *IFEES*, www.ifees.org.uk; details of Christian groups, http://bit.ly/Christian-Ecology.
5. *They Work for You*, http://www.theyworkforyou.com/.
6. *Avaaz*, www.avaaz.org; *38 Degrees*, www.38degrees.org.uk; *Change*, https://www.change.org/; *350*, www.350.org.
7. *The Climate Coalition*, http://www.theclimatecoalition.org/; *Stop Climate Chaos Cymru*, http://stopclimatechaoscymru.org/; *Stop Climate Chaos Scotland*, http://www.theclimatecoalition.org/scotland.
8. *Friends of the Earth*, www.foe.co.uk; *Greenpeace*, www.greenpeace.org.uk; *World Development Movement*, http://www.wdm.org.uk/.
9. The *Campaign Against Climate Change*, www.campaigncc.org.
10. *Plane Stupid*, www.planestupid.com; *Climate Rush*, www.climaterush.co.uk; *The Climate Justice Collective*, www.climatejusticecollective.org; *Coal Action*, www.coalaction.org.uk; *Coal Action Scotland*, www.coalactionscotland.org.uk; *Frack-off*, http://frack-off.org.uk/.
11. *The Carbon Trust* provides information and support for businesses in reducing carbon emissions, www.carbontrust.co.uk.
12. "There are many people who go from denial to despair without pausing on the intermediate step of actually solving the problem." Al Gore, in the 2006 film *An Inconvenient Truth*.

Index

action,
   collective, 4, 92, 146, 190
   personal plans for, 37-38, 91-93, 118, 124, 146-147
   political, 4, 191-192
affluence, 138
air travel, 83, 97, 98
ambivalence, 171, 181
anxiety, 12-13, 35, 106, 151, 164-165, 175, 181

behaviour change, 12, 163
biofuel/biomass, 17, 60, 65, 80

capitalism, 8, 133
car ownership, 76-77
car travel, 76, 82
carbon budget, 17
Carbon Conversations groups, iv, 2-3, 22, 154, 190
carbon dioxide, 6
   embodied, 132
   equivalents, 104
carbon emissions, 7
   direct, 22
   fair share, 15
   in food, 107-111
   in goods and services, 142-144
   in housing, 32
   and income, 141-142
   indirect, 22
   per person, 15-16
   in travel, 83-84
carbon footprint,
   average, 16
calculation, 22-3
carbon offsetting, 98
carbon rationing/allowances, 18, 82
carbon reduction, iv, 22, 134, 166, 175
carbon trading, 18

change,
   and complex systems, 89
   process of 22, 94-95, 154
childhood, 34, 176, 183
climate change iv, 1, 5, 11, 162
   the basics, 6-8
   and water, 103, 119
cognitive approach, 179-181
communication, 164-165, 185, 189
congestion, 76, 77, 82, 99
conversations, 53, 77, 97, 154, 175
   difficult, 161-163
   levels in, 167-169
creativity, 14, 140, 146, 154, 189

decarbonisation, 33, 134
defences, 162, 181
denial 11, 162, 174, 185
despair, 174, 177, 178
disavowal, 11, 162, 185
disruption, fear of 54
droughts, 7, 26, 119

economic growth, 131-5
economics,
   conventional, 134, 148
   and environment, 132
   steady-state/ecological, 131, 135, 158
economy, circular 148-149
ecopsychology 185, 186
electric and hybrid vehicles, 80-81, 99
emotional security, 34-35, 77-78, 123
emotional support, 94, 176-179
empathy, 165, 169-171, 176
energy,
   demand, 7, 33
   efficiency, 7, 80, 135
   generation, 33
   renewable, – see renewables
   saving, 55
exploitation, 153

family 34, 104, 122, 166
financial help, 51, 63
financial crisis, 133-134
floods, 7, 119-120
food,
   choices, 104
   place in our lives, 105
   sovereignty, 107, 129
   system, 103, 104, 121
force field analysis, 89-91
fossil fuels, 5-6, 104, 135
fuel poverty, 52

GDP, see Gross Domestic Product
General Progress Indicator, 19
geo-engineering, 16
Global Commons, 132
global,
   scenarios, 20-21
   systems, 10-11
   warming, 6
GPI, see General Progress Indicator
Green Deal, 51, 69
Green New Deal, 134
greenhouse effect, 6
grief, 55-56, 177, 184
Gross Domestic Product, 19, 133
guilt, 12-13, 147, 153, 177

heat pumps, 69
heritage buildings, 52, 63, 69
home, meaning of 34-35
hope, need for 175, 177-8
housing,
   comfort, 35
   renting, 37, 43-45, 47-48
   survey, 40-41
   upgrading, 42-50
   zero-carbon, 74
hurricanes and typhoons, 26

identity 1, 78, 121, 122, 137, 164, 180
income, correlation with carbon emissions 141-142, 155,
information trap, 1-2, 163-164
inner conflict, 171, 181
insulation, 32, 41, 59, 62, 70
integrated transport, 81
international families, 78
investment, 82

justice and equality, 2, 8, 14, 55, 135, 136, 153

lifestyles, 10, 93, 97,
living, patterns of 81
loss, 19, 24, 154, 173, 186
low-carbon,
   diet, 113-115
   future, 5, 15-21
   goods and services, 144-146, 147, 155
   housing 37, 42-50
   society, 2
   travel, 79-83

markets, 17, 134
monitoring and diary keeping, 38-39, 59, 63, 91, 112, 188
motivation, 13-14, 174, 181

natural world, 13, 18, 132-133
   connection to, 13, 151, 180
nuclear power, 16, 60,

payback times, 55
photo-voltaics, 33, 60
planetary boundaries, 8, 143
planning permission, 63, 71
policy,
   housing, 33, 39, 62
   national and international, 9, 17-19
   travel, 76-77, 81-83, 101
   workplace, 58, 96
poverty, 133, 135
projection, 164-5, 174
psychology of climate change iv-v, 1-3
psychosocial approach 185, 186
public transport, 76-77, 81, 82, 101

rebound effect, 18, 52-53, 95, 121, 146, 155
recycling, 151-152,
regulation, 17, 21, 33, 81
   upstream and downstream 17
relationships, 53, 166, 186, 188
renewables, 64, 80,
resentment, 55-56, 174
resistance, 171-2, 181, 182
responsibility,
   personal, 9, 79
   shared, 9
   role models, 190

safe space, 23, 24, 165
self efficacy, 174-175
self-esteem, 94, 137
self interest, 14, 179, 180
   corporate, 76,
sense of self, 89
shame, 13, 137, 151, 153,
social practice, 35
solar hot water, 60, 73
splitting, 164
star ratings, 22
status, 77, 137

taxation, 17, 82, 175
technology, 16-17
temperature increase, 6-7
therapeutic approach, iv, 10, 162, 165
travel,
   changes in, 76
   choice, 78, 79, 95, 97
   comfort, 78, 94
   infrastructure, 95,
   options, 79-83
   patterns, 76, 77
   smarter, 92, 96
truth, avoiding 11, 133

values based approach, 180, 186
ventilation, 40, 59, 73
visions of the future, 19-21, 84-85, 159

waste,
   problem of, 148, 157, 159
   feelings about, 150-151
water,
   in the UK, 120
   virtual, 119
wind power, 74
wood, 60, 74
work places, 25, 56-57, 95-97, 124-126, 154-155